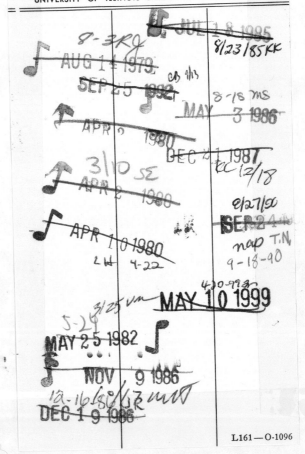

L161—O-1096

# Learning Fundamental Concepts of Music

# Learning Fundamental Concepts of Music:

## AN ACTIVITIES APPROACH

**Second Edition**

# Virginia Austin

*State University College, Buffalo, New York*

**KENDALL/HUNT PUBLISHING COMPANY**

2460 Kerper Boulevard,
Dubuque, Iowa 52001

To Beatrice Krone, whose writings in music education pointed the way for me, and to my mother, who kept telling me I had a book to write.

# Preface

If you are: (1) a student learning the fundamentals of music, (2) studying to become a classroom or music teacher, (3) a teacher of future classroom or music teachers, (4) teaching anyone music, this book is offered to you in the hope that it will suit your needs.

The book attempts to approach the fundamentals of music from several perspectives, namely activity, discussion, music making and participation. It includes complete lessons, not just lesson plans. Throughout the book a constant attempt has been made to recreate the learning situation: to show the step by step, word for word procedure from first faint dawn to full comprehension.

As a student of music you will often find yourself assuming a multiple role: that of the student, that of the new teacher acquiring new skills and that of your pupil. The book attempts to address you in all three of these roles, to illuminate your interaction with them.

Though it is suggested that certain parts of this book could best be studied in the sequence offered, each chapter is an entity in itself and the instructor may select at any point, those individual chapters he may particularly wish to deal with.

Practically everything explicated here has been tested and proven in the classroom. It is humbly offered to all those engaged in learning and teaching the language of music.

# Acknowledgments

Mrs. Elsa Long, of New Jersey, former student and sometime colleague, to whom I am indebted for the part of the lesson on the staff which begins with one line.

Mr. Walter Lenahan of Laurel, Maryland, publisher of *Classroom Method*, and manufacturer of melody flutes, for his generous cooperation and support.

All my students with whom I exchanged ideas, and who taught me as I taught them.

# Contents

Contents

# Chapter 1

# The Beginnings of Rhythm

## WHAT YOU NEED TO KNOW FOR THIS LESSON

Nothing!

## BASIC FACTS YOU WILL LEARN

| | | |
|---|---|---|
| walk = | quarter note ♩ = | 1 count = 1 beat |
| walk-hold = | half note ♩ = | 2 counts = 2 beats |
| walk-hold-hold = | dotted half note ♩. = | 3 counts = 3 beats |
| walk-hold-hold-hold = | whole note o = | 4 counts = 4 beats |
| run = | eighth note ♪ = | ½ count = ½ beat |

eighth notes often go in pairs; 2 eighth notes = 1 quarter ♫=♩
2 quarter notes = 1 half note ♩ ♩=♩

accent = loud beat = | bar or bar-line = downbeat = count one
bar-line = a picture of an accent = the musical symbol of an accent
the end (a period) . = || double bar
measure = the space between bars          Sometimes measures are called bars.
measure signature = the counting numbers which tell how the music is counted and beat and conducted

THERE ARE ———— QUARTER NOTES IN EACH MEASURE, OR SOME-
THING THAT EQUALS IT.

counts=an even numbering of beats.    Count one on accent.    Counting must be steady, even.
beats = even equal units of time—a physical picture of counts
conducting = a physical picture of the counts or beats

## WHAT THIS LESSON CAN LEAD TO

1. Further reading skill.
2. Further dictation skill.
3. The ability and tools for composing and self-expression.

---

This lesson is a formal introduction to note values. We will hope that it has been preceded by the numerous kinds of physical and creative responses described so well in the many fine Methods books, which encourage students to respond to music with parts or all of themselves: tapping, clapping, patschen (slap knees), running, jumping, skipping, bowing, swaying, twirling; keeping time with instruments, all kinds of dancing and dramatizing. (In the case of older students, as many of these as their inhibited adultness can tolerate.)

These experiences are provided by teachers so that students may actually "feel" music; particularly its rhythm, although other components of music can be "felt" too — tempo, mood, meter, form, etc. The term, "feel" the rhythm is often used glibly by those who do not really believe the term or realize what it means. We must indeed actually "feel" the rhythm deep inside ourselves to produce or reproduce it in music, and to appreciate or understand it. Our muscles and viscera and nerves should actually feel and react to rhythm. Counting of itself won't do it. Who among us has not witnessed some one counting aloud crookedly and unevenly? Counting aloud in rhythm reflects an inner feeling.

It is for this precise reason that many music educators are against beginning the study of rhythm through mathematics. Indeed, although rhythm is based on a mathematical foundation which the students must clearly understand eventually, this should follow visceral and muscular mastery of rhythm and not precede it. Besides, suppose the student is poor in mathematics, or too young to have learned it? With fractions, this can well be the case.

*Beware the pie;* the famous pie or apple so beloved by unwary teachers. Although the musical pie is a much used institution, it presents a false analogy, and must surely leave as many unanswered questions in the bewildered mind of the student as it solves. A pie or an apple always has four quarters. If you want to use only one or two, how do you explain away the remaining quarters? Or in $\frac{2}{4}$ or $\frac{3}{4}$ meter, what happens to the remaining quarters? So, back to a way which is simple, clear and successful.

## INTRODUCTION TO NOTE VALUES THROUGH PHYSICAL MOVEMENT

TWINKLE, TWINKLE LITTLE STAR                                                    French

Teacher plays the song (fl., Her: 41).* Teacher can play it at the piano, or on a record, or sing it, or have all the students sing it. He asks a leading question which provides a controlled choice or almost suggests the answer.

*fl. indicates that the composition mentioned is in the book *Classroom Method for Melody Flute* by Frederick Beckman, published by Melody Flute Co., Laurel, Maryland.
Her: refers to the page number on which this composition will be found in the *Heritage Songster* by Leon and Lynn Dallin, published by the William C. Brown Co., Dubuque, Iowa.

**Is this good skipping music? Or running music?**

No. If the answer should be yes, he asks the student to get up and try to run or skip to the music. It is always a good technique to help the student prove or disprove to himself his answer. Otherwise, how does he know *why* his answer is wrong? Just because teacher says no? If the student had not thought his answer correct, he would not have given it in the first place. Now just because he is told no, he knows no more about why he is wrong than before teacher said no. Trying out his answer shows him immediately.

Of course we are all aware of the frequent cases of "dreamers" who answer without thinking. Requiring such a student to get up and test his answer has at least two good consequences:

1. It jogs him awake and into thinking and exercising some judgment and becoming more involved in the learning situation.
2. The prospect of having to prove his answer makes him consider what he says more carefully in the first place.

It also has an undesirable consequence of inhibiting the lazy or timid from even venturing answers, so the resourceful teacher must be a step ahead, and, anticipating such escapes from the business of thinking and learning, use such devices as **Let me see you all run with your feet** (while seated, or standing in place). **I want each of you to decide whether this is good running music.**

**Try moving your feet to the music.**

If there is room (there ought to be for rhythm lessons, but even a small aisle is enough) he gets some students up, if not all, to move to the music. Sitting in place and moving the feet ought to be the minimum physical experience.

The answer is usually quickly forthcoming. Walking. Some say marching. It could be either, but if marching is mentioned, teacher can play the music again in an exaggerated martial style to show that in contrast this is more like comfortable strolling down the street; maybe window-shopping as you walk. Incidentally as this technique unfolds, teacher or students may decide they prefer the term march, which will be entirely suitable. **Let's see how you would walk to this music.**
A common response is this:

Of course this is not wrong, but it will not build the particular concept we are leading to and it won't help to make the desired point. It is certainly correct in that it is a way of walking in time. In the light of our discussion above, the teacher should certainly not imply that this response is incorrect. But what the teacher is aiming at is a response from the student in which he moves as the music does. Teacher should follow up such a case by asking **When would a person be likely to walk like this?** Usual answers are funeral, ceremonial occasion like commencement, hesitation walk as in wedding. To direct the response better the teacher might ask, **Are you moving your feet every time the music moves? Do it again to see. You are moving your feet on "Twin" but how about "kle"?** Usually a student then realizes he has not been walking on every musical note and now does.

If teacher is working with many persons, or if adults feel silly to get up before others and move to the music, he can suggest they walk with their fingers. **Listen carefully to the music and see what your feet do. Does the music always walk?**

No, on "star" it pauses, stops, waits (some of the words students use). **What do your feet do?**

They don't move; they hold their previous position, taken on "star." This could be compared to the childhood game of "Statues" in which the player is swung around and then freezes in the position he finally reaches. The walker *holds* his position because the music holds. The word "stop" implies silence; in a way "pause" does too. Since the words and music are sustained, the word, "hold" seems more appropriate. Could we not call the action on "star" a WALK-HOLD? Following the window shopping analogy a little further, the walk-hold could be the time when the window shopping stroller stops to admire something in the window.

Some teachers prefer to have the student *step-bend* on the sustained notes. The very action of the *bend* focuses attention on the sustained tone as well as its length. It has an exact duration, of course, which we can soon aid the student to see for himself.

**Now let's walk through the entire song.**

**Say the words of the song, then say "walk" or "walk-hold." Or some say or sing the words of the song, and others say the action words.** It will come out like this: Everyone will sound a little bit like a cackling hen, but it's an important step.

TWIN - KLE     TWIN - KLE     LITTLE     STAR
walk          walk      walk      walk   walk   walk   walk-hold

HOW     I     WON - DER     WHAT     YOU     ARE
walk    walk    walk   walk     walk      walk     walk-hold

## Apply the New Skill

The minute you have come this far, you are equipped with enough musical vocabulary to use it to communicate. The clever teacher will use it immediately, in some of the following ways.

1. Teacher plays a series of walking notes on a tom-tom or improvises at the piano or plays suitable excerpts:
   Haydn's Surprise Symphony, second movement.
   Lightly Row (fl., Her: 271)
   Children's Prayer from Hansel and Gretel by Humperdinck (fl., Her: 173)
   middle section of Chopin Nocturne in G Minor (Chapter 12 on Minor)
   March from Album of the Young by Schumann.
2. Play a percussion instrument. It is particularly suitable in this activity because it produces pure rhythm without pitch. Get up and walk, or walk with your fingers.
3. You and teacher do the same with walk-hold notes.
4. Teacher mixes them up. He tells the students to listen first, then walk them. For example:

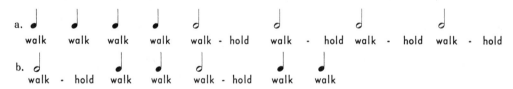

Of course this activity can be varied by echo-clapping or patschen (knee slapping), with teacher or student presenting a pattern and other students echoing it. This is part of the techniques of both Orff and Kodaly, except that in their systems the student does not always know, or need to know any name for the notes he is clapping. Here in this situation, he does. Both experiences are important and have their respective values and functions.

### Dictation

What can we call this procedure? It is very important for us all to realize its significance and to recognize it as DICTATION. When one imitates accurately what one hears, or translates sounds into another language (actions and words in this case) one is doing dictation. Often regarded as a difficult and fearsome skill, this is an easy and pleasant way to begin it. It should be noted however that in the case of a lesson such as this, the skill of dictation is *not* the goal, but merely a teaching tool, a learning experience, with its goal the comprehension of note values and rhythm.

Use rhythm sticks or drum sticks and play the patterns after hearing them played by teacher. Use a whole rhythm band.

Teacher should encourage students to make up their own patterns. Vary the experiences: hear them, play them, say them, sing them, walk them, create them.

After activities such as these, these sounds and terms should have real meaning to you and you now have some solid knowledge.

The next step is particularly rewarding. Not only is it successful, the experience is usually a source of delight to the student and therefore to the teacher.

### Let's make a picture of this song.

If teacher asks for ideas he will get an assortment of usable suggestions. A common one which is used by some of the basal song series as well as many teachers is the employment of short and long dashes to indicate WALK and WALK-HOLD: — and ——. This is an excellent system but it won't work for our purposes. He may in the end have to direct that you use a dash for a WALK (—) and a circle for WALK-HOLD (O). Not walk-hold = — O, but walk-hold = O. To clarify, teacher should draw several circles while saying walk-hold, walk-hold, walk-hold. Singing or playing the song again rather deliberately, you should arrive at this picture: — — — — — — O — — — — — — O — — — — — — O — — — — — — O — — — — — — O — — — — — — O.

Notice there is a definite order to our procedure; first a physical response (walking or finger-walking) and secondly a written picture of what was heard and physically portrayed.

### More Dictation

Here again, as in the previous step, you should experience many dictation activities. Only now, in addition, you can write what you hear; on the chalk-board or flannel board or chart, or each on your own paper. A series of patterns which teacher beats on a drum, for instance, should look like this: (Teacher must choose the patterns carefully and try to avoid complications or confusion). He asks: **What is the drum saying?**

Beginners of any age may not be able to do a whole pattern without help. Teacher may have to ask questions like this. **What kind of step came first, walk or walk-hold?** (Notice he does not use the word, "note" yet.) **How many walks came first?** He may have to play it again; students may have to count how many steps there were. Although later on students should not be counting NOTES, but rather BEATS, at this stage it doesn't appear to hurt and some seem to need this assistance. **Then what**

came next? **How many?** Remember the best solution if you give wrong answers or are stuck is to walk or finger-walk as you hear the pattern. You really can get very close to 100% accuracy this way. And it is fun. It takes on the aspect of a game, and it provides a small success to entice you a step further. It also opens the door to another procedure, even more significant.

### Reading

Keeping the column of circle—dash patterns displayed, teacher now tries a new procedure. He points to one of the patterns the students have written and asks, **Can you beat this pattern? Or walk it?** Because these signs are so meaningful, and because you have followed a clear procedure which you understood, to arrive at these patterns, it is usually a simple matter to sound out these patterns. Here again is an extremely significant procedure of which the teacher should be fully aware, although it is not yet the proper time to bring this to the attention of the students. What is this procedure? Is it not the first steps of MUSIC READING? Notice that Dictation came first. If a student can *name* it and *write* it, he ought to be able to *read* it. Is not READING the reverse of DICTATION? In dictation, an unrehearsed sound must be mentally analyzed (assisted perhaps by such processes as finger walking), and then translated into the agreed-upon picture language:

?    ?

∿∿∿∿   ——————▶   — — O

sound

In reading, a pattern of symbols of recognizable meaning is translated into sound:

— — O   ——————▶   sound ∿∿∿∿

How to help students to read is one of the stickiest challenges. Here in this procedure lies a passage-way. The very nature of the response indicates whether or not the student knows what he is doing, and both the student and the teacher are aware of this.

**What am I doing on some of the notes?**

Using tom-tom or piano, teacher plays the song again with a very strong obvious accent on the first note and every other note, as follows:

Young children rarely answer "accent" or "emphasize." Older children and grown students are more likely to. Some answers are "it's heavier," "harder, louder, lower (?), stronger." Words like this get all mixed up by children, so instead of verbalizing too much, they should do something. Warning: some students say "longer." This can be a confusion of words, or of the ear. Always test it or prove it. You should then see that your feet or finger-steps move evenly; that one step is not longer. Also, the answer "lower," is wrong.

If students walk to it, some will most likely STAMP on the accented tones. But stamping is not what we are really getting at now. Teacher says, **this time do something with your arm. Drop your arm every time you hear the loud tone. Don't strike your desk, just swing your arm down. Don't forget to lift your arm for the next down swing. Start with your arm high, ready to swing down.** And since you have to lift it up in order to swing it down again, you will usually fall into a good rhythmic swing of down on the accent, up on the unaccented tone.

### Conducting

Teacher plays or sings the song through, giving the students plenty of time to feel this motion. **What are we really doing?** (If a hint is needed—Lawrence Welk does it the same way. So does

Leonard Bernstein or James de Priest.) Answers are usually keeping time, beating time, leading. **Yes, LEADING or CONDUCTING.**

Now that you are a conductor, let's see you really lead. Let your wrist be loose and relaxed (shake it) and bounce a little at the bottom of your stroke. Hold a rhythm stick if you want to. What could we add to our picture to show that some dashes and circles are loud? Make it a picture that is similar to the motion we make when we conduct: a vertical line. What teacher wants is to arrive at a picture like this: | − − | − − | − − | O. As the music sounds again, teacher asks the students to draw this vertical sign on their pattern: − − − − − − O. Some may do this: | − | − | − | − etc. It is merely a mechanical error, a misunderstanding as to what each dash represents, and what the vertical line represents. Remember that each dash represents a walk, and not all the walks were loud. The vertical line indicates which walks *are* loud. The picture should come out like this: | − − | − − | − − | O | − − | − − | | − − | O | − − | − − | − − | O | − − | − − | − − | O | − − | − − | − − | O

## Music Notation

*Now comes the magic moment.* Watch to see what happens. Using the side of the chalk, the teacher should quickly fatten the dashes | •    •    | •    −    | and add stems to all the signs:

| ♩ ♩ | ♩ ♩ | ♩ ♩ | ♩    | ♩ ♩ | ♩ ♩ | etc.

(If using the flannel board he should make the appropriate changes and additions.)

It is the rare student who doesn't comprehend what has happened; not merely the transformation of these signs into musical notes, with which he may or may not be familiar, but the complete significance of what these notes represent. To make sure, it helps to make a chart together.

We started with a walk, and made a sign for it, a dash. That turned into a musical note. Do you know its name? QUARTER NOTE. We also had a walk-hold and its sign was a circle. What is the name of the note it became? HALF NOTE. We also had a sign for an accent. In musical language it is the same but it has another name—BAR or BAR-LINE. In our written language, how do we say "the end"? A period. In musical language we use two bars close together and call it a DOUBLE BAR.

| WALK | − = ♩ QUARTER NOTE |
| WALK-HOLD | O = ♩ HALF NOTE |
| ACCENT | | = | BAR or BAR-LINE |
| PERIOD THE END | • = ‖ DOUBLE BAR |

## Apply and Prove

Notice now that we have moved through the third and final step of the procedure:
1. from physical action
2. to a picture
3. to the actual musical symbol.

Each step of the way the student understands what he is doing and what these signs mean. The teacher must now reinforce this. Again dictation first and then reading, using the real musical symbol. Teacher beats: ♩ ♩ ♩♩♩♩ . Student walks or finger-walks, discusses or answers leading questions, and then reproduces ♩ ♩ ♩♩♩♩ . A flannel board is highly effective here as the notes can quickly be manipulated. It takes so long to draw them! Madeleine Carabo-Cone gives her young pupils signs of quarter notes or half notes to wear and carry as they step the values. Effective is any kind of echo game teacher can devise in which the sounds are made and the appropriate term spoken and written.

*Reading:* ♩ ♩ ♪♪♪♪ pupil speaks the action-words:  WALK-HOLD,  WALK-HOLD,  WALK, WALK, WALK, WALK; does the action; claps or beats the rhythm.

## Counting

Let's go back to conducting this music. Remember another term we used for conducting was beating time. Sometimes our arm beats down, other times up. But we always dropped our arm down on . . . ? The ACCENT. This beat is also known as the DOWNBEAT. The other beat would be called . . . ? The UPBEAT. This time as you conduct the music, say out loud on every DOWNBEAT, ONE— ONE—ONE—. Fill in the other numbers now as you beat. Say as many more numbers after "one" as you need until you get to "one" again. It is usually obvious to most that it will be ONE-TWO, ONE-TWO;

however it is effective not to tell this but to have the students arrive at this themselves. This is to make sure that they understand and are not just copying. If some say ONE-TWO-THREE etc. teacher should remind them that every loud note (which the teacher should exaggerate) is to be called ONE. It comes out:

It helps to write out this diagram with the students. **How are we counting to this music? How does the music count?** One-two. In twos. **If the music counts in twos, why don't we put a 2 in front of the music?**

$$2 \ | \ ♩ \quad ♩ \ | \ ♩ \quad ♩ \ | \ ♩ \quad ♩ \ | \ ♩ \quad | \text{etc.}$$

**What does the 2 tell us?** That the music counts in twos. And lo! We are at the portals of measure signature.

We could write two equations. The bar-line is always just one thing, a picture of an accent which we name COUNT-ONE, and indicate by a DOWNBEAT. Therefore:

> **BAR-LINE = ACCENT = COUNT-ONE = DOWNBEAT.**

Another equation would be:

> **WALK = QUARTER NOTE = ONE COUNT = ONE BEAT.**

## MEASURE SIGNATURE

Have some fun and learn at the same time. Teacher says, **Conduct as I play.** He can use a tom-tom or play selected music at the piano; better still, improvise. (It allows more freedom.) When the students settle into a good one-two pattern, without any warning, he slips into a 3-pattern. *This is an inside joke which everybody gets!* No need for explanation. Those arms sticking foolishly up there at the wrong time, or coming down when they have no business to, tell the whole story. Everybody laughs and enjoys the joke on themselves, and then someone can tell teacher that the music goes in THREES.

Some people may slip naturally into a beat like this:  which is perfectly suitable unless teacher wants to teach the authentic conducting beat: Down, over and up.

Often curious students will *ask* how three is conducted—a beautiful sound to a teacher's ear.

**Count as you conduct: ONE-TWO-THREE . . . The music counts in . . . ? THREES. What number would go before the music?** 3. **How would you place the bars in the following?**

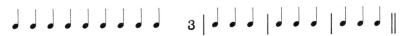

(Teacher can with-hold for the present the fact that the first bar-line is assumed but not written. It only confuses the issue and halts the learning momentum—the momentum of success.)

Conduct again. Some students will be happily tricked again; others may be wary. When there is a good 3 going, teacher slips into 4. All should count and conduct: 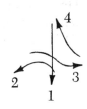 Teacher may show the authentic beat:

Down, sweep-the-floor and-up; down, sweep LEFT, sweep RIGHT and up. He may improvise, going from one count to another judging students' reaction by their conducting beat. The conducting beat is very effective here because it is a *picture* of the student's reaction and judgment. It shows him and his teacher, immediately, whether or not he understands. Teacher shouldn't hesitate to do 5 and 7 and 9. Count, conduct (the simpler pattern) and put the correct number on the chalk or flannel board, i.e.:

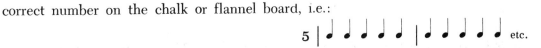

**The downbeat or bar or accent does what to the music? Doesn't it really "mark off" or "measure out" the music? That may be why the space between two consecutive BAR-LINES | ⌣ | is called a MEASURE. The number at the front of the music also indicates how to measure off or count the music.**

**If we refer back to the picture of Twinkle Twinkle which we made earlier**

we said the "music counts in twos." Two what? Two beats. Yes. Two counts. **Yes. There are two WHAT in each MEASURE?** Two quarter notes. **Yes. Then let's add that sign to the COUNTING NUMBER 2 . And what does it tell us?** There are **2 → 2** in each measure.

quarter notes → ♩

**Is that true? Are there two quarter notes in every measure?** No, at "star" there is another kind of note, a half note. **But maybe you noticed that on the word "star" you beat down *and* up, and counted**

ONE-*TWO*. What can you conclude? That one half note takes the same number of beats or counts as two quarter notes. We can say one half note equals two quarter notes. If you think of money, you know that two quarters equal one 50-cent piece. Or if you know fractions, $\frac{1}{2} = \frac{2}{4}$ . Then, coming back to the counting numbers we can say the sign tells us there are two quarter notes in every measure, or something which equals it. Teacher can point to the numbers, as the arrows indicate, while stating the definition: There are **2 → 2**

quarter notes → ♩

Instead of the note ♩ we could use the number 4 for quarter note, so the counting numbers would look like this $\frac{2}{4}$ . In the beginning stages we'll use them interchangeably.

Students sometimes ask about the upside-down note ♩ instead of ♩ , or do not recognize the first note to be similar to the second. This is a good reminder to us teachers who sometimes forget how very difficult and complicated the musical language appears to the uninitiated. A simple explanation about putting the stem where there is most room seems to suffice at this time.

The numbers at the front of the music indicate how to measure off or count out the music. So might they not be called a MEASURE SIGN? Because the numbers tell us how to beat or count the music, it sometimes is called a TIME SIGN or METER SIGN. Sometimes the world SIGNATURE is used instead of SIGN. If you put down all the possible names, you would have:

| MEASURE | SIGN | | MEASURE | SIGNATURE |
|---------|------|--|---------|-----------|
| TIME | SIGN | | TIME | SIGNATURE |
| METER | SIGN | | METER | SIGNATURE |

**In our lessons we will call it MEASURE SIGNATURE.**

Here the author would like to make a strong plea for a simple definition, such as the one presented here, for the measure signature. The traditional definition is a terrible mouthful, and it is not easy to understand: "The top number tells how many beats in a measure and the bottom number tells the kind of note which gets one beat." There have been faint signs from certain quarters in favor of a change, but there is great resistance, or indifference, to a simplified definition. Just because a term is traditional doesn't mean it can't be improved. Maybe the traditional jargon is one reason so many have given up trying to read and understand music.

From here on the study of note values and measure signature is so inter-related that it would be hard to keep them under separate captions and so we won't. Also, it would be perfectly possible to introduce the quarter and half rest at this time. Kodaly does. This text is going to reserve them for a place slightly later in the order of things, but the techniques presented then could be used at this point. See p. 17.

## Apply the New Concept

Now we need to reinforce the concept of MEASURE SIGNATURE. Here are some game drills:

### Place Bars

Place a series of notes on a flannel board or chalk board: ♩ ♩ ♩ ♩ ♩ ♩ ♩ ♩ ♩ ♩ . The teacher plays tom-tom or piano with exaggerated accents, students count and conduct to themselves and then

place bars in correct locations and place proper measure signature:

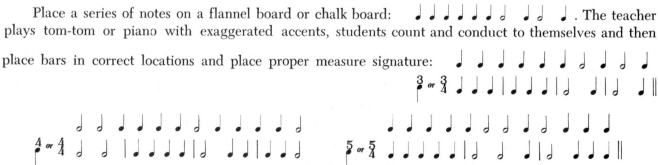

### Dictation

Dictation is always very effective. Teacher plays $\frac{2}{4}$ | ♩ ♩ | ♩ ♩ | ♩ ♩ | ♩ ♩ ‖ and asks **What is the measure signature?** If answer is correct, students write it on blank paper, or on the chalk board or the flannel board or on little personal flannel boards which the students can make themselves. **I am going to change one measure. Which?** $\frac{2}{4}$ | ♩ ♩ | 𝅗𝅥 | ♩ ♩ | ♩ ♩ ‖ The second. **How is it changed?** There is now a half note. **Is it correct? Does it fit?** Yes, because one half note equals and can replace two quarter notes.

Expanding the scope of the Dictation this way helps to circumvent the common error of counting NOTES instead of BEATS. This mistake can't be completely avoided. Whenever it occurs, teacher should always come back to this question, "What is the measure signature?" It is always the first and most important question. Teacher plays: $\frac{4}{4}$ | ♩ ♩ ♩ ♩ | ♩ ♩ ♩ ♩ ‖. If answer is correct, **write it.**

**I am going to make some changes. How many can you identify?**

$\frac{4}{4}$ | ♩ ♩ 𝅗𝅥 | 𝅗𝅥 ♩ ♩ ‖ The answer may have to be arrived at one measure at a time. It doesn't matter. The important point is that the student is handling the musical language correctly and the sound he hears communicates meaning to him which he can translate accurately into the appropriate sign.

Then the teacher should try dictating mixed patterns immediately, with the students always identifying the measure signature first, then the note values. It is always harder to start with a note longer than one beat. The counting and beating tends to falter.

$\frac{2}{4}$ | ♩ ♩ | 𝅗𝅥 | 𝅗𝅥 | ♩ ♩ ‖  $\frac{2}{4}$ | 𝅗𝅥 | 𝅗𝅥 | ♩ ♩ | ♩ ♩ ‖  $\frac{3}{4}$ | 𝅗𝅥 ♩ | ♩ ♩ ♩ ‖

$\frac{3}{4}$ | ♩ ♩ ♩ | 𝅗𝅥 ♩ | ♩ ♩ ♩ | 𝅗𝅥 ♩ ‖  $\frac{5}{4}$ | ♩ ♩ ♩ 𝅗𝅥 | ♩ ♩ ♩ ♩ ♩ ‖

$\frac{4}{4}$ | 𝅗𝅥 𝅗𝅥 | ♩ ♩ ♩ | ♩ ♩ ♩ ♩ | 𝅗𝅥 𝅗𝅥 ‖  $\frac{4}{4}$ | ♩ ♩ ♩ | ♩ ♩ ♩ ♩ | 𝅗𝅥 ♩ ♩ ‖  $\frac{6}{4}$ | ♩ ♩ ♩ ♩ ♩ ♩ | 𝅗𝅥 𝅗𝅥 ♩ ‖

### Reading

Then take these very patterns which have been placed somewhere for all to see and READ them back as individuals or in groups, clapping or tapping rhythm sticks on a desk or floor or book. Count aloud steadily and then start to play. Teacher should impress upon his students that they are actually reading music; reading rhythm and meter. Whenever there is difficulty, go back to walking or finger-walking. The familiar action usually straightens out the difficulty. Walk it, say it, play it. Slightly change the patterns as they are written, or write completely new ones. Read those. Do them backwards.

*Note*: the measure signature is *not* a fraction. It should not be written $\frac{2}{4}$ $\frac{4}{4}$ etc. Notice there is no horizontal line between the numbers of the measure signature: $\underset{4}{2}$ $\underset{4}{3}$ $\underset{4}{4}$

## NEW NOTE VALUES

Going back to a familiar activity, teacher plays walk notes on a tom-tom. **Are these walks or walk-holds?** (He is using the various languages interchangeably for a while.) The student should always prove his answer by walking or finger-walking. Add counting or conducting. (Although it may be hard to finger-walk with one hand and conduct with the other, it isn't hard to *walk* and conduct.)

### Trick Question

Teacher plays three-beat notes and asks, **Are these walks or walk-holds?** Students are usually right with the teacher and can't be fooled, because they have such clear machinery for determining the duration of a note. **What do your feet (or fingers) do?** WALK-HOLD-HOLD. **How many counts?** Three. If someone knows, teacher can have them tell how to write a 3-beat note, and what to call it. Otherwise, teacher shows—a half note with a dot called a dotted half note. Teacher need not make any further mention of the dot at this time, unless he wishes. It is not necessary. There is further mention made later. (See Chapter III, The Dot.) The dotted half can be added to the chart: (on p. 7 )

> walk-hold-hold = dotted half note = 3 counts = 3 beats.

Now the students are primed for what follows. **What kind of note?** Teacher plays on the tom-tom some whole notes. Students can use the routine and can answer. A 4-count note. A whole note. It is added to the chart. Of course a tom-tom can't sustain sound, but the question of rests hasn't been introduced so may not confuse. If there is any confusion, teacher should resort to the piano or any instrument which does sustain sound, or sing on some neutral syllable.

> walk-hold-hold-hold = whole note = 4 counts = 4 beats

## Apply and Use

**Now we know four kinds of notes:** ♩ ♩ ♩. 𝅝 **Which are these?** Teacher should play a group of one kind. Students finger-walk or count, or beat and identify. The teacher mixes them up. This is dictation of note-values *without* a measure signature. It is good to start with quarters to set a beat. Drills

♩ ♩ ♩ ♩ ♩ ♩ 𝅝 ♩

like this will probably be solved a few notes at a time with repeated hearings necessary. This doesn't matter. Remember it is not the acquisition of dictation skill we are concerned with, desirable though it may be, but the understanding of note values.

♩ ♩ ♩ ♩. ♩. ♩ ♩

*Talking about* this aspect of music is not nearly so fruitful or meaningful as *doing* it.

♩ ♩ ♩ ♩ ♩ ♩ ♩

Sometimes it is good to provide a stick for every student so they can echo play the pattern immediately. This helps to retain and to identify. Then as soon as the pattern is correctly before the students, they play it again, this time *reading* it.

Teacher plays: → ♩ ♩♩♩ ♩ ♩ ♩.   ♩

Students echo → ♩ ♩♩♩ ♩ ♩ ♩.   ♩

it takes form         ♩ ♩

♩ ♩♩♩                 ♩

♩ ♩♩♩ ♩ ♩.            ♩

Several more playings, then everyone plays it again while "reading" it from board or chart. Of course it is at least partly a rote procedure as a result of all the hearings, but it is establishing and reinforcing proper skill-building steps in their proper order.

Since a drum cannot sustain a tone, a final long note cannot be distinguished unless teacher indicates with silent arm beats that the tone is still continuing, or always concludes the pattern with a 1-beat note. Teacher might also play these rhythms in improvisations at the piano where the sustained tone can be heard, and then lift his hands from the piano in a large obvious gesture to indicate the termination of the sound. Dictation and reading of note-values within a meter should now follow.

## MORE DIFFICULT DICTATION AND READING

The problem to expect is that students will confuse counting *notes* with counting *beats*. In this case it helps to point out something that really hasn't been presented until now because it hasn't seemed necessary: beats move evenly and steadily and equally. From the equation, walk = quarter note = 1 count = 1 beat, this is implied, but now that things are more complicated it needs to be defined again. Like our heart beat, or the drip drip from a faucet or the click click of the 2nd hand on the school clock, beats move steadily. Picture a string of box-cars all the same size, slowly moving through your town. Those are the beats. On the other hand, NOTES can be long or short (rather than fast or slow, which implies TEMPO or SPEED rather than DURA-TION); and the only way—*THE ONLY WAY*—to determine exactly how long or short a note is, is to

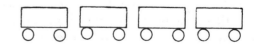

*count the beats* in each note, or to walk it. Therefore in working with the following dictation game-drills, it is best that the measure signature be determined first.

**What is the measure signature?** Teacher sets up beat: **Here are the beats going by.** Tom-tom: beat, beat, beat . . . 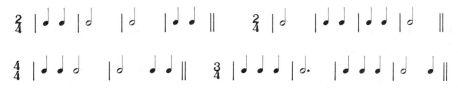 The music goes in threes. The measure signature is ¾ , meaning, there are three quarter notes in every measure or something that equals it. **What are some of the notes? Tell any you can identify.**

1.  It ends with a 3-beat note—a dotted half note.
2.  It starts with some walks . . . etc.

Teacher plays it several times until it is all determined. Students write using any of the techniques mentioned earlier. Other typical dictation patterns:

## EIGHTH NOTES

Teacher improvises on piano or tom-tom. **Are these quarter notes? What do your feet (or fingers) do?**

Everyone can tell. Run. **These are RUNNING** notes.

A delightful touch is for teacher to try to find a girl or two who wears her hair in a pig-tail or pony-tail, and have her run to the music. Teacher says **Here's a way to remember how running notes look: This is a quarter note or walk note.** ♩ When the girls ran, their hair flew out behind them like this ♪ **and that's the way a RUNNING NOTE looks.** ♪ It has a **TAIL** flying out. Sometimes it's called a **FLAG.** Boys can picture running with a flag. What's the name in musical language for a run note? **EIGHTH NOTE.**

Teacher at the piano improvises as follows:

**What is the music doing; running or walking?** Neither answer is totally correct. Teacher can say each answer is partly right, until someone detects what is happening. If no one discovers it, he can help by exaggerating hand motions at the piano and suggesting students watch his hands, or by playing more loudly with one hand while subduing the other. One hand is playing running notes, the other walks. **Yes. Clap the eighths. Clap the quarters.** He divides the students, some clap eighths, others quarters, then exchange. Using finger-walking, some walk, some run. Some students try to beat (or patsch—(slap the knee) quarter notes with one hand, eighth notes with the other. All of this activity is directed toward solving the question, **In the time that it takes to walk once, how many times do you run?** Two. A frequent answer is four, and it needs to be demonstrated that during four runs, there are *two* walks.) This is a much better way to determine this equivalent—through experiencing it—than through fractions. But now is a good time to point out that if we divide 1/4 into two equal parts, we get 2/8. **Therefore we can say**  ♩ **= ♪♪ = 1 beat = 1 count. Because it takes** *two* **eighth notes to make a complete beat, they more frequently travel together in pairs. Sometimes they are written this way** ♫ **as if holding hands.** Add it to the chart: run = ♪ eighth note = ½ count = ½ beat The eighth note can now be added to the Dictation and Reading drills. They can be done first without accents and measure signature. Teacher can mix up the notes. **What do your feet want to do? What do you hear?** Walk it.

> Clap it.
>
> Beat it.
>
> Count it.

Students can make up their own dictation patterns.

As it gets more complicated, remind yourself again about the difference between BEATS and NOTES. Use the analogy of the train of box-cars again: beats are units of time—boxes of time. Within each beat or box-car can be varied contents, small or large—the note values.

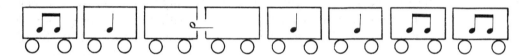

## Dictation and Reading

Here are some typical patterns for dictation and reading. With patterns as complex as these, some further guidelines are helpful. When notes are short, the key questions are How many notes to a beat? Even or uneven? When a note is long, the question is How many beats to the note? Always determine the measure signature first. This is a good time for teacher to point out that in music writing, we just assume that first accent, and so do not need to write the first bar-line before the beginning note.

## Common Danger Areas

1. A pattern most likely to give trouble is this: ♫♩ Students will say it sounds like three eighth notes. It *does* sound like three short even equal notes, doesn't it? We could explain it mathematically. 3/8 does not equal 2/4, but that does not explain to the student *why* he made his most logical mistake. The best way is to walk and run the pattern, (or finger-walk—less good). The student soon sees that the third note does not run. Remember that a running note always keeps running. It runs on to the next note. If it doesn't, it isn't a run note. It may have been *run into* ♪♪ → ♩ , but that note itself doesn't run on into the next note. Much stepping of the pattern run-run-walk, run-run-walk, helps to clarify this quite difficult pattern. Also playing a continuous string of each pattern ♫♪ sounds this way: ♫♪♫♪♫♫♫♫♫♫♫ ; ♫♩ sounds this way: ♫♩ ♫♩ (hold) ♫♩ (hold) ♫♩ (hold).

2. Remember also that long starting notes make a dictation pattern harder because the beat or count tends to falter. Students must count and beat strongly, firmly and confidently, ALOUD.

3. A habit which sometimes develops is stopping at a bar-line, or waiting or hesitating from measure to measure. A bar-line has no time value. It does only one thing: it indicates that the next note is count-one, the down-beat. Practice playing the pattern as if there were no bar-lines. Remove them if necessary. Teacher can play the pattern with the student.

4. Students often play a string of eighth notes this way:
Several solutions:

a. Teacher should play the rhythm the way the student is playing it and have him run.
b. The student should run and then play his runs.
c. Teacher runs with limps the way student is playing.
d. Teacher can tell him they must be even notes. But just telling him probably doesn't help him understand. The student already thinks he *is* playing even notes. He must be helped to hear and visualize and feel what he is doing.

5. Students sometimes play pairs of eighth notes this way:
Those are two quick short notes, aren't they? The remedy is the same as for the previous fault.

6. The musical pie. The trouble with the pie is that it fits only $\frac{4}{4}$. Of course one can easily see that four quarters make a whole pie, and two quarters make a half. But in $\frac{2}{4}$ or $\frac{3}{4}$ there is *no whole note* and there is room for only two or three quarters. What happens to the rest of the pie . . . ?

When you can read well patterns like those in this lesson, and you will, you have become quite good beginning readers and your teachers should tell you so. Students realize this already and are quite thrilled to be able to read and comprehend this previously unintelligible musical language.

## A Little More Complicated Dictation

1. Teacher beats. **Here are the beats. They are like what kind of note?** Quarter.
2. **You chant: beat, beat, beat, beat, beat. I'll play.**

Beat, beat, beat, beat, beat, beat, beat, beat, beat, beat, beat, beat.

3. **Instead of saying "beat" this time, beat a finger. Say "one" on every loud note. Start beating.**

One       One       One       One

4. **Add the other numbers:**

1 - 2     1 - 2     1 - 2     1 - 2

5. **The music goes in . . . . ?** Twos. **The measure signature is . . . . ?** $\frac{2}{4}$.

6. **What kinds of notes do you hear?** Quarters, eighths, halves.
7. **What kind of notes are at the beginning? At the end? Etc.**
8. **You write them down. I'll put them here on the chalkboard. In front of every loud note we put a . . . . . BAR. What says "The end"? DOUBLE BAR. Here is the finished product:**

*Chapter* **2**

# Additional Rhythmic Concepts

## WHAT YOU NEED TO KNOW FOR THIS LESSON

Basic Note values: whole, dotted half, half note, quarter, eighth

Meter and measure signature; accent and bar-line

Conducting

## BASIC FACTS YOU WILL LEARN

Rests are periods of silence which are measured by beats as carefully as notes.

Rests take their names from the notes to which they correspond in duration:

a two-beat note is a HALF note; a two-beat rest is a HALF rest.

### Basic Facts - - -

| | | | | | |
|---|---|---|---|---|---|
| ɣ | eighth rest | = | 1/2 count | = | 1/2 beat |
| ₹ | quarter rest | = | 1 count | = | 1 beat |
| ▬ | half rest | = | 2 counts | = | 2 beats |
| ▬· | dotted half rest | = | 3 counts | = | 3 beats |
| ▬ | whole rest | = | 4 counts | = | 4 beats |

(or one complete measure of silence regardless of measure signature)

Sometimes music begins with an UPBEAT (PICK-UP or ANACRUSIS). It consists of part of a measure; the first accent doesn't occur until the next measure.

Music does not have to begin with an accent.

## WHAT THIS LESSON CAN LEAD TO

Ties, slurs, dots. Then §8 and other compound meters.
Further reading and dictation skill.

## RESTS

Teacher plays at the piano and asks, **Is there any difference in the sound?**

Students usually do not notice any difference.

Helps from the teacher:

1. teacher sings on duh or other neutral syllable. Optional: students can echo.
2. teacher plays again at the piano and at the rests lifts his hands high from the keyboard in exaggerated motion.

Students can then usually recognize that there are silences. If they can't tell the name of the silence, teacher tells them it is a REST.

**Where did the silence occur? Locate it.** Students count *aloud* while teacher plays again.

**On what counts was there silence?** Two and Four.

**Say it—first without silences, then with the rests:** walk-hold    walk-hold
walk REST    walk REST

**Is this the way to indicate the music just heard?** $\frac{4}{4}$ ♩ ♩ ♩ ♩ | ♩  ♩  ‖

**No, every beat must have a sign representing either a sound or period of silence.**

**How many counts long are the rests in this pattern?** One.

**If a 1-count note is called a quarter note, what do you suppose a 1-count rest is called?** A quarter REST. **It looks like this** 𝄽 **or** ⌇ **(a Z backwards).**

**The equation would read** | ♩ = 𝄽 or ⌇ = quarter rest = 1-count = 1 beat |

A student writes in the correct rests in the correct places. A flannel board and flannel-backed notes and rests help greatly.

$\frac{4}{4}$ ♩ ♩ ♩ ♩ | ♩ 𝄽 ♩ 𝄽 ‖

Now the QUARTER REST can be incorporated into the dictation and reading game-drills. On the rests, say aloud the word, REST and separate the hands widely when clapping. Or see further suggestions on p. 18. Teacher will have to use a piano or some other sustaining instrument (his voice?) rather than the tom-tom now.

$\frac{4}{4}$ ♩ 𝄽 ♩ ♩ | ♩ 𝄽 ♩ 𝄽 ‖
walk REST walk walk  walk REST walk REST

$\frac{3}{4}$ ♩. | ♩ 𝄽 ♩ | ♩ ♩ 𝄽 | ♩ 𝄽 ‖

$\frac{3}{4}$ ♩ 𝄽 ♩ | ♩ 𝄽 ‖

$\frac{2}{4}$ ♩ 𝄽 | ♩ ♩ | 𝄽 ♩ | ♩ ‖

Teacher plays the following pattern: $\frac{4}{4}$ ♩ ♩  | ♩  ‖  $\frac{4}{4}$ ♩ ♩ – | ♩ – ‖ Through the usual questions students can find that there is silence on beats 3 and 4 in both measures. **How can we indicate this 2-beat rest and what would it be called?** HALF REST. **A little bar on top of a line. Write it in and add to the table.**

| ♩ = – = HALF REST = 2 counts = 2 beats |

More game-drills: $\frac{4}{4}$ ♩ 𝄽 ♩ ♩ | ♩  –  ‖
walk REST walk walk  walk - hold REST REST

Make up some. $\frac{3}{4}$ ♩ – | ♩ 𝄽 ♩ ‖

Teacher plays the first pattern again: $\frac{4}{4}$ ♩ ♩ ♩ ♩ | ♩ ♩ ‖

Then he makes a new change. **How is it changed now?** $\frac{4}{4}$ ♩ ♩ ♩ ♩ |  ‖
The second measure is completely silent. **How do we indicate the silence and what is it called?** A WHOLE REST. **A little bar beneath a line:** ▬

**Write it in and add it to the table.** $\frac{4}{4}$ ♩ ♩ ♩ ♩ | ▬ ‖

| ○ = ▬ = WHOLE REST = 4 counts = 4 beats |

The whole and half rests look much alike. How can we distinguish between them? How are they alike?   bars attached to line

> both in third space on musical staff (easier to remember this than which rest is attached to which line)

**How different?**   half rest sits on top of the line
> whole rest hangs below the line

Similes:  Think of a full bucket of water, which is heavy and hangs from something—the WHOLE REST.
> An empty bucket is lighter and can be placed upside-down—the HALF REST.

There is another special function of the **WHOLE REST**. It can indicate a whole measure of silence in any meter, even if the measure signature is $\frac{2}{4}$ or $\frac{3}{4}$. There should be the usual dictation and reading game-drills.

Teacher plays the following:

A 3-beat silence. **How write? How name? Like the 3-beat NOTE, it is called a dotted half REST.** The three-beat rest can use a dot ▬· seen more in instrumental music. It is seen just as frequently this way: ▬ ⁊   a combination of a 2-beat rest and a 1-beat rest.

> | 𝅗𝅥· = ▬ ⁊ = dotted half rest = 3 counts = 3 beats |

Teacher plays the first pattern and then the other: **Any difference?** Students often hear none, so exaggerated arm lifting helps *show* the silence. Some think this to be the solution 𝅘𝅥 𝅘𝅥 𝅘𝅥 𝅘𝅥 . They are not really wrong—it is a matter of attack, release, touch. Teacher can say, "If it is not staccato either, then what?" Students can then usually arrive at a solution.

> | ♪ = ⁊ =   eighth rest   = ½ count = ½ beat |

The eighth rest looks like a number 7. Notice it still has a tail or flag. But on the rest, the tail always flies to the left—⁊ ; on the eighth note the tails always flies to the right ♪ 𝅘𝅥𝅮 .

## Special Helps

There are many times when gimmicks appear to be more of an intrusion than a help, but in the case of rests, clever gimmicks can be used to good advantage. Even advanced musicians are careless concerning rests and sing or play through them or past them. Here are some ideas for you to consider.
1. say shhhhh or snore zzzzzzz on the rest.
2. silently place fingers to lips on rest.
3. while counting aloud for notes, count silently or in a stage whisper for rests.
4. say the word REST aloud and separate the hands widely when clapping and counting or chanting the music.
5. use a song like Bingo in which the letter is either whispered, said silently or replaced by a clap— or all of these.

> 𝅘𝅥 = 𝄽 = ⁊ B I NGO ⁊I NGO ⁊I NGO

Scotland

There was a far-mer had a dog and Bin-go was· his name-o (B) I N G O

(B) I N G O (B) I N G O and Bin-go was his name - o.

6. a "no-sound" instrument. An instrument which plays nothing! It might be a party favor which un-curls when you blow it ⌇⌇⌇

One student devised a kind of "bazooka" of the cardboard tubes which come inside rolls of paper towels. Blow into it on rests. Or use two tubes, one sliding inside the other like a trombone.

This is where percussion instruments are extremely effective because they can reproduce an exact sound-picture of the musical symbols using sound without pitch. Use the rhythm band. Wherever dictation and reading game-drills are suggested, use rhythm instruments sometimes rather than clapping or tapping.

1. Play the rhythm patterns on one or many instruments.
2. When reading such patterns, use a different instrument to play each note value: ♩ cymbals ♩ sticks ♪ shakers or tambourine

*Words*
Use words to locate the rest: § ♫ ♫ ♩ ♪  ² ♫ ♫  ⁴ ♩ ♩ ♩ ♩

Chris - to - pher Ro - bin    Ro - bin Red - breast    One two three four

Clap and chant all together. **Now chant the words softly, while I clap. On which word-syllable do I not clap?** ♫ ♪ **On "Red." Then we need to substitute for the eighth note an . . .?** An eighth
Ro - bin breast

rest: ♫ 𝄾 ♪ **Where is the rest now?** ♪ 𝄾 ♫ **On "bin."** ♪ 𝄾 ♫ **Where now?**
Ro - bin breast                    Ro - bin Red - breast

§ ♫ ♫ 𝄾 ♪ **On "Rob." So for the quarter note we substitute a quarter rest. Clap and chant.**
Chris - to - pher Rob - in

♫ ♫ 𝄾 ♪ **Where now?** ♩ ♩ 𝄾 ♩ **On three. Replace the missing quarter note with a quar-**
One two three four

ter rest: ♩ ♩ 𝄾 ♩

**Here is a song you know well. Listen to how it sounds if we replace every note on the first beat with rests.** Teacher plays America with a quarter rest on every first beat:

*[musical notation]* etc.

**Here is another song on the board. I've put a rest on every second beat. Can you even recognize it? Clap it, chant it, use syllables, play it on your bells. What is the song?** Deck the Halls With Boughs of Holly.

*[musical notation]*

An activity like this helps to bring home the impact of a rest—the necessity of observing rests—their effect. It also is a good reading drill.

## THE RHYTHM BAND

This marvelous teaching tool has fallen into neglect and disfavor. There have even been printed statements against it, listing the many corruptions of its use. Many teachers think that it belongs only in Kindergarten, perhaps first grade, as a fun thing, or at the most to teach how to keep time.

On the contrary, the author believes that in the rhythm band we have a versatile, most effective and appealing teaching tool. Its possibilities are numberless; its potential unlimited.

An important part of every learning experience is the application of newly acquired skill or knowledge. How do I use what I have learned? In the case of pure rhythm, which is measured sound without controlled pitch, what better mode of application than the percussion instruments comprising the Rhythm Band?

1. As mentioned previously, assign a different instrument to each note value. Make a picture-score of it: (See Figure 2-1)

2. *echo-playing* a la Carl Orff. Teacher plays pattern on an instrument (drum, sticks, etc.) and students echo (one or many) on their instruments.

This is really dictation—*aural* and *oral*, rather than written down.

3. *Create* a rhythm band score. Then try to write it down using pictures, notes, or any system you can devise. (Figures 2-2, 2-3) The challenge to put this instrumental score into musical notation is much greater, of course, but fully within the skill of students who have come this far. It utilizes the skill of dictation combined with the knowledge of meter and note values.

It demands of him all his rhythmic resources and skills: he must use the instruments creatively and appropriately and then be able to use his knowledge of theory and dictation skill to notate what he has composed. The teacher merely asks the same questions: How many beats does the tambourine shake, the triangle trill? On which beats? On which beats is there silence? What kind of rest should we write? Etc. (Figure 2-4)

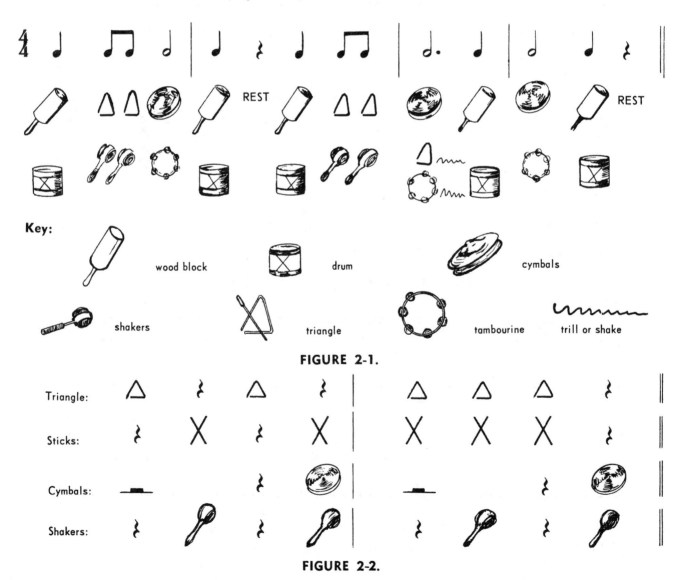

**FIGURE 2-1.**

**FIGURE 2-2.**

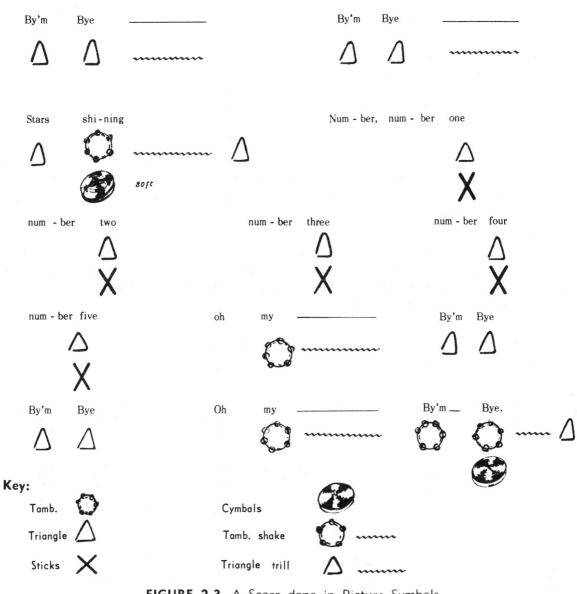

**FIGURE 2-3.** A Score done in Picture Symbols.

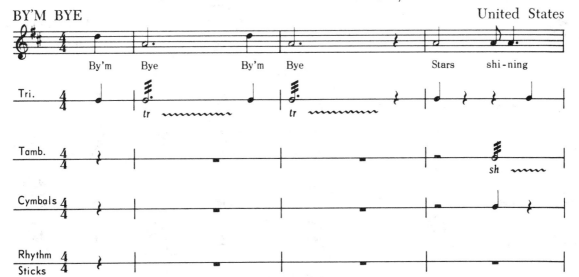

**Figure 2-4.**

4. *Reading* a rhythm band score. This activity is currently not in vogue, but it is one of the most effective teaching tools available. It is a legitimate application of newly learned skills. Students *must* count, they *must* listen, they *must* know the meaning of the symbols. Rhythm band is highly motivating because the students *want* to know so they can play. (The age doesn't matter; all ages love this.)

There is no hiding and faking. The teacher can *see* and *hear* immediately who knows what he is doing and who doesn't.

The meaning of rests is made eminently clear because it requires of the players the hardest thing of all to do: NOT play!

It makes students somehow willing to do what they almost always otherwise resist: COUNT ALOUD.

Each player has a score only for his instrument. It may look like this:

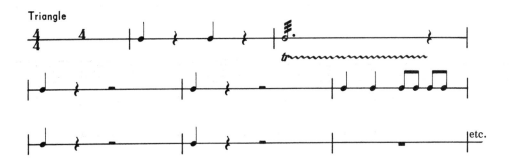

Since he is familiar with most of these symbols and has indeed read such patterns he can read and play this. The occasional symbol he may not know he can learn, such as the 4 in the beginning which means to be quiet for 4 full measures. He will have to count like mad! Teacher can tell him that so must the musicians in the San Francisco Symphony Orchestra, the Philadelphia Orchestra, and the U. S. Army Band.

The Carl Orff system combines percussion instruments with pitched instruments, uses percussion instruments in pure rhythm drills, and in combination with dancing, and other physical responses.

The Vandevere scores are an excellent collection for reading. Yet you have only to look at the illustrations to realize these date back many years; and it has not seemed necessary to bring the illustrations up to date. Not everything old is obsolete. The rigid rote teaching of scores such as these was discarded long ago. But there are now better uses. If scores like these are not so much used as they should be it could well be because not enough people are learning enough about music reading to be able to use them. Try them.

Also to be recommended are "Melody, Rhythm and Harmony" by Slind, published by Mills; "Melody Makers," arrangements published by Van Roy Co.; and "Music Making in the Elementary School" by Burakoff and Wheeler, published by Hargail Music Press. In these, percussion instruments are combined with melody and harmony instruments most effectively, and are intended to be read from score. Frederick Beckman has contributed some exciting arrangements to the Ginn series, and it is common now to find in most of the basal song series, arrangements for percussion instruments. These instruments are indeed beginning to enjoy a deserved renaissance in fresh roles.

In summary, rhythm band is a marvelous tool which offers many musical benefits, to say nothing of social and psychological values. Through it we can experience rhythm in all its dimensions—mathematical, visceral, kinesthetic, tactile, aural, oral, visual. The rhythm band requires a student to *count* and makes clear *why* he must count. It teaches and reinforces meter and measure signature, note values and the time value of rests. Because they must be executed by the player, the meaning of many symbols and terms is taught:  ⊲ :‖ ⌢  ⟍⟍⟍  ritard, crescendo, allegro, pianissimo, etc. The rhythm band involves the student: in participating he hears himself and others. It demands reading skill and develops ear training. And it is fun.

## USE OF WORDS

Another highly effective device for teaching rhythms is the use of words. It is not new in this country, but probably has received renewed impetus from the surge of interest in the systems of Orff and Kodaly. The basis for the use of words is the fact that words are a familiar staple of every day life and they have a basic built-in rhythm, accent and proportion which is indisputable. Everybody knows that the word TOGETHER is pronounced to geth'-er. If we used the musical symbol for accent instead of ', it would look like this: TO |GETH -ER. Other words would be as follows:

| | | |
|---|---|---|
| COLOR | CO' LOR | \|CO LOR |
| EXCEPTIONAL | EX CEP' TION AL | EX \|CEP TION AL |
| COMPLETE | COM PLETE' | COM \|PLETE |
| DESCRIPTION | DE SCRIP' TION | DE \|SCRIP TION |
| INSECURE | IN SE CURE' | IN SE \|CURE |
| DARKNESS | DARK' NESS | \|DARK NESS |
| INCONTROVERTIBLE | IN CON TRO VER' TI BLE | IN CON TRO \|VER TI BLE |

Certain syllables of words are longer or shorter, although this does probably vary a bit with speech habits. ASTRONAUT has three short syllables and if it were "walked" would be ♪ ♪ ♪ or perhaps ♪ ♪ ♩ . CAPSULE has two even syllables and could be either ♪ ♪ or ♩ ♩ , but it certainly would not be ♪ | ♩ for instance. Likewise with such space words as ORBIT, COUNT-DOWN, BLAST-OFF. Words like PERIMETER, SUB-ORBITAL go this way:

PER | I-ME-TER  } ♪| ♪ ♪ ♪
SUB | OR-BIT-AL

MISSIONARY IS | MIS-SION-A-RY | ♫ ♫

Moving even closer to home, names of persons or places provide useful rhythmic material. What is the rhythm of *your* name? What kind of notes are in your name? How would you play it? Write it? Where is the accent? Say it and chant it and clap it or tap a toe; walk it and play it.

Eva
Jerry
Jimmy    } ♪ ♪          Smith }    ♩
Johnny                   Jones }
Mary

Catherine
Barbara  } ♪ ♪ ♪        Pettinichi   } ♫ ♫
Cynthia                  Rothenberger }
Jonathin

                         Rosenthal    ♫ ♩

Joan  }    ♩
Jean  }                  Mason        ♪ ♪
Mark

Names like the following contain complicated patterns we haven't dealt with yet.

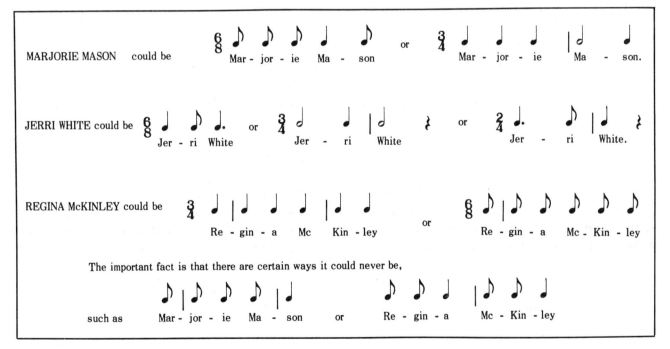

Words *can* be said more than one way. Usually it is the meter which could be varied, thus causing certain variations in the rhythmic values.

Why not? students sometimes ask. Because a bar implies accent and we wouldn't say MAR JOR′ IE or MC′ KIN LEY.

Yet when students are attempting to notate original poems or songs this is one of their commonest mistakes, and one of the hardest concepts to get across. It is hard because it hasn't had proper preparation such as:

1. reciting much poetry
2. chanting many jingles, and lyrics to songs
3. marking off accents and meter of a song or jingle like this:

1.
Where o where is dear little Nellie
Way down yonder in the paw paw patch

2. $\frac{2}{4}$ Where o | where is | dear little | Nellie |

| Way down | yonder in the | paw paw | patch ||

3. $\frac{2}{4}$ Where o | where is | dear little | Nellie |

| Way down | yonder in the | paw paw | patch ||

4. $\frac{2}{4}$ Where o | where is | dear little | Nellie |

| Way down | yonder in the | paw paw | patch ||

What are the rhythms of our streets, our town, our state?

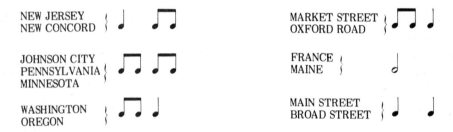

| NEW JERSEY NEW CONCORD | MARKET STREET OXFORD ROAD |
| JOHNSON CITY PENNSYLVANIA MINNESOTA | FRANCE MAINE |
| WASHINGTON OREGON | MAIN STREET BROAD STREET |

Play listening-guessing games.    Whose name        am I beating?
What street
What state
etc.

Make a parade of names; everybody chant each name twice; that is, speak the name in its natural rhythm very clearly.

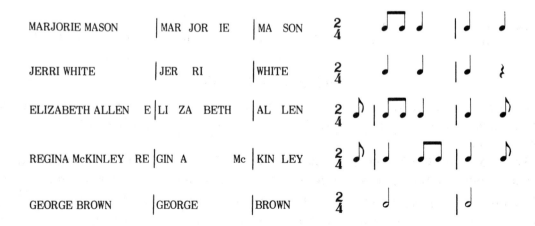

| MARJORIE MASON | MAR JOR IE | MA SON | $\frac{2}{4}$ |
| JERRI WHITE | JER RI | WHITE | $\frac{2}{4}$ |
| ELIZABETH ALLEN | E LI ZA BETH | AL LEN | $\frac{2}{4}$ |
| REGINA McKINLEY | RE GIN A | Mc KIN LEY | $\frac{2}{4}$ |
| GEORGE BROWN | GEORGE | BROWN | $\frac{2}{4}$ |

(You can refer to this page later when studying anacrusis: A -NA|-CRU - SIS    ♫ | ♩  ♩ )

Chant each name twice, then go to the next.

Walk (or run) each name twice, then go to the next.

Make a big circle, or lead a line snaking up and down rows.

Tap it with a pencil; clap it, snap, patsch it (slap knees).

Beat it with sticks.

Make a chorus. Assign one name to each of four or five sections.

Chant all the names simultaneously.

Walk them; tap, clap, snap or patsch.

Orchestrate them: first name played by sticks

second name played by wood blocks

third name by triangles

fourth by tambourine

fifth by tub drum

etc.

Make a round. This requires more independence and stability from the students and more skill and control from the teacher. Do first name twice, then second name enters; do second name twice and third name enters, etc. Chant it, walk-run it, tap, snap, clap it, orchestrate it.

## Mystery Rhythm

Use a device like the *Mystery Rhythm.* The rhythm alone of music is so strong that often we can recognize a song just from hearing the rhythm. Listen.

Teacher claps, taps, beats the rhythm of songs like America, Alouette, any song he knows is very familiar to the students. Usually some can recognize the song. This is dictation, of course. Other students can take turns beating out their own choice.

Write a mystery rhythm out on a board or chart. This involves reading and dictation. We must beat out the rhythm (reading) and listen to ourselves (dictation) in order to identify the song.

$\frac{3}{4}$ ♩  ♩  ♩ | ♩  ♫ ♫ | ♩  ♩  ♩ | ♩.      (Lavender's Blue) (fl., Her: 169)

$\frac{4}{4}$ ♩  ♩ ♩ | ♩ ♩ ♩  | ♩ ♩ ♩ ♩ | ♩ ♩ ♩      (Fairest Lord Jesus) (Her: 16)

$\frac{2}{4}$ ♫ ♫ | ♫ ♩ | ♫ ♫ | ♩      (Jolly Old Saint Nicholas) (fl., Her: 88)

## THE ANACRUSIS

**Let's review your conducting. See how quickly you can recognize the meters and the meter changes.** If teacher is uncomfortable improvising at the piano he can always beat a tom-tom, giving a good strong accent.

**Now listen to "The Star-Spangled Banner." What is the meter? Threes. All right, start counting and conducting: one-two-three, down—over—up.** Teacher begins to play or sing the song as the students count and conduct, but manages it so that the word, "Oh" falls on the downbeat: $\frac{3}{4}$ ♩. ♫ ♩  ♩ |
It's quite a funny feeling to find your arm way up in the air when your ears detect    Oh,— say  can

a strong downbeat, meaning a down-stroke for the arm. Maybe the song is not in threes. **No, the music is in three, and you were counting and conducting in threes. What was the matter?**

This time instead of starting ahead of the music as you did before, **try to start conducting with the music.** It may take several tries, but finally some may discover the music doesn't start on "one"! **It doesn't start with a downbeat. If you don't understand this, check it this way. Stamp your foot as soon as you hear a loud note.** Teacher plays or sings the opening phrase. **What word in the song was accented?** SAY. **How many words before SAY?** One—OH. **How many notes?** Two. **How many beats? Start beating and counting before the music starts.** One beat. **Do you see that if there is one beat BEFORE the accented beat, the music doesn't start on the accent or downbeat? There is no rule that says music has to begin with a downbeat, or on an accent.**

What do you suppose we call a beginning beat which isn't a downbeat? Well, what is your arm doing just before it comes down for the accent? Conduct and see. It is sweeping *up.* So we call it an **UPBEAT. And when music begins with an upbeat we have to indicate this in our conducting and counting. If we want to conduct "The Star-Spangled Banner" correctly, we will have to start the song by conducting the upbeat. We could do that several ways.**

Start conducting down-over-up, down-over-up and start singing on the upbeat.

Move your conducting hand out to a position from which you can sweep up for the upbeat.

**On what count does the song begin?** We found there is one count before ONE, the downbeat. The music goes in threes so . . . it begins on count 3.

| 3 | 1 | 2 | 3 | 1 | 2 | 3 |
|---|---|---|---|---|---|---|
| Oh,— | say | can | you | see —— | | By |

When music begins on an upbeat and you are not sure how many beats are in the upbeat, just go backwards from the downbeat.

Lots of words don't begin on an accent either. We noticed that when we were discussing meter. The word TOGETHER is an example. It isn't | TO-gether. It is to | GETH-er. How about CONTINUE? It isn't | CON tin-ue; it is con | TIN-ue. How about your name? We saw that a great many names begin with an accent, but here are a few which begin with an upbeat:

| Patricia | Pa | TRI cia |
| Virginia | Vir | GIN ia |
| Regina | Re | GIN a |
| Victoria | Vic | TOR ia |
| Cinderella | Cin der | EL la |
| Anita | A | NIT a |
| Jeanette | Jean | ETTE |
| Bettina | Bet | TIN a |
| Christine | Chris | TINE |

Sometimes the upbeat is referred to as a **PICK-UP.** There is a fancy musical term for the pick-up also: **ANACRUSIS.** The word itself has an anacrusis: A na | CRU sis. See if you can tell by listening which of these songs begin with an anacrusis. Listen and count and conduct.

| We Wish You a Merry Christmas | (Her: 95) | | Yes |
| We Three Kings | (Her: 92) | (p.146) Chapter 12 | No |
| Prayer of Thanksgiving | (fl., Her: 177) | | Yes |
| I'm Goin' to Leave Ol' Texas | | | Yes |

| Jingle Bells | (fl., Her: 149) | | No |
|---|---|---|---|
| Erie Canal | (Her: 256) | (p.200) Chapter 17 | Yes |
| Polly Wolly Doodle | (Her: 241) | (p.198) Chapter 17 | Yes |
| Amaryllis by Ghys | | | Yes |

AMARYLLIS

How quickly can you look at a song and determine:

1. Whether it begins on an anacrusis.
2. How many and which counts go to the anacrusis.
3. Where in the conducting pattern you would start conducting the song.

There are several hints:

1. If a song begins with an anacrusis, the printed music will probably indicate an incomplete measure—just a piece of a measure. It will contain fewer notes and may not be as long as a full measure.

2. The ending measure is very significant. It may not have enough beats! Music is very symmetrical and usually mathematically exact. When there is an anacrusis, the last measure compensates for this extra piece of music just dangling there at the beginning, and contains only the number of beats necessary to make a complete measure in combination with the anacrusis. The following are examples:

| | | Opening measure | Heritage | | | Last measure |
|---|---|---|---|---|---|---|
| | 4 | Downbeat | | | (p. 156) | complete |
| Charlie Is My Darlin' | 4 | | | | | |
| | 4 | Downbeat | 51 | fl. | (p. 83) | complete |
| Joy to the World | 4 | | | | | |
| | 4 | Mine \| eyes | 26 | | (p. 199) | marching \| on — \|\| |
| Battle Hymn | 4 | 4 ← \| ↓ | | | | \| 1-2-3 |
| When Johnny Comes | 6 | When \| Johnny | 179 | fl. | (p. 44) | marching \| home |
| Marching Home Again | 8 | 6 ← \| ↓ 1-2 | | | | \| 1-2-3-4-5 |
| | 3 | The \| first | 86 | fl. | (p. 83) | Is-ra- \| el |
| The First Noel | 4 | 3 ← \| ↓ | | | | 1-2-3 \| 1-2 |
| | 6 | What \| child | 10 | | | \| Ma-ry |
| What Child Is This | 8 | 6 ← \| ↓ | | | | \| 1-2-3-4-5 |

You can see this more clearly if, on a chart, we write out the whole song on one staff like this:

The __ first__ no - el the __ an - gels did say     King __ of Is - ra - el.

Then bring the two ends together by making a ring and you will see that the "tail end" of the song, together with the anacrusis, make one complete measure.

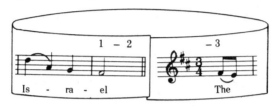

As indicated on p. 14, so much music does begin with an accent that the custom has developed *not* to write in the first bar-line as long as the music does begin on the accent. If the music begins with an anacrusis, then of course, a bar will indicate the first accent. Instead of

as we wrote earlier in the chapter, it should be:

## SUMMARY

The best tools and activities to teach rhythms are:
1. words—sounds familiar to us all—something we know viewed a new way
2. physical reaction—something we all do naturally as part of living; a natural response to rhythm utilized to teach a new concept
3. rhythm instruments—an expansion of physical activity which can be heard and seen and combined with other sounds.

When learning new symbols for rhythm a good order of procedure to follow is:
1. physical response
2. a picture—sometimes made in the air using part of ourselves; always written down
3. the musical symbol.
Approach the skill of Reading through Dictation. It is the reverse of reading; and although sometimes regarded as the harder of the two skills, in this case it is easy and makes reading clearer.

Try a simpler definition of measure signature: THERE ARE ————— QUARTER NOTES IN EACH MEASURE OR SOMETHING WHICH EQUALS IT.

A rest is a period of silence as clearly definable and measureable in duration as sound. In music every single beat of time must be accounted for in terms of sound or silence, and represented by a symbol. The names for the rests correspond to the names of the notes of similar duration. Note value has to do with duration. Should we refer to eighth notes as fast, or short notes? Are half notes long or slow? Since note values deal with duration and not TEMPO, the correct terms should be short and long.

To determine the duration of a tone or rest ask yourself one of two questions:

If it is a long note—HOW MANY BEATS TO THE NOTE?

If it is a short note—HOW MANY NOTES TO THE BEAT? EVEN OR UNEVEN?

A BAR or BAR-LINE is a picture of an accent. It separates the music into measures. That's all it does. It has no time value. Do not stop or wait at the bar.

Dropping the arm on the accent begins the concept of accent and bar, and begins the useful physical response of conducting.

Music does not have to begin on an accent. When it does not, we call the beginning an UP-BEAT, or PICK-UP, or ANACRUSIS. The final measure in such music will not be complete. Instead of all the beats indicated by the measure signature, it will have that number minus the beats in the anacrusis.

Sometimes we confuse one musical term with another because of laziness, carelessness or ignorance. The following are often confused.

| *beat* | *rhythm* | *accent* | *meter* | *pulse* |
|---|---|---|---|---|
| unit of measure | the mathematical arrangement of notes. | the loud or strong beat, represented by the bar-line | the mathematical arrangement of beats from one accent to the next | Sometimes within one measure there are other lesser accents, besides on count one. The other beats group themselves around these accents—primary and secondary, and each accent could be referred to as a pulse. |
| | note values, duration, long-short, fast-slow, even-uneven | | | |

## WHAT YOU CAN DO WITH THIS KNOWLEDGE

1. You can now start to read music.
2. You can use your ears and your knowledge to recognize and identify what you hear.

## SUGGESTED ACTIVITIES OR ASSIGNMENTS

1. Sight read simple songs or rhythm scores, using sticks, clapping, drums, etc.
2. Notate the rhythm of songs you already know in your head.
   use circles and dashes
   use music notation
3. Conduct music you are listening to on your radio or stereo or TV.
   determine the correct pattern and meter
   determine whether it begins on an accent or on an anacrusis
4. Step out a song you know well; identify your foot actions with words.
   WALK WALK WALK | WALK RUN RUN RUN RUN | WALK WALK WALK |
   WALK-HOLD-HOLD     (Lavender's Blue)
5. Tap out out the rhythm of a well-known song for others to identify. Use any kind of song; show-tune, symphonic theme, hymn, etc.

# Chapter 3

# Some Accessories of Rhythm

## WHAT YOU NEED TO KNOW

Basic note values: 𝅝 𝅗𝅥 𝅘𝅥 𝅘𝅥𝅮𝅘𝅥𝅮

Rests

Measure signatures

General reference is made to ⁶⁄₈ and to the dotted quarter ( 𝅘𝅥. ) which aren't formally presented in the book until later. If you wish you can skip over that part and return to it later.

## BASIC FACTS YOU WILL LEARN

1. A Tie is a curved line joining two or more notes of the same pitch into one note whose duration equals the sum of the tied notes.
2. Only notes on the same pitch can be tied.
3. Sometimes the tie is the only way to construct a tone of certain duration:

   a tone lasting longer than the number of beats provided in a measure ¾ 𝅘𝅥. ⌣ 𝅗𝅥    ⁴⁄₄ 𝅝 ⌣ 𝅗𝅥

   a tone beginning in one measure and extending into the next ¾ 𝅗𝅥. ⌣ 𝅗𝅥

   a tone of a length for which there exists no other way in musical language to write it

   ⁴⁄₄ 𝅗𝅥 ⌣ 𝅘𝅥𝅮𝅘𝅥𝅮𝅘𝅥    ⁴⁄₄ 𝅗𝅥. ⌣ 𝅘𝅥𝅮𝅘𝅥𝅮𝅘𝅥    ⁶⁄₈ 𝅘𝅥. 𝅘𝅥 𝅘𝅥𝅮
   
   2½ beats          3½ beats          5 beats
4. A Slur is a curved line joining two or more notes of different pitch. It has to do with the articulation of the notes: when two or more notes go to one word-syllable or when only the first tone of several is to be articulated when playing an instrument.
5. The Dot is a musical shorthand, often replacing a tied note. The Dot adds to a note one-half the value of the note it dots. 𝅗𝅥 ⌣ 𝅘𝅥 = 𝅗𝅥.    𝅘𝅥 𝅘𝅥𝅮𝅘𝅥𝅮 ⌣ 𝅘𝅥𝅮 = 𝅗𝅥. 𝅘𝅥𝅮
6. The dotted quarter and eighth 𝅘𝅥. 𝅘𝅥𝅮 is a typical dotted rhythm pattern—uneven, long-short, limping. It is musical shorthand for 𝅘𝅥 𝅘𝅥𝅮𝅘𝅥𝅮

## WHAT THIS LESSON CAN LEAD TO

1. Growing skill in reading music and in aural recognition
2. ⁶⁄₈ meter
3. Compound meters

Down    in    the    val - ley,    Val - ley    so    low _____

## TIES AND SLURS

Let's play "Down in the Valley" (Her: 8 fl.) from our flute books. Now sing it. What does the measure signature say? $\frac{3}{4}$ Count aloud while just this group sings. One-two-three-One-two-three . . . Now just listen while I sing the song again. Count lightly to yourself as you listen and tell us how many counts go to the word "low" in the phrase "valley-so-low." One-two-three One-two-three - Six! How

LOW . . . . .

is this note, equal to six quarters, written in the music in our book? Look. Two dotted half notes. Do we sing or play each of those notes? Do we sing Low-Low? No. Well, what is there to make the song sound as it does? A curved line connecting the two notes. Yes. What does the curved line do? It seems to make one note out of the two, and the one note is as long as the two together. The curved line joins the two. It TIES them together into one note as long as the two notes formerly were. We can tie together any notes we like, even more than two. Let's tie some.

Jeff, you come up and hold this half note from our flannel board set. Harry, you hold a quarter note. The rest of us will clap the beats and chant the rhythm—

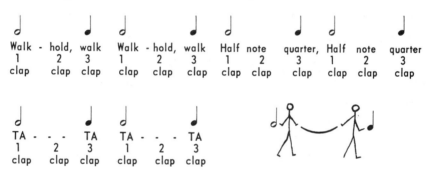

Now each of you hold an end of this rope. Now how long a note will they make?

Half note = two beats  
Quarter note = one beat  
―――――――――――  
total = three beats

Clap and chant again:  Walk-hold-hold, Walk-hold-hold, TA - - - TA - - -  
1 2 3    1 2 3    1   2   3    1   2   3  
clap clap clap  clap clap clap  clap clap clap  clap clap clap

Why not use a three beat note? What would it be? A dotted half note.    We could if the measure signature is $\frac{3}{4}$ or $\frac{4}{4}$: $\frac{3}{4}$ 𝅗𝅥. |  $\frac{4}{4}$ 𝅗𝅥. 𝄾 | But if the measure signature was $\frac{2}{4}$, could we use it?

Three beats wouldn't fit into a 2-beat measure: $\frac{2}{4}$ 𝅗𝅥 . We can't draw a bar-line through a note.
1 2 3

A better way to have a 3-beat note if the measure signature is $\frac{2}{4}$ is to tie a half note over the bar-line to a quarter note. John, you hold a yard stick here to be the bar-line between the half and quarter notes. This is how it would look.

Jeff—half-note        John—yard stick        Harry—quarter-note

Let's do another. Sarah you hold a quarter note, Jane an eighth. Hold the rope. How long is the note they make?

one quarter = 1 beat
one eighth  = ½ beat
total       = 1½ beats

Is there another way to write such a note? Yes, the dotted quarter. ♩. This is a clearer, easier way to write this note value.

## Six-Eight

Sing the song "When Johnny Comes Marching Home Again" (fl., Her: 179) without looking at the music. Can you remember or can you feel now what the measure signature is? Yes, it has the swinging, skipping effect which we have said is typical of ⁶⁄₈. Now I want you to count in sixes and find out how long the word-syllable "rah" is, in the word "Hur-rah." One-two-three-four-five-six, One-two-three-now-sing-When John ny comes march ing home a gain, Hur rah        Hur rah        We'll

6      1      2  3      4  5    6 1  2 3 4 5    6    1 2  3 4 5    6    1 2 3 4 5    6

"Rah" is five counts long. And since we are counting eighth notes, this word-syllable RAH is equal to five eighth notes. Is there a note equal to five eighth notes? No. Then we will have to construct one by tying two notes together. Use the notes commonly used in ⁶⁄₈ —do you remember: ♫♪  ♩.  ♩ ♪  ♩. ♩.

Now from these notes how can we make a note equal to five eighth notes? Here is a hint. Start with the longest note possible. Is ♩. possible? No, it is equal to six eighth notes which is too many. How about ♩. ? Yes, it equals three eighth notes. How many more eighth notes do we need? Two. What kind of note then? A quarter. Tie the dotted quarter to the quarter: ♩. ♩ That leaves an eighth note for "Hur"

♪ | ♩. ♩ ♪ | ♩. ♩
Hur - | rah ——— Hur- | rah ———
6   | 1 2 3 4 5 6  | 1 2 3 4 5

What can we say then about the tie? THE TIE IS A CURVED LINE WHICH JOINS TWO OR MORE NOTES, MAKING ONE NOTE EQUAL IN DURATION TO THE SUM OF ALL THE NOTES TIED. Here are examples of more than two notes being tied:

SLEEP OF THE INFANT JESUS                          French Carol—arr. Gevaert*

Hov - er  all  a - round  the  lit - tle  Lord  of      love,  Sleep _____ etc.

GOIN' HOME ON A CLOUD                               United States*

I'm  go - in'  home     on      a     cloud _____

LISTEN TO THE LAMBS                                    United States

Lis - ten  to  the   lambs _____   Lis -ten  to   the  etc.

THE  LONE  STAR  TRAIL                                  United States

Sing - in'  Ki   yi   yip - pi  yap - pi  yay _____

(a different version is in Her. p. 82)

Here is an example of the tie being the only way to write the note: Cielito Lindo. (fl., Her: 12)

In this song A is a two-beat note, but since we can't put a bar-line through a half note, $\phi$ we tie one quarter across the bar-line to the other quarter: ♩‿♩

## SLURS

**Here is a curved line joining two notes. Is it a tie? Sing it:**

Oh _____  say  can  you   see

Do we make only one sound from the two notes? No, there are two separate pitches. Why is there a **curved line then? Maybe you've noticed, there is only one word-syllable. "OH," on two separate pitches. The curved line helps to bring this to our attention. It's not called a TIE, but a SLUR. How many notes should be slurred here?**

When  love  is    kind _____

**Four notes. It should look like this:**

kind _____

**Here is another example from our flute book. This song has no words. What does the curved line mean here?**

**This concerns how we use the tongue when playing the flute—tonguing. If the curved line were not there, how would we tongue?**

too    too      too    too   etc.

**But with the SLUR, we tongue:**

tooooooo      tooooooo

Here is a question to make you think. In this example we just referred to from the Carnival of Venice, are all the curved lines SLURs? No. The curved line connecting the two Ds is a TIE. What makes the difference?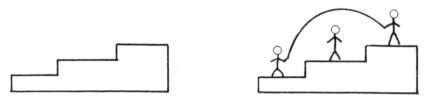

A tie concerns duration and can connect only notes on the same pitch. A SLUR IS NEEDED AND USED TO INDICATE HOW TO SING OR ARTICULATE NOTES OF DIFFERENT PITCHES.

Here are some steps—props from the drama department. If we place a person on each step and have the first and last persons hold the rope, what do they represent? A SLUR. If we take our identical twins and stand them flat on the floor holding the rope, they represent—the TIE. If two students hold the flannel-board letters A and C, and the rope, what is the rope? A SLUR. Different pitches. If two students hold a half note and an eighth note, and the rope, what is the rope? A TIE. It concerns note *duration.*

## THE DOT

Let's begin with a song we know well, the Thanksgiving Prayer (fl., Her: 177).

THANKSGIVING PRAYER                                                                    Netherlands

As we look this song over, we find it consists mainly of what kind of note? Quarter notes. But some of the quarter notes have something else attached to them, a dot. What does the dot do to the quarter note?

Chant the words in rhythm, while we clap the quarter note beat:

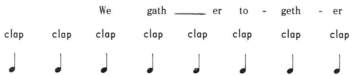

It appears that "GATH" is longer. How much longer? Chant the words again; this time this group clap quarters and this group tap eighth notes with your pencils. Remember, two eighth notes to each quarter.

WE | GATH - ER | TO - GETH - ER | TO
clap   clap   clap   clap   clap   clap   clap   clap

tap tap tap tap tap tap tap tap tap tap tap tap tap tap

How long is "GATH" on the dotted quarter? Three eighth notes long. **How much longer than a quarter note?** One eighth note more. **Or, one half of a quarter note longer.**

## Reinforcing Activity

Let's beat with drum sticks some basic rhythms: ready, drum.

2/4   walk   run run   walk   run run       This time, while you beat, chant.

Now watch how I change it and be ready to chant. Since the eighth note is tied, substitute the word TIE for the first run note. Ready, go.

Now, TA it.   2/4   walk  tie  run  walk  tie  run
                    TA_____  TA  TA_____  TA

Are you TA-ing both eighth notes? No, the first is tied to the quarter note. What does that do to the quarter note? Makes it longer—BY AN EIGHTH NOTE. Yes. Isn't that what we just decided the dot did to the quarter note? Yes. Then let's substitute the dot for the tie. Beat and chant.   2/4   walk dot run  walk dot run

Now just beat this pattern with your drum sticks. You could say   "GATH—ER"   or   walk dot run   to yourself while you beat. It helps if teacher improvises the same rhythm at the piano in a steady tempo, not too fast at first. **Stop chanting but continue to beat and listen to yourselves. What physical action could be done to this rhythm? LIMPING.** Yes, some of you get up and imagine you have a stiff knee and walk with a limp to our drumming. Some of you can do a limping walk with your fingers.

limp - ing limp - ing limp - ing

Now I'll pick up the tempo at the piano—you follow; and what does it sound like now? A horse— **What else?** You could skip to it. Yes. Get up and try.

gal - lop gal - lop gal - lop gal - lop     skip - ping skip - ping

So just as we have notes that walk (♩) or run (♪) or walk-hold (𝅗𝅥) here is a pattern which fits gallop, skipping, limping. Listen to it again. Teacher plays or drums or TAs. What words could describe how these notes go? LONG — SHORT  LONG — SHORT. Yes. Notice there is one single eighth note, instead of the two we are used to seeing in pairs. Chant and clap. Where does the eighth come?

walk  dot  eighth   walk  dot  eighth
walk      walk      walk      walk

After the walk. *After* the BEAT. Or you could say IN-BETWEEN THE BEATS. It's almost at the very last moment—as if we almost forgot that poor little eighth note and he came running after the dotted note crying, "Hey! Wait for me!"

Let's have a clap-snap orchestra. This group patsch (slap knees) quarter notes. This group tap eighth notes with your pencils and this group snap with your fingers the dotted quarter and eighth note. Ready, go. This time play finger cymbals on ♩. ♪ wood blocks on ♩ ♩ and sand blocks and sticks on ♪ ♪

Always do Dictation and Reading. Sample patterns follow. Refer to the lessons on Rhythm for specific techniques.

Read from actual songs containing the dotted pattern. For instance:

HUSH, LITTLE BABY                                                                     United States

Descant

Hush            lit  -  tle  ba - by                Hush            lit  -  tle  ba - by

Hush  lit - tle  ba - by      don't  say  a  word    Mam - my's goin' to  buy   you  a   mock - ing - bird

Hush, Little Baby. **Look at the measure signature. Look at the descant. Find the dotted pattern. Now leave out the dotted pattern and chant and clap the rest. One two three four:**

**Now include the dotted note pattern:**

**Now chant the words while you clap.** Teacher unobtrusively plays the tune of the descant at the piano as they chant.

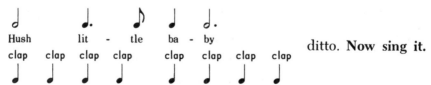

This way the students have *sight-read* the *rhythm*, but learned the tune by rote. If it isn't too tedious, they can be helped to sight read the tune using syllables or whichever technique teacher prefers. (Refer to Chapter 9 on syllables.)

## THE MATHEMATICAL FACTS

It is the inclination of most teachers to teach first the mathematical composition of a rhythmic pattern like the dotted note. It really is not the best way. *Telling about* something is not teaching. *Reciting about* something is not learning. Most students will be able to recite the facts correctly, but unable to *execute* the rhythm. Rather, they should learn to *do* first with understanding, then later learn the mathematical why. Even so, a dotted pattern like this is difficult for many a student to master.

**Earlier on p. 31 we noticed that the dotted quarter is equal to three eighth notes, or one more than the quarter note is equal to. Then how much of the quarter note is the dot equal to?** The **dot is equal to half the quarter note or one eighth note.** In this case the **DOT IS EQUAL TO ONE HALF THE VALUE OF THE NOTE IT DOTS. Is this always so? Do we know another dotted note? The dotted half note .We know this is to be a three-beat or three-count note. How many counts go to the half note without the dot? Two. Is the dot then equal to one half the value of the half note? Yes.**

$$\text{half} = 2 \text{ quarters}$$
$$\text{dotted half} = 3 \text{ quarters}$$
$$\text{dot} = 1 \text{ quarter} \quad \text{or } \frac{1}{2} \text{ of two quarters}$$

This definition of the dot will always be correct. It is possible to dot any note. What is the value of these notes:  dotted whole   4 beats plus ½ of 4 = 2    Total 6 beats

dotted eighth   ½ beat plus ½ of ½ = ¼    Total $\frac{3}{4}$ beat

More is said about dotted eighth in the lesson on and its derivatives, Chapter 17 . A dot is a short-hand. It replaces the slightly more cumbersome method of using a TIE.

Try some simple dictation and reading, with patterns like these.

## SUMMARY

Ties are sometimes the only way we can indicate notes of certain duration:

1. A note which is 2½ beats long is usually written this way:

2. In $\frac{6}{8}$ a note equal to 5 eighths can be written best this way:
   (see Chapter 4 )

3. In $\frac{4}{4}$ a note which is 6 beats long is written this way: The musical language doesn't provide another way, except by using a tie.

4. A note which is equal to two quarter notes could be written this way: but it would be simpler to write it this way: However, if the two-beat note occurs across a bar, it has to be written this way:

5. A table of dotted notes:

| | | |
|---|---|---|
| dotted whole | = | 6 beats |
| dotted half | = | 3 beats |
| dotted quarter | = | 1½ (in simple meters) |
| dotted eighth | = | 3/4 beat |

Of these new symbols, the dot is by far the hardest to master; especially the dotted quarter. Although the novice student will ignore a tie or slur until he learns their meaning, these symbols are usually quickly learned. Patience, practice, time and experience will help you master the dot.

# Chapter 4

# The Six-Eight Meter

## WHAT YOU NEED TO KNOW

1. Measure signatures $\frac{2}{4}$ $\frac{3}{4}$ $\frac{4}{4}$ and conducting beats for these meters.
2. Accent, bar.
3. ♩ ♪ ♩. = ♫ ♩. = ♬
4. Dot as used in ♩. ♩. ♩. ♪
5. Tie
6. All the notes which go to the same beat are often connected to the same beam: ♫ ♬
7. Eighth notes usually travel in pairs: ♫ "hold hands"

## BASIC FACTS YOU WILL LEARN

Six-eight is much different from simple meters in LOOK, SOUND and MATHEMATICS. Yet it does not forsake the basic equations of music. There are still two eighth notes in a quarter ♫ = ♩ three eighth notes in a dotted quarter ♬ = ♩. and so on, but they are used and counted and arranged differently.

1. In $\frac{6}{8}$ a beat or pulse is often divided into 3 parts, which is not common in simple meter.
2. In $\frac{6}{8}$ the beats are measured in eighth notes, rather than the more usual quarters; each eighth note gets one beat.
3. In $\frac{6}{8}$ when the eighth notes move quickly, the beats or pulses are measured in dotted quarters (♩.) which never happens in simple meter.
4. In $\frac{6}{8}$ notes are combined in rhythmic groups different from those in simple meter: ♬ ♩ ♪ ♩.
5. Music in $\frac{6}{8}$ creates a very characteristic and recognizable musical effect: swaying, rocking, flowing.

## WHAT THIS LESSON CAN LEAD TO

1. The tools to create.
2. More advanced reading skill.

## INTRODUCING SIX-EIGHT

The various steps of this lesson don't have to be in this order. They are all suggested ideas for making the point. If this particular order *is* followed, the growing suspense creates rising interest, an atmosphere of fun, a spirit of growing curiosity and search for the solution. If the whole lesson can't be taught in one meeting, it won't hurt to stop at places just short of the answer so that the student just "bursts" to know the answer!

## Plan A Trap

Teacher asks: **What meter is this music in, $\frac{2}{4}$, $\frac{3}{4}$, or $\frac{4}{4}$?** Teacher plays excerpt. A record can be used, but the piano is preferable. Teacher doesn't tell title. "Barcarolle," from *Tales of Hoffman* by Offenbach.

If answer is $\frac{2}{4}$ teacher has students count aloud to the music, and conduct. It will work.

**How many notes do you hear to count-one?** Teacher plays 2nd measure, 1st beat
ANSWER: 3

**How do we write this? When we divide a quarter note into two equal parts, we call them eighth notes:** ♫ ♪♪. **What kind of notes are they when a quarter note is divided into three equal parts— 3rd notes, 12th notes? It's not possible.** (Secret: a way to do this is triplets (see Chapter 17) ).

If no one mentions this, the teacher shouldn't either; if someone does, teacher should admit that triplets *are* a way, but can suggest assuming we didn't know about them. This helps to keep the students in suspense. Teacher doesn't give the answer yet. They go on.

If the answer is $\frac{3}{4}$ teacher has the students count aloud and conduct. It will work.

Teacher asks: **What *one thing* is missing to make us doubt it is $\frac{3}{4}$?** Accents on the notes with asterisks. Teacher plays again to show there are no accents at those places.

An answer of $\frac{4}{4}$ is incorrect because of frequency of accents. Teacher asks those who know the name of this composition to keep it a secret for the present.

Question to rest of students: **What could you imagine this music is meant to depict?** If necessary, teacher plays again, and emphasizes with his body and the music the swaying characteristic. Water, dancing, swaying, boat.

Additional or alternate question: **What characteristics does this music seem to have? How would you move?** Smooth, flowing, graceful, swing and sway, rocking.

**Swing and sway is good. What other sets of words might fit?** Rock and roll; back and forth; to and fro, etc.

Teacher should encourage the students if they are not too inhibited, to enact these motions with arms and body. He still keeps the "secret," but points out that we are accumulating lots of information about this.

Teacher plays Looby Loo (Her: 233), or an excerpt.

Same as opening question — **What Meter?** Teacher must be sure to give the stated choices of $\frac{2}{4}$, $\frac{3}{4}$, or $\frac{4}{4}$ — this is part of the *planned trap*.

If answer is $\frac{3}{4}$, count and conduct it. It works, but seems clumsy; too fast. Again, there are no accents at the asterisks.

If answer is $\frac{2}{4}$ count and conduct. Then the same question as with Barcarolle—**How many notes are on the first beat in the first measure?** 3 notes.

**How would we write it?** No solution. Teacher plays another part of the song; he sings it too and invites the students to sing:

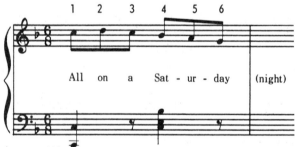

**How many words or parts of words (word-syllables) do we sing before the next accent (in other words, in one measure.)** 6.

If there are students who have known the answer and teacher has held them off, now is the time to let them give the solution. If no one knows, teacher shows that sometimes music counts in 6, as was just answered. Since a quarter note is usually the bottom figure, it could be $\frac{6}{4}$ or $\frac{6}{4}$. Often, however, for easier reading and perhaps because the notes are likely to move quickly and lightly, the measure signature is written $\frac{6}{8}$ or $\frac{6}{8}$.

ALTERNATE SOLUTION: Teacher doesn't even have to tell this step to the students. He can help them conclude this themselves, using familiar techniques they already know. Referring to "All-on-a-Sat-ur-day," he asks, **What kind of notes are the notes on these words? Use the way to find out which always works so well and so clearly—get up and step out the words; or walk with the fingers. What are your feet or fingers doing?** Running. **What kind of notes are running notes?** Eighths. **Then in this measure, there are six runs—six eighths. So, as our measure signature we can write—? $\frac{6}{8}$ meaning? There are six eighth notes in each measure, or something which equals it.**

This is called COMPOUND METER (the others are called SIMPLE METER) because:
1. it can be reduced into a count of two
2. it contains components of $\frac{2}{4}$ as well as of $\frac{3}{4}$

Therefore, those who answered $\frac{2}{4}$ or $\frac{3}{4}$ weren't really wrong—they were both partly right!

We should always be able to recognize music which counts in $\frac{6}{8}$ when we HEAR it because of the characteristics already noted: 3 notes to one beat (or PULSE might now be a better term); and the swing and sway. Now is the time for someone to mention the title of the first selection: "Barcarolle," from an opera, *Tales of Hoffman*, by Offenbach. **WHAT IS A BARCAROLLE?** A boat song. **Naturally** there would be a swing and sway. All barcarolles are boat songs. Almost all boat songs are in $\frac{6}{8}$. **All** music in $\frac{6}{8}$ will swing and sway (or maybe skip, if very fast).

## DISCOVERING THE COMMON PATTERNS IN $\frac{6}{8}$

Taking "All-on-a-Sat-ur-day" teacher asks, How many of these words or word-syllables go to the first beat—to count one? Chant, sing, count, conduct to get the answer. All-on-a. We said these were all eighth notes, so these would be ♪ ♪ ♪. A very good rule to observe in music is that usually, all the notes which go to one beat (or in this case, PULSE) are placed on the same BEAM like this: ♫ All three notes are "holding hands."

If you limited yourself to a walk, how would the walk go? Teacher plays the music or sings it while some try the walk. It would be ♫♫ a steady walk, which illustrates the way $\frac{6}{8}$ reduces to two pulses, or a count of one - two.

Listen to this part of Silent Night (fl., Her: 223) and count. Start counting: $1-2-3-4-5-6$, etc.

How many words are in the second measure? One—Peace. How many *notes* on that word, peace? Two. How many counts to each note? Three. They are each the same length. How can we write a note which is worth three eighth notes? (A half note is too many—it contains 4 eighth notes; a quarter note is too few—it contains 2 eighth notes.) What sign will add one eighth note to a quarter note? A dot. A dotted quarter note equals 3 eighth notes. (♩.) The 2 notes for peace are then ♩. ♩.

How about the last phrase, when the words go this way?

How many notes on the word peace this time? One. How many counts? All—six. How can we write one note which equals 6 eighth notes? (Do it by quarter-note equivalents if you have to: ♫. ♪)

Another way would be just to take the two ♩. ♩. and tie them: ♩.⌣♩. . This is really the better picture because it matches all the other patterns in ⁶⁄₈ which show in their pictures the division of the measure into 2 equal parts. Could a whole note be used in ⁶⁄₈? No, it equals 8 eighth notes, too many. **Could a half note be used in ⁶⁄₈?** Mathematically it would fit, but its picture doesn't fit:

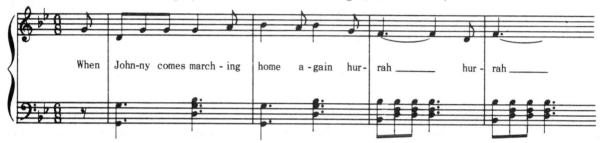

**We've said there are 6 eighth notes in a measure (6 word-syllables) or their equivalent. Let's take this song and explore.** Teacher plays, class and teacher sing: (fl., Her: 179)

**This time, some of you count while others sing. Count quickly like this: 1-2-3-4-5-6 (3 counts to a walk or ♩. ). What I want you to find out is this—in the second measure, the second time you count 1-2-3-4-5-6, What are the exact word-syllables being sung?**

Home a-gain Hur   (rah). **How many word-syllables?** Four. **They take up the whole measure, but can**
1    234 5  6     1

they all be eighth notes? No. We would need six word-syllables. Are they all the same length? No. **Which word-syllables get more than one count?** Count, sing and chant to find out.   ♩ Home   ♩ How gain.
                                                        1 2         4 5

**many counts do we say to each of these words?** Two. **What kind of note is worth 2 eighth notes?** A quarter note. **Then HOME and GAIN must be quarter notes. How many counts do the other word-syllables get?** One each. **Then they are eighth notes.** Home a-gain Hur

**Listen as I play the pattern of quarter—eighth (♩ ♪ ).** Teacher improvises on piano, or beats on tom-tom, or claps. **What words can we use to describe this sound?** Long-short. **This is a very common pattern in ⁶⁄₈. Try walking *every* note in the pattern—what happens?**   ♩ ♪ ♩ ♪   **A limping**
                                                                                 limp - ing limp - ing
**walk. Try walking with a stiff leg or as if you had a sore toe or a sprained ankle. All these actions help you to "feel" the rhythm inside yourself. If you do "Johnny" faster, you will find yourself skipping. In the previous chapter we noted there are other rhythm patterns to which we could skip or say "long-short." Two patterns are ♩ ♪ and ♪⌐♩ (See Chapter 17). If possible teacher should improvise these rhythms at the piano, or on a tom-tom, and have the students move and chant to them to see that this is so. But there is a difference between the *"long-short"* which characterizes these rhythms and the "long-short" of ⁶⁄₈. See if you can tell the difference from experiences in moving, chanting and listening. The ⁶⁄₈ long-short should be more lazy, flowing, stretched-out, smooth. Find some words for yourself. These patterns ♩ ♪ and ♪⌐♩ are sharp, angular, abrupt. The short note is *very* short. (Mathematically of course, the short note receives a smaller amount of time proportionately to the long note). If you can feel and note these differences, there is hope you can play and sing these small but important rhythmic differences more correctly.**

    **Look again at "When Johnny Comes Marching Home Again"** ♪ |? ♪ |   ♪ |   **If the *Hur* gets one**
                                                               Hur rah        Hur rah
**beat, the previous *rah* must get how many?** 5 beats. **How write it then? Begin with** ♩. **which**

equals 3 eighth notes and TIE to it a note which equals two more eighth notes—

How then could we indicate a note worth four eighth-note-beats? A tie helps here again. Take the largest denomination of note which fits the "picture" $\frac{6}{8}$ (♩.) and TIE to it as many more beats as are needed: ♩. ♪ . Remember, here again, a half note equals 4 eighth notes, but doesn't fit the "picture."

## Rests

WHAT ABOUT RESTS? Let's set up a picture of some common patterns to remind us:

Could we use a whole rest ( ▬ )? Yes, because a whole rest has 2 functions. It equals 4 quarter notes of silence (8 eighth notes—too much); but also a whole measure of silence, no matter what its measure signature. Thus is correct. Could a half rest be used? No, for the same reason that a half note shouldn't be used—its picture doesn't fit. How would we indicate half a measure of silence? Three eighth notes worth of silence? One answer is in the question—3 eighth rests ɤ ɤ ɤ. Also possible is a dotted quarter rest. ƺ. Most common is ƺ ɤ . It is also common to see ƺ ɤ ƺ ɤ indicating a whole measure of silence.

## HOW SIX-EIGHT LOOKS DIFFERENT FROM SIMPLE METERS

It helps to make a list of how music in $\frac{6}{8}$ differs in LOOK from music in simple meter.

### COMPOUND

eighth notes are grouped in threes—three on one beam

a dotted quarter often appears alone because it accounts for a full half measure, or a complete pulse

an eighth note can stand alone since it represents one of six equal beats.

$\frac{6}{8}$ ♩ ♪ ♩ ♪
     1-2 3 4-5 6

$\frac{6}{8}$ ♩ ♪
     1-2 3

$\frac{6}{8}$ ♩.
     1 2 3 4 5 6

### SIMPLE

eighth notes are grouped in pairs— two on a beam

♩.        ? needs something more
1 & 2 (and?)

a dotted quarter always needs to be completed by an eighth note in order to complete a beat—the dot represents ½ a beat (most likely ½ of a quarter note) requiring an eighth note to complete it. We rarely see one eighth note ♪ by itself in simple meter since it represents ½ a beat. In the pattern ♩. ♪ always think of that poor little eighth note running after the dotted quarter ♩. shouting, "Hey, wait for me!"

$\frac{2}{4}$ ♩        ♪ ?
   1 and 2 (and) needs something more to complete the measure

$\frac{3}{4}$ ♩        ♪ ?
   1 and 2 (and 3 and) also here

$\frac{3}{4}$ ♩.
   1  2  3

In each case the dotted half fills a complete measure. That is why we often see a full measure in 𝟨𝟪 written this way:

𝟨𝟪 ♩. ⌣ ♩. Just because the *picture* more clearly belongs to 𝟨𝟪.

HOW MANY COUNTS DOES A DOTTED QUARTER GET IN EACH METER?

𝟨𝟪 ♩. = 3 counts                                     ♩. = 1½ counts

But each still equals 3 eighth notes.

WHAT KIND OF NOTE GETS 3 COUNTS IN EACH METER?

𝟨𝟪 ♩. = 3 counts                                     ♩. 3 counts

WHAT KIND OF NOTE EQUALS ONE COUNT IN EACH METER?

𝟨𝟪 ♪. = 1 count                                     ♩ = 1 count

The three most common patterns we will encounter in 𝟨𝟪 look like this:

But rarely will we see them just that way in simple meter. (Of course students love to find exceptions to a flat rule, so you might make a game of finding cases where such patterns *do* appear in simple meter.)

Notice beams are different

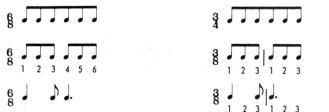

Each has six eighths grouped differently. Most important of all, they are counted and accented differently. Even if they should appear as below, the different measure signatures imply the differences.

𝟨𝟪 ♪♪♪♪♪♪                               𝟥𝟦 ♪♪♪♪♪♪

𝟨𝟪 ♪♪♪ ♪♪♪                               𝟥𝟪 ♪♪♪|♪♪♪        Here the bar and the accent it represents account for
   1 2 3 4 5 6                             1 2 3 1 2 3         a difference.

𝟨𝟪 ♩ ♪♪.                                 𝟥𝟪 ♩ ♪|♩.          Here also.
                                           1 2 3 1 2 3

Say this little couplet with good strong rhythm:

| Six to a measure is | what we are studying

| Six to a measure will | feel just like two.

## HOW SIX-EIGHT SOUNDS DIFFERENT FROM SIMPLE METERS

How can we describe the outstanding characteristics of 𝟨𝟪 in *sound* so as to distinguish it from simple meter?

1. Slow 𝟨𝟪 will always have a SWING AND SWAY. **What other words could we use to describe this?**
   ROCK AND ROLL                          TO AND FRO
   BACK AND FORTH                         LONG-SHORT, LONG

2. A fast 𝟨𝟪 creates a fast, snappy, "skippy" march. If the band seems almost to skip down the field, you can be pretty sure the music is in 𝟨𝟪. If you listen hard and try to determine how many sounds or notes go to one beat (or pulse), you will find that often there are 3 sounds to a beat—another sign of 𝟨𝟪.

3. Notice how often ⁶⁄₈ music seems to SKIP. Play or sing some of the following:

Bring a torch — Jean-nette Is-a-bel-la

Good Chris-tian men re-joice _____ with

Bring a Torch, Jeannette Isabella (Her: 70)
Good Christian Men Rejoice
Here We Go Looby-Loo (Her: 233)
When Johnny Comes Marching Home Again (Her: 179)
Or sway:
It Came Upon the Midnight Clear (Her: p. 20)
Silent Night (Her: 223 fl. )
Drink To Me Only With Thine Eyes (fl.)
Song to the Evening Star from Tannhauser by Wagner (see Chapter 11)

It came up-on — the mid-night clear

Drink to me on-ly with — thine eyes — and I ___ will pledge with mine. _____

Teacher should encourage the students to respond physically to the music. Besides swaying and skipping, what other actions fit the music? A gallop or limp is a good one:

The Wild Horseman from Album for the Young by Schumann illustrates this.

Italian Tarantellas are good examples; for instance Funiculi, Funicula. Or Irish Jigs, or the kind of gigue Bach wrote. The opening of Mendelssohn's Symphony No. 4 in A major (Italian) is a brilliant pell-mell ⁶⁄₈ and Mozart wrote a slow ⁶⁄₈ for the Andante of his Symphony No. 40 in G minor. You could play this on xylophones.

SYMPHONY IN A MAJOR, NO. 4     *8va*            Mendelssohn

A MERRY LIFE (Funiculi Funicula)                                                                Luigi Dénza

SYMPHONY NO. 40, G MINOR                                                                          Mozart

It is interesting to note that novice composers of any age often create in $\frac{6}{8}$ without necessarily realizing this or deliberately selecting this meter. The teacher, who has to identify and perhaps notate the song may be the only one aware of this fact. It is probably the sing-song effect of the swing and sway of $\frac{6}{8}$, matching the chant of jingle or verse, which causes this.

However, when students are engaged in a formal study of $\frac{6}{8}$ teacher can capitalize on this natural inclination by making them aware of how their composition would be notated.

# APPLY AND PROVE WHAT HAS BEEN LEARNED ABOUT $\frac{6}{8}$

### Dictation

1. Using the 3 basic patterns ♩. ♩. ♩ ♪♩ ♪ teacher tells the students he will play a measure on a tom-tom of one of the 3 patterns. They should be able to identify which pattern teacher is playing and write it down.

2. Teacher tries two measures, using only one pattern to each measure.

3. Combines 2 patterns in one measure.

4. Expands to 2 measures as in 3.

5. Invites students to make up and dictate patterns of their own.

6. Dictates a skipping pattern and has the students determine whether the pattern is the $\frac{6}{8}$ ♩ ♪ skipping pattern, or ♫ .

7. Try to write down a song you know is in $\frac{6}{8}$. This is purely a dictation problem. Do it a measure or two at a time. It helps to chant the words or beat the rhythm.

## Compose

Create an original musical composition in $\frac{6}{8}$ by ear, with words or not, individually or in a group, and then attempt to notate it. The steps would be as follows:

1. chant the words or music, finding the natural accents. Let the word help you or the music—don't try to *make* the accents. They are built naturally into the music, even the music you compose yourself. This is always the hardest step. (See the final chapter on composing and notating your own music.)

2. Beat out or chant the music a bit at a time, keeping a steady beat of 6 or pulse of 2, and try to identify which of the 3 basic patterns is used. Occasionally, of course, a pattern other than these basics will be used. Teacher may have to help here. (See final chapter on Creativity.)

## Reading

1. Teacher places patterns of two or four measures on a chalk or flannel board and sets some students to counting, some to beating; individual students or groups beat out the patterns.

2. Combines several patterns to be played simultaneously—a sort of rhythm chorus. Use either patschen-clapping-tapping activities, or a group of percussion instruments.

3. Tackle a new piece in $\frac{6}{8}$ for bells, or flutes, or recorders. Find the basic patterns, review them and tap them and count them, then try to read the selection through on the instrument. Teacher should avoid assisting in the actual reading, because then it is not reading but rote.

4. Try singing a new song as in 3, reading the rhythm first and then teacher helping with the pitches.

5. Teacher gives every one a percussion instrument and they try reading actual rhythm band scores. Or combine pitched instruments with rhythm instruments and read from scores arranged for such a combination. Several very good publications are "Rhythm, Melody and Harmony" by Lloyd Slind, published by Mills, "Melody Makers" published by Van Roy Co., and "Music Making in the Elementary School" by Gerald Burakoff and Lawrence Wheeler, published by Hargail Music Press.

## Try These Games

1. All the students are wearing Carabo-Cone hats either ♩. or ♩ or ♪ or ♩ or ɤ . They are seated in a circle. The teacher or a student selects one or more persons from the circle to make a partial $\frac{6}{8}$ pattern. They are placed inside the circle. Only one person is allowed to complete the group to make a com-

plete $\frac{6}{8}$ measure. At a signal, the players seated in the circle are free to go to the group to complete the rhythm pattern. Those left behind get points against them. Shuffle and play again. Those who

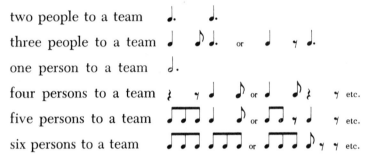

get 3 points against them are out of the game. Thus a gradual elimination of players. There should always be more people seated in the circle than patterns to be completed.

2. Send teams of students to make a $\frac{6}{8}$ measure. *What are the possibilities?*

two people to a team

three people to a team          or

one person to a team

four persons to a team          or          etc.

five persons to a team          or          etc.

six persons to a team          or          etc.

Six-eight meter is a world quite different from simple meter; it even uses its own musical language. To the student who has had a struggle mastering the fundamentals of simple meter, it is quite a shock to encounter $\frac{6}{8}$. Even though students make good progress, they can be detected avoiding an involvement in this meter. And yet it is a meter close to the heart of the Child in all of us. Six-eight has an irresistible swing and beat—rock and roll. So teacher and student alike should be patient with themselves and encouraging to each other.

# Chapter 5

# Pitch

## WHAT YOU NEED TO KNOW

A good concept of high and low.

The concept of high and low can be established by many experiences in the kinds of procedures found in all good methods manuals:

1. Indicating pictures of pitch with our hands, our bodies.
2. With pictures of objects in up—down relationships à la Kodaly and others.
3. Contour lines.
4. Echo games on xylos à la Orff and others.
5. Singing and playing good tone matching games.

## BASIC FACTS YOU WILL LEARN

1. A staff consists of 5 adjacent lines and the spaces between them.
2. The lines and spaces of the staff are a way of indicating exact levels of pitches.
3. A clef is a sign used to show us which lines and spaces, of them all, are being used in a particular staff. We say the clef names the lines and spaces, usually assigning its name to a particular line.
4. Although it is often customary to teach beginners first the treble clef and staff   some contemporary musicians have expressed disapproval of this custom, saying that the student then experiences unnecessary difficulty when he makes the acquaintance of the F and C clefs and learns that the 5 lines and 4 spaces of the staff can have many names. 

    Bass   Tenor   Alto
5. The Law of Stems: Stems go up on the right, down on the left.
    Stems on notes on B or below go up, on B or above go down.
6. Leger lines are short horizontal lines added above and below the staff to extend it.
7. The musical alphabet consists of the first seven letters of the alphabet, A-G.

## WHAT THIS LESSON CAN LEAD TO

1. Whole steps, half steps, other intervals.
2. The scale.
3. Key signatures.
4. Reading readiness and reading melody.
5. Aural and visual identification of melody.

There are several good approaches to the staff:
1. Begin with the Grand Staff.
2. Begin with one line and add to it.
3. Present the 5-line staff immediately.

## THE CONCEPT OF UP AND DOWN, HIGH AND LOW

Sing a familiar song of limited range, or of decided contrasts in range; large leaps, etc., or with strong lines in one direction. ("Hot Cross Buns," "Row, Row, Row Your Boat," "Twinkle, Twinkle, Little Star," "Joy to the World")

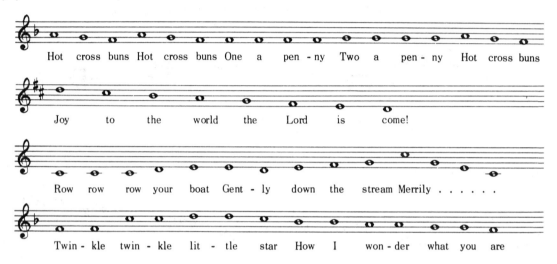

Teacher asks, **How does the** *melody* **go? Show me with your hands.** (Students don't always listen carefully. Some may beat out the *rhythm*. These terms are not always clear in their minds. They need repeated clarification and use. This is a good time to make this clarification.) Rhythm has to do with— WHAT? Answers usually are: time, beat, accent, long and short (duration), heavy and light.

Teacher can add: **it is a horizontal on-going characteristic, a moving forward ⟶ through TIME. This second, this minute will never be here again. What then is melody? It is the pitch, tune, high and low, up and down. It is a vertical ↓↑ passage through SPACE.**

**Now, can you show with your arms this vertical aspect of the song we just sang?**

Students show pitch levels with their arms and hands. **Now make a picture of it.** Notice: first a physical representation. Next a picture—a visual representation. Finally will come a translation into musical notation.

Examples: *Joy to the World* (fl., Her: 51)          (Shockers:)

*Hot Cross Buns:*
(fl., Her: 89)

If we have pictures for a flannel board or chart, it might look like this:

*Row, Row, Row Your Boat:*
(fl., Her: 27)

What words are these? ........................ ( Merrily )

*Twinkle, Twinkle, Little Star:*
(fl., Her: 41)

It is hard for a picture to be exact. How can we be sure just how far away, how high the third and fourth stars are from the first and second stars? There is a way to work it out which is a good learning experience and helpful for the ear. **Sing the last word of the phrase represented in the picture—ARE. Now sing the first "twinkle". How do they compare?** If you can't tell (some cannot) one group of students sing "twink" and another group sing "are." These pitches are—the same. So "Twink" and "are" must be on the same pitch level, and their stars will be placed on the same level on the flannel board. What about the pitches on the words just before "are"? How I wonder what you —. Write them on the board the way they would go: HOW I

       WONDER             Down by step, two word-

           WHAT YOU          syllables on each pitch.

               ARE.

Stars on the flannel board would make the same picture. Now sing the first part of the song and stop on "star." Twinkle, twinkle little star. **Hold it.** Now sing, "How I" and stop. Where should we place "star," in relation to "how"? "Star" is a little bit higher:  STAR.

             HOW I

Now sing to "little" and stop. Now "star." How does "little" relate to "star"? **"LITTLE" is just a little bit higher:**     LITTLE

             STAR

              HOW  I

Start the song and stop at "little." Where is "little" compared to the second "twinkle"? Twinkle is just below. Sing "Twinkle little star"—can you tell that "Twinkle" is on the same pitch as "star"?

          LITTLE

      TWINKLE ←——→ STAR

           HOW I

Now we have placed all the stars correctly.

Well, we know what these signs or pictures stand for, but if someone else were to see this for the first time, would *they* know? We could even make notes:

"Twinkle" ♩ ♩ ♪ ♪ ♪ ♪ ♩ ♪ ♪ ♪ ♪ ♩ ♩ ♩ ♩ ♩

Hot Cross Buns ♩ ♩ ♩ ♩ ♩ ♩ ♫ ♫ ♫ ♩ ♩ ♩ ♩

but it still would not always be clear.

# THE STAFF: HOW TO INDICATE PRECISE PITCH LEVELS

How was it finally decided to indicate pitches clearly? A series of horizontal lines was devised to divide empty space into levels of pitches—or *degrees* of pitches. It is called a STAFF. When STAFFS or STAVES were first used, they were made up of many different numbers of lines. A staff which we still use today is the GRAND STAFF, using many more lines and spaces than you are used to seeing: eleven lines.

Can you imagine trying to keep your place on *that* staff? And of course each line and space had to have a name. What did they use?—letters of the alphabet, but only the first seven. A way to remember the number of letters in the musical alphabet is to think of the week—seven days in the week, seven letters in the musical alphabet.

Where should we begin naming the staff?—at the beginning or bottom. In music, the beginning place is usually the bottom. Starting at the bottom, and at the beginning of the alphabet:

Sometimes someone asks why the letters naming the grand staff don't begin on the bottom *line* instead of the bottom space. The answer is that even this great big staff is only a piece, so-to-speak, out of the middle of the piano keyboard, which can be considered to be a picture of the entire range of musical pitch. If we look at the very lowest note on a piano, we see its name is indeed A, the first letter.

It still isn't easy to find your way on this big staff, is it? However, if your voice is high, or you play a high instrument (flute, violin) you use only the top part of the staff; and if your voice is low, or you play a low instrument (bassoon, string bass), you use only the lower part of the staff. So it was decided to divide the Grand Staff in half and make two staffs, or staves. If you've counted the lines you will see there are eleven lines which doesn't divide evenly in half. One line is left over: C is left in the middle on its own personal private line.

If it is to be included with the bottom staff, it will appear above the staff: But if it is included with the top staff it will appear below, but it is the same C. And that C sitting there on its personal private line is everybody's friend, *middle C*, which everyone knows is just to the left of the name on the piano. It is usually easy to remember C.

Now notice what happens if we place the lower half of the Grand Staff next to the top half:

For example, the 3rd line has a different name on each staff. So do all the lines and spaces. Take the 2nd line; on the bottom half it is named B, on the top half it is G. The 3rd space is named E on the bottom half; C on the top. And so on. Everyone is different. Of course, piano players know this already. Their left hand must learn one language, their right another. The two hands must read and play these different languages at THE SAME TIME. Maybe they have wondered what person could think up such a mean diabolical scheme! Now you can see it just *happened* as a consequence of dividing up the Grand Staff. Nobody did it deliberately out of meanness. But it does complicate matters. When the Grand Staff is divided in half, each half consists of 5 lines and the 4 spaces in between—the size we are more familiar with. Which half is this, the bottom or the top? Whichever answer you gave, you are as much right as wrong. The truth is, we can't tell until we have an identification tag which labels or names the staff. We need a sign. What is it called and where does it go? It is called a

CLEF and it goes at the beginning of the staff. What was once an old-fashioned flowery kind of G has turned into 𝄞 . And what was once an old-fashioned kind of F has turned into 𝄢:

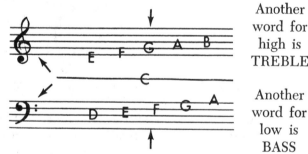

Another word for high is TREBLE

Another word for low is BASS

So 𝄞 is called the TREBLE CLEF or G CLEF which curls around the line G and 𝄢: is called the BASS CLEF or F CLEF which seems to single out the line F for attention.

## C Clef

Suppose one wanted to use only the middle lines and spaces of the grand staff—some instruments do (viola, trombone, bassoon). There is a way to build a staff around the middle C. Refer to our pictures of the grand staff or the other staves to answer these questions: Put middle C literally in the middle —C . If the staff has 5 lines, how many go above C? Two. What will their names be? E and G above: Which two below? A and F below And since C is so important in this arrangement of lines and spaces, the clef is called – – ? C CLEF. It looks like this:

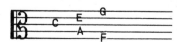

## Learning the Names of the Staff Degrees

What are some ways to get to know the names of the lines and spaces of the staff (known as DEGREES)—for the present, the treble staff?

Well, there is good old reliable  or Every Good Boy Does Fine which

isn't as good grammar; and F A C E.

A good fun drill is to spell words with notes:

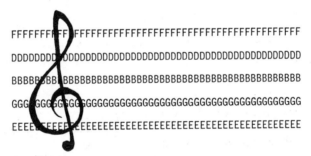

C A G E D     F A C A D E     B A G G A G E

Sometimes start with the words and fill in the notes; other times start with the notes and fill in the letters to make words. Have teams and contests and work sheets and homework, etc.

The best way is to learn them just by using them. Resonator bells or tone blocks are excellent because one single bell can be held in the hand, its name is printed clearly on it, and it must be played when its picture appears on the staff. Plenty of experience with these bells, or xylophones, or flutes as indicated in the many fine Methods texts and basal song series will help to make the names more familiar. The best way to learn almost any aspect of music reading is through these instruments. Singing drills can help too especially if they are related to playing experiences, and not overdone so as to spoil the singing experience.

Use the Carabo-Cone version of the treble staff.

FFFFFFFFFF FFFFFFFFFFFFFFFFFFFFFFFFFFFFFFFFFFFFFFF

DDDDDDDDD DDDDDDDDDDDDDDDDDDDDDDDDDDDDDDDDDDDDDDDD

BBBBBBBBB BBBBBBBBBBBBBBBBBBBBBBBBBBBBBBBBBBBBBBBBBB

GGGGGGGGGGGGGGGGGGGGGGGGGGGGGGGGGGGGGGGGGGGGGGGGGG

EEEEEEEEEE EEEEEEEEEEEEEEEEEEEEEEEEEEEEEEEEEEEEEE

From "How to Help Children Learn Music" by Madeleine Carabo-Cone and Beatrice Royt. Copyright 1953, by Cone-Royt Publications. Reprinted by Permission of Harper & Row, Publishers.

Sing a familiar song from the score (from the written page or chart or chalk board) but on letter names. Since the tune is *familiar,* all the concentration can be applied to letter names. This won't work with an unfamiliar song, at least without plenty of preparation.

Switch constantly from playing to singing. Play a short song through on instruments, sing it on letter names, play it, beat the rhythm, chant the words, sing it on letter names, or numbers, or on syllables, or words, play it, etc. In this way the more-easily-mastered instruments create a rote-note learning situation regarding the singing; and enough experiences like this build readiness for, and lead to actual sight *singing.*

## The Law of Stems

There is a rule about writing notes on the staff. It is meant to keep the notation *on* the staff rather than extending off. The rule says stems go up on the right, down on the left; up when the note is below or on the 3rd line, down when the note is above or on the 3rd line.

wrong          correct

## ANOTHER WAY TO INTRODUCE THE STAFF

Another way to introduce the staff is to begin from the opposite end; from nothing to one line to two, etc. After making a picture of a song such as Hot Cross Buns, as in the previous procedure on p. 52,  teacher can ask, If I divide this empty space this way, Here $\frac{above}{below}$ how could we arrange the three notes? above here below Suppose we used two lines, how then would we arrange it?

here
line - space - line

Using one line, how could we place the words of Au Claire de la Lune ? (Playing to Pierrot)

Or the notes?

Using two lines?

The next step would be a 4-note song, such as Chairs to Mend

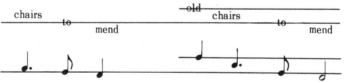

A 5-note song could be Jingle Bells:

And so on. When teacher leads a student to build this system step by step, as if it were his own, there is a much better chance that he will really understand it.

A 6-note song is All My Little Ducklings, or the first part of Long Long Ago (Her: 204) (Chapter 6).

Similar procedures to these listed here can be applied to the bass staff and to the C clef, and can be introduced at this time or when desired; which might be much later. The important thing is to teach it when it is pertinent and meaningful. If students will have no further immediate use for the knowledge, it seems inappropriate and unnecessary to go further than the material here covered. The teacher should wait until the situation requires it or students inquire about it. (Of course, the teacher can always manage to **make** the situation "require" it.) What might such situations be?

## MOTIVATING INTEREST IN THE BASS STAFF

Those students who play orchestral instruments can provide the motivation for further exploration. Either they make inquiries or are used as illustrations by the teacher for further development of the topic.

If Orff instruments are being used in the classrom, the tympani, bass xylophone and other drums may provide the stepping off place for the teacher to provide reasons for learning to read the bass staff. Instead of playing by ear and rote which is the Orff approach, pose the problem of writing out the notes they play, and the problem of clef is presented.

From 6th grade on up, there is the very real situation of the boys' voices changing. Their voices are "falling off" the treble staff and down onto the bass staff just as we saw it in the Grand Staff. A simple harmony part or descant for these voices (such as one finds in the excellent Kjos publications of descant books by the Krones) is just the solution here. The boys really have to go through several brand new learning experiences: how to handle an entirely new and different singing voice; how to read and recognize the music written for this new voice. To illustrate, pose a problem to the students; or trap them!

1. Start a song which is being sung for fun by memory, in such a low key that the girls and younger boys complain that it is too low, but the changed or changing voices can handle it. This helps us understand something about range and lends a bit of badly needed prestige to the boys, to whom some puzzling things are happening.

2. Listen to some bass instrument being played, live or recorded, and set out to find what range on the piano corresponds to its range, and how to write the notes. The trial and error method enables any student to participate.

3. Attempt to write down the notes those boys are singing. Or take a simple descant they know and try to write it. It is sometimes fun to take a song or descant which descends by step, and deliberately pitch it so that a writing problem develops.    For instance, take  Marching to Praetoria  in the key of C or B or B♭. Use a descant:     do    ti    la    so         Suggest the students find and write
                                                                Marching,   marching etc.

the correct notes for the descant, either by using syllables or by the "hunt and peck" system at the piano, resonator bells or xylophone. Immediately the problem arises that the notes are "falling off" the staff and are too low for the girls to sing. It introduces or re-introduces LEGER (sometimes spelled ledger) LINES, extra lines added to the staff (refer to end of this chapter), which are not easy to read. What is an easier solution? Why don't we remember the Bass staff as it came from the Grand Staff and use that?

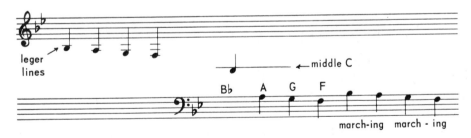

4. Find the notes on the piano or bass xylo, label them, and there is the basis for further drill like those words and spelling games suggested on p. 56.

5.  Or what could be more simple but clever than the staff of letters devised by Madeleine Carabo-Cone:

## C Clef

Instruments which play in a similar range to the Praetoria descant might just as well extract those lines and spaces from the Grand Staff to use as their staff. We noted that the clef which is used singles out C, and is called the C clef. The staves would look like these:

Alto        Tenor

## Related Listening

Appropriate related listening would be examples from the various albums on Instruments of the Orchestra by a number of companies; Second movement, second theme (for string basses) from Beethoven's Fifth Symphony; Knight Rupert from Album for the Young by Schumann; the Elephant theme from Carnival of the Animals by Saint-Saens.

## LEGER LINES

Teacher poses a problem to the students. **Let's learn a descant to Marching to Praetoria.** (Whatever song he uses should be one his students already know.) **The descant goes this way:**

do   ti   la   so      do   ti   la   so
marching  marching  marching  marching

**What direction?** Down. **How?** By step. Teacher deliberately places the song in a key which will take the descant off the staff, and hopefully out of the range of the girls' voices and that of boys with unchanged voices. Only those boys with changing voices will be able to sing the descant. Teacher must not let the girls use their "blues" chest voice. **Here is some music only some of our boys can sing. Let's see where the notes would go.** Teacher sets up the key of D. Several ways to proceed from here:

1.  If our descant starts here, use the hunt and peck method on piano to determine the remaining notes.

2.  If the students know syllables well or can read some music, teacher can ask: **In this key, what notes would we use for the syllables of our descant, do, ti, la, so.** Answer: D, C♯, B, A.

3.  **If the descant goes down by step, would it look like this?**
    here

**We seem to have run out of staff, and the notes are "falling off the staff." What note do we know that has its own private personal line?** C. **Why don't we use that?** Who has some more ideas to make the descant clearer? Why not add more extra lines? After all, the Grand Staff has many more.

Just like a rope ladder we are letting out a window—say, out of the D space:

Notice we add the extra lines only as we need them, and don't forget to use the spaces in between.

How can we know what to name those lines? Several ways:

1. Refer to the picture of the Grand Staff.
2. Use middle C as a point of reference—the space under C would be B, then the next line would

be A, and so on.

There is a name for these extra lines—LEGER LINES. They can be used at the top of the staff as

well—picture an extension ladder: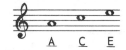

For instance, if we were to write out a scale beginning on B, the top notes would be "lost in space"
if we did not use leger lines:

Leger lines are short horizontal lines added above or below the staff to extend it.

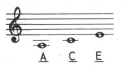

## SUMMARY

The staff is a way to divide space into specific levels of pitch. Theoretically we can use any five
adjacent lines we wish; in practice certain groups of lines are used more than others. These we identify by means of signs called clefs. When more than five lines are needed we just borrow them from
the Grand Staff and add them to the staff, calling them leger lines.

## SUGGESTED ASSIGNMENTS

1. Spell words on the treble staff.

   A   C   E

2. Spell them a second time using leger lines.

   A   C   E

3. Spell words on the bass staff.

   A   C   E

## WHAT YOU CAN DO WITH THIS NEW KNOWLEDGE

1. Learn about steps and half steps.
2. Learn about other intervals.
3. Move to other reading readiness and reading experiences.
4. Learn about the scale.
5. Begin to identify melodic movement visually and aurally.

# Chapter 6

# Introduction to the Scale

## WHAT YOU NEED TO KNOW

This chapter is organized with the absolute beginner in mind. However, even the more experienced pupil will appreciate the review as an opportunity for refreshing and clarifying his memory. And even the so-called beginner has now lived enough years surrounded by music from radio, TV, church and school to have acquired a reservoir of musical vernacular whether he is aware of it or not.

Stored somewhere in his knowledge there is likely to be the fact that the musical alphabet goes from A to G, that music is written upon lines and spaces called a staff and is sometimes arranged into something called a *scale*, whose sound is recognizable to him.

If educators are participating in the laying of this foundation, the student may be reinforcing this knowledge by playing a keyboard, percussion or blowing instrument of the pre-orchestral variety—xylophones, rhythm band, tonette, flutophone, etc.

## BASIC FACTS YOU WILL LEARN

1. Any distance between two notes can be called an interval.
2. The shortest distance between two notes is called a half step. This can be seen most clearly on the keyboard, where the shortest distance between two keys is a half step.
3. Any note a half step higher than a given note is called the sharp of it.
4. Any note a half step lower than a given note is called the flat of it.
5. A whole step is the sum of two half steps.
6. The several names of any given tone are referred to as enharmonic.
7. Leger lines are extra lines added above or below the staff to extend it.
8. A sharp can be sharped, a flat flatted; they are called double sharp or double flat.

## THE CHARACTERISTICS OF A SCALE

1. Eight notes moving consecutively by step in one direction.
2. Starts and ends on the same letter—a letter and its first reoccurrence.
3. Using all the letters of the musical alphabet in order from the starting letter from which it gets its name.
4. No lines and spaces (degrees) of the staff are skipped or repeated.
5. No letters of the musical alphabet are skipped or repeated.

## FREQUENTLY RAISED QUESTIONS WHICH WILL BE ANSWERED

1. Why would the note A also be called G double sharp?
2. Why can't we always call it A?
3. How do we know which name to use for a note?

## WHAT THIS LESSON CAN LEAD TO

1. Scale structure.
2. Tetrachords.
3. The circle of fifths.

## THE SCALE

The novice teacher who embarks on a project of teaching scales by beginning with scales themselves is in for some surprises. He may find himself backing up a number of times to teach certain concepts which must be clear *before* a student can understand scales.

In this chapter the teacher's prerogative of over-simplification is going to be exercised and reference will be made only to "scale" rather than "major scale." Study of the scale is difficult and demands of the student all his staying power. He is better able to give his best efforts if he doesn't know that this scale is just one of several. It would be too much to bear if he thought he had to go all through this again several more times with other scales! As a matter of fact he won't have to. Once he masters the difficult concepts necessary to understand one kind of scale he will be able to understand them all, with just the few modifications necessary for each of the others. Of course a teacher may call it THE MAJOR SCALE from the beginning if he prefers.

Some of the material which follows immediately is a duplicate of material in the beginning of the section on Staff. It is repeated here because it is just as effective an approach to the topic at hand. The teacher can use it or skip it as he wishes. This approach need be used only once with the same group of students, either as an introduction to Staff, or when beginning Scale. It is natural for the two topics to follow each other and blend into one large unit of learning anyway.

Teacher plays Joy to the World. **Tell me about this. Describe it.** Typical answers: its name; it starts high and goes down. Teacher should be aware that not everyone will be able to describe the direction as starting high and going down. **Draw some pictures in the air with your hand to show how the melody goes. Draw some pictures on the board.** Typical responses:

Yes, all these pictures do describe how the song goes; you could say it consists of a — —? It goes down the — —? Most students can supply the word SCALE. We hope they have heard and used the word many times; probably have heard it defined. If they have not, or if teacher is not sure, here are some optional activities to reinforce the concept of SCALE, its look and sound.

### The Scale by Eye and Ear

Here are some scale songs.

Taffy Came to My House
I Know a Little Pussy
Anywhere I Wander
Joy to the World (fl., Her: 51)
The First Noel (fl., Her: 86)

1. Play the excerpt from the song, Anywhere I Wander on the diatonic 8-bell xylophone as previously learned by rote, letter, number, or note, with the music before the students.

ANYWHERE I WANDER                                                          Frank Loesser

C  C  B  A  G  C  A  A  G  F  E  C  D  E  F  G  A  B  C  G  F  E

An - y - where I  wan - der  An - y - where I  roam  When I'm in the arms of my  dar - ling once more

From ANYWHERE I WANDER by Frank Loesser. (©) 1951, 1952 Frank Music Corp., 1350 Avenue of the Americas, New York, N. Y. 10019. International Copyright Secured. All Rights Reserved. Used by permission.

2. **Can you find a place in the song where you strike the lowest and biggest bell and then play each bell to the right, each one in order till you run out of bells? How many bells did we strike? Eight. All in one direction with no skips or repeats? Yes. Then we can call this a — — SCALE.**
3. **Sing just the scale part of the song, either on the words of the song or the letter names on the xylo.**
   C      D      E      F      G      A      B      C
4. **Who will frame it [              ] on the chalk board or flannel board?**
5. **Let's hold the xylophone vertically and play only the scale that way when we come to it** in the song as we sing it.
6. **When we come to the scale in the song, play the scale on step bells.**

7. **When we sing the song and get to the scale part, show the pitch levels with your hands. Sing the scale section on the Do Re Mis.**

8. Teacher can make a HUMAN SCALE of the students. They can play the song on resonator bells, and those persons who play the scale section can arrange themselves in order according to their size, short to tall.

### The Scale by Ear

Only after repeated experiences like the above during which the ear is attuned to the sound of the scale and assisted by the eye might you try game-drills like this: (The music should NOT be in sight of the student.)

A WONDERFUL GUY                                             Rogers and Hammerstein

No    more    a    smart lit - tle  girl with no  heart I'm  in  love with a  won - der - ful  guy
C     C      C      C    D    E    F    F    F    F    G    A    B    C    B    A    G    E    D

Copyright © 1949 by Richard Rodgers and Oscar Hammerstein II. Copyright renewed. Used by permission of Williamson Music, Inc.

1. **Can you hear a scale in this song? Where and on what words? Is it changed in any way from the scales we've been playing? How?** There's a scale on the words, *No more a smart little girl with no heart, I'm in love,* but some of the notes are repeated.

*Optional*—On which word-syllables are there repeated notes?

No-more-a-smart                                    girl-with-no-heart

**Well, once you know that, you can play the scale passage on your bells. Start on C and say the words or sing them so you know where to play the repeated notes: C C C C D E F F F F G A B C B A G E D**

2. *Long, Long Ago.* **There is almost a complete scale in the beginning of this song. On what words?** Tell me the tales that to me were . . .

**It stops on what Latin syllable?** La. **On what letter?** A. The top two notes are missing and some notes are repeated.

*Optional*: **See if you can tell which are the repeated notes. Sing it over to yourself or try it quietly on your bells.** The repeated words are TELL-ME and TALES-THAT. **Now try starting on C and playing it on your bells. Someone who is not a pianist go to the piano to try it there.**

3. *My Romance.* **This song begins with a piece of scale but something is missing. Who can tell? Sing DO or C and sing to yourselves and experiment with the bells.** This is a song which starts with a complete scale except that the two bottom notes are missing. The next line is a complete scale except for the two top notes. **Try playing the song that far on the bells.** (By ear with the help of knowledge.)

Rodgers-Hart

Copyright 1935 T. B. Harms Company. Copyright renewed. Used by permission.

4. *I'm in the Mood for Love.*—this is a complete scale counting the end of one phrase and all of the next; or just within the second phrase it is a complete scale minus the first note.

"I'm in the Mood for Love" by Jimmy McHugh and Dorothy Fields. Copyright 1935 (renewed 1963) Robbins Music Corp., New York. Used by permission.

*Optional*: **Try playing by ear as in the previous examples.**

5. *The Bells of St. Mary's.* **Is this a scale?** Almost. The fourth note is skipped—Fa or F; and there are repeated notes.

Copyright © 1917 by Ascherberg, Hopwood & Crew, Ltd. Copyright renewed. Used by permission of Chappell & Co., Inc.

6. *Lady of Spain.* **This song moves up and down the scale, but uses only pieces. Try to pick it out by ear, starting on the high or smaller C.**

7. *Beautiful Dreamer.* This song has a complete descending scale with repeated notes and no top note.

Beau-ti-ful dream - er      wake un - to   me

8. Row, Row, Row Your Boat (fl., Her: 27). No scale.
9. Fly Me to the Moon. Only pieces of scale.
10. Joy to the World. The first line is a complete descending scale.
11. The First Noel. The first phrase has a complete ascending scale in it.
12. Saint Paul's Steeple. This song contains a complete descending scale.

ST. PAUL'S STEEPLE                                                England

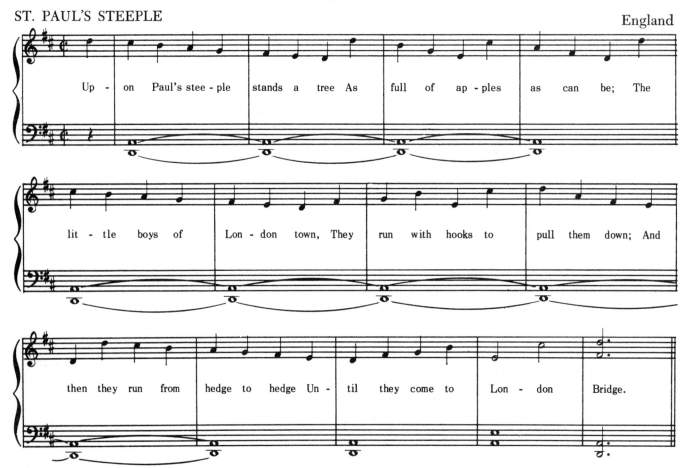

From "First Solo Book," by Angela Diller and Elizabeth Quaile. Copyright by G. Schirmer Inc., New York.

## More About the Look and Sound of the Scale

**Well then, what is a scale?** Here teacher can play that old effective game of taking the not-so-specific words and teasing the students with literal illustrations of their definitions. A device like this livens the lesson, gets them smiling and laughing, but *tantalizes the curiosity*. Students will BEG teacher to tell them.

Typical responses:

1. A series of notes that go up (or down).

   **Like this?** Teacher plays a random series in odd intervals—more or less than eight notes.

   *Note:* some may say, notes that go from C to C. (This is right but often students think of C as the beginning and end of all music.) Teacher should respond as above.

2. Eight notes which go in order.

   Teacher plays eight notes "in order" but varies the steps and half steps, or plays them in random order—anything but the right order.

3. They all go by step.

   Teacher plays a whole tone scale: C D E F♯ G♯ A♯ C D.

4. They are all consecutive—next to each other.

   Teacher plays a chromatic scale—EVERY note, black or white, from C to G.

By this time the students will be teased and frustrated enough that they really want to know.

## What Makes a Scale?

Teacher places on the chalk board or flannel board, part of the song, Joy to the World, The First Noel, or any other scale song which is familiar to all. In this case it will simplify matters to use the scale of C.

Someone indicates exactly where the scale is in the song and marks it off somehow—"frame" it, brackets, etc.

If the students can read this music on the bells, or learn it by rote to play on the diatonic 8-bell xylo, or color xylos, or step bells, they will be able to deduce some helpful facts from looking at the music and their instrument.

On a keyboard facsimile, in view of all, someone marks the scale with letters, or colored letters, or magic marker, or with colored tape, etc. All play the song and sing it, first on words and then whatever other language is comfortable—maybe on lu, la, duh, doo, numbers, Latin syllables, etc.

**Let's list all the things we can notice about the scale by looking at it and listening to it.**

1. **Describe its direction.** It goes in one direction only.
2. **How many notes?** It has eight notes.
3. **What about the letters of the musical alphabet?** It ends on the same letter which begins it. Every letter of the musical alphabet is used. None are skipped; none are repeated (except the beginning letter which then ends the scale eight notes higher up). The letters of the musical alphabet go in order (A-B-C) from the beginning letter, in this case C.

   A way to remember that the musical alphabet consists of the first seven letters of the English alphabet might be to compare it to our week—seven days in a week.

4. **What about the lines and spaces of the staff?** If the scale begins on a line it ends on a space and vice versa; it goes line-space-line-space, etc. The scale does not skip any lines or spaces, but no line or space is repeated.

   Someone may finally say there is a special arrangement of steps and half steps—or be able to give the correct pattern. If teacher knows or can sense that certain students already do know this fact, he shouldn't let them tell it until now or they'll spoil all the fun—and the motivation. On the other hand it is frustrating to those students who know, not to be allowed to tell, so at the proper moment (this is it) they should have the chance to give the correct answer. Now it is a problem all the students want to solve, and at this point we must digress to certain other basic matters.

## Teaching Aids

First, a word about the time-honored ladder. Perhaps time-WORN could express it better. Has anyone really ever taught the scale with this confusing device? For example, is the first note on the first rung, or on the ground? One can get lost before getting started. The similarity in appearance of the ladder to the staff is only misleading because on the staff we use the spaces as well as the lines; on the ladder our feet go only on the rungs. Also, the rungs on a ladder are evenly spaced; in the musical ladder they are not.

A flight of steps is not much better. Why use these confusing devices? There is no need for these when the tool which can show us so clearly these intervalic relationships is the actual keyboard of the piano itself, or a facsimile. In the case of chromatic bells or an actual piano, both of these will even provide the sound. Schirmer makes an excellent wooden keyboard; Vandre makes an excellent plastic interlocking keyboard. Madeleine Carabo-Cone has a clever lettered staff (see Chapter 5) and other aids. Xylophones can be used. A keyboard can be placed in a vertical position. Use should be made of all the genuine visual aids possible.

## THE INTERVALS, HALF AND WHOLE STEPS

Every student should now have a lettered keyboard for himself; at least one keyboard in use should belong to an instrument which can be sounded.

1. **Put your thumb on a C**—teacher shows the students—mentions it is the white note directly to the left of any two black notes.
2. **Put your little finger on the A above the C. What might we call the distance or space between these two keys?** An INTERVAL. Teacher shouldn't tell if he can ask and get the answer; but there may be no reason on the other hand to expect the term would be known. **Interval has to do with space, distance. We speak of an interval of time, a space of time. This is a space of distance.**
3. **Put your thumb on a C and go the shortest distance, or the shortest interval to the right, which you can go.** The word "right" is clearer than "up" since all students don't know that on a keyboard to go up is to go right. On the violin it is a different direction, on the flute different, on the recorder, on a stairway—all different.

Not all students will land on a black note. Some don't really seem to notice the black note and go to D, the next white. It helps to cover the lower half of the keyboard and to do all the measuring of intervals on the upper half where it is easier to see that black keys do indeed come between white ones.

**The answer to the directions is that the shortest distance to the right from C is the black note to its right. Prove it out. Everyone put your thumb on C and pointing finger on D.** Teacher shows by sliding his finger over the black note intervening, that to reach D one must first touch the black note and therefore it is closer to C. ⌨ **What could we name this interval—this distance?** If the students can't tell, teacher tells them—a HALF STEP. **How can we define it?**

> The shortest distance between any two notes is called a half step.

With the students fingering their keyboards, teacher directs them in finding some other half steps, either up or down. They can go first from white to black, or black to white. It is not necessary yet to name the black notes—just call the black notes a half step higher than G, etc. Examples:

With your finger on G, go to the black note a half step higher.

With your finger on G, go to the note a half step lower. **What color?** Black.

With your finger on the black note to the right of C, go up a half step. **What color?** White. **Its name?** D.

With your finger on the black note to the left of A, go down a half step. **What color?** White. **Its name?** G.

Now put your finger on **B**. Go to the right a half step. BIG SURPRISE. **We land on a white key. What is the interval?** A half step. Many students are surprised that between B and C there is a half step. There is a misconception that half steps occur only between white and black notes. They can be reminded then of the definitions of half-steps. There is nothing but a crack between B and C—it must be the shortest distance. They'll find the other similar interval—between E and F.

## SHARPS

**Put your finger on C again. Go higher, or right a half step. By what name can we call the black note?** C SHARP. **How then can we define a SHARP? Here is a definition which uses simple words.**

| Any note which is a half step higher than a given note is called the sharp of it. |

**What actually does the sharp do to the note?** It causes the tone to sound one half step higher. Many people say it raises the tone a half step.

Find and finger some sharps. These should be sounding also at bells or piano.

Thumb on D—pointing finger on black note a half step higher—D sharp.

Thumb on G—pointing finger on black note a half step higher—G sharp.

Thumb on E—pointing finger on the note a half step higher—to the right.

**What color note?** White. **Its name?** Some will answer F. **It looks like F, it sounds like F, and often is called F, but according to our definition, any note a half step higher than a given note is called the sharp of it. This note should be called E sharp.** Consternation! THIS IS ANOTHER BIG SURPRISE. A white note can be a sharp. A common misconception is that only black notes are sharps. Also, at this point a glimmer of a puzzle begins to show on some faces; some hands fly up. Teacher knows what the questions are: "How can the same note be called E sharp and F? When do you know which to call it?" Teacher might want to wait until these questions are further developed and until more students are asking the questions, so he can tell the students he expected their questions and persuade them to wait just a bit until they've covered more facts. (Enharmonic might just as well wait until flats are covered also.) Find the other interval like E to E sharp, B to B sharp.

**Notice how a sharp looks. It is something like a TIC-TAC-TOE but a bit different.** ♯

**Two long lines close together** ||. **Two short heavy slanting lines further apart.** ⌇ ♯

**Notice where the sharp goes. Even though we say F SHARP, when we write it, the sharp comes first. Why do you suppose?** So we see it in time before playing or singing it. This should look strange to you. Now what's wrong about this? Maybe you did not notice but we must be very careful to place the ♯ on the very same line or space as the note it sharps— like this How can you tell what line or space the sharp is on, since it is so big? By the line or space which goes through the little box. **Practice drawing a few sharps before notes:** Here's a way to remember what a sharp does. If somebody sat on a tack or pin, the *sharp* prick would make him jump *up*.

## Double Sharps

Put your finger on F♯.

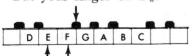

Can F♯ be sharped? Move your finger up a half step. Where do you land? **It looks like G and sounds like G and often is called G but according to our definition, it is the sharp of F♯. Is it F SHARP *SHARP?*** Most commonly it will be called **F DOUBLE SHARP.**

Put your finger on E. Sharp it; go one half step higher—to the right. Its name? E♯. Put your finger on E♯ and sharp it. Its name? E double sharp.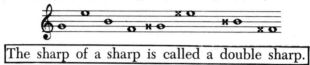

A double sharp looks like this. ✸ Sometimes it is written this way ✶ with fewer dots. You are not likely to encounter double sharps until the music gets more complicated, but here is some practice. Place a double sharp before these notes, making sure it is on the same line or space as the note.

> The sharp of a sharp is called a double sharp.

## FLATS

Flats can be presented in the same way as sharps so we will not duplicate some of the details. Students don't need it. **Put your third finger on a B. Go to the left one half step. What color note?** Black. **What do we call it?** B flat. **What then could we say a flat is?** Definition:

> Any note which is a half step lower than a given note is called the flat of it.

What actually does the flat do to the note? It causes the tone to sound one half step lower. It lowers the tone one half step.

Find and finger some flats. These should be sounding also.
3rd finger on A—place pointing finger half step lower—A flat (Black)
3rd finger on E—place pointing finger half step lower—E flat (Black)
3rd finger on D—place pointing finger half step lower—D flat (Black)

**3rd finger on F. A half step lower is a white note. Its name?** Some will answer E. **It looks like E, sounds like E, often is called E, but according to our definition of a flat, the note is called F flat.** Here the puzzled faces return and hands fly furiously. With students begging for an explanation, it would be foolish to miss the opportunity, the pupils are "ready." Teacher can put them off a few minutes while they finish with flats and then help them to discover ENHARMONIC. **Notice that again a white note is a flat.** Find the other "white" flat—C flat. **Notice how a flat looks. Half a heart ♪ and a long line**

♭ ♭ . Not the letter b. Not all scrooched up but a long sign crossing many degrees of the staff. We say **B flat, but write the flat** *before* **the note on the same line or space as the note, with that degree going**

through the "half-heart."  Here's a way to remember what a flat does. When a tire gets a

nail in it, it goes FLAT—it goes down, it *deflates.* (de-FLAT es.)

### Double Flats

**Can we flat a flat? Yes. Put your finger on B♭. Go one half step to the left. We land on a white note which looks like A, sounds like A, often is called A, but in this case can be called B DOUBLE FLAT. In the case of double flats, we do use two flats—♭♭. And as in the case of sharps, flats and double flats can be on both black or white keys. Find C♭♭.**

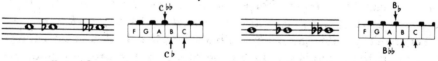

Once a sharp or flat (these are sometimes referred to by the mouth-filling name, pitch-modifying signs) has been placed before a note, it affects every recurrence of that note in the measure. If F is sharped, every other F on the same degree, in that measure, is sharped. In this example, the two Es after the first E♭ are flatted, the last E is not. In the next measure, no E is flatted: The bar-line ends the influence of the flat:

We could say, a second function of the bar-line (the first is to indicate accent) is to nullify the effect of any previous pitch-modifying sign in the previous measure.

## ENHARMONIC

You have noticed that some of the notes on the keyboard are called by more than one name. In fact, all of them have more than one name. See for yourself.

Put your finger on B. It is a half step lower than C, so it is also C♭.

Put your finger on F♯. It is also a half step lower than G, so it is G♭. And so on. But there is more!

Put your finger on B♭. Suppose you wanted to flat B♭. Remember that although it looks like A and sounds like A and is often called A, in this case it is called B double flat. Why on earth would we ever want to call a note B double flat when it would be so simple to call it A? There is a reason. Notice first a bit more. Consider note A can also be written and called G double sharp as well as B double flat. C♯ can be written and called B double sharp or D flat. When this happens, as it can with every note on the keyboard, we say the notes are ENHARMONIC—they sound the same. (Notice part of the word HARMONY.) The notes are written differently, named differently, but sound the same—and they are the same note on the keyboard. What is a comparable word to describe two or more different words which mean the same thing? SYNONYMOUS. Enharmonic is the term applied to tones which sound the same although having different names.

Why would we ever write or call a note G double sharp if we could call it a simple A? Here is an analogy. Take yourself. If you are female,

| | |
|---|---|
| you are someone's | DAUGHTER |
| you are someone's | GRAND-DAUGHTER |
| maybe you are someone's | GREAT-GRAND-DAUGHTER |
| or even | GREAT-GREAT-GRAND-DAUGHTER |
| you might be someone's | SISTER |
| or | AUNT |
| or | GREAT AUNT |
| or | COUSIN |
| or | COUSIN-ONCE-REMOVED |
| you are someone's | CUSTOMER |
| or | PATIENT |
| or | PUPIL |

If you are male, you can think of the corresponding names for yourself. Look at all the different names you have. And you can't change them at will and select the name you prefer or take the shorter name if you wish. You can't possibly be your mother's SISTER. You can't be your GREAT-GRAND-MOTHER'S AUNT. Even if the name is a long tongue-twister, if you are with your great-grandmother, then you are her GREAT-GRAND-DAUGHTER, and that is the name you must use. When? What determines which name you are called? Of course—the RELATIONSHIP. How you are related to the other person determines how you are named. It is exactly the same with these notes. Their relationship to other notes determines how they are called. And the relationship has to do with SCALES, which is what started all this in the first place.

# WHOLE STEPS

Put your thumb on C—put your pointing finger on the black note to the right of C, and now move it to D. What is the interval from C to D? It consists of two half steps or—a **WHOLE STEP.**

> A WHOLE STEP IS THE SUM OF TWO HALF STEPS—OR EQUALS TWO HALF STEPS.

It is wise to measure out every WHOLE STEP by measuring two half steps, to avoid confusion. Find some and finger them and you will see that sometimes whole steps involve two black keys, sometimes two white keys, and sometimes a black and a white key.

> thumb on D, pointing finger right a half step to black note, then to white note E
> D - E          white to white
>
> thumb on B, pointing finger right a half step to white note C, then to black note C♯
> B - C♯          white to black
>
> thumb on F♯, pointing finger right a half step to white note G, then to black note G♯
> F♯ - G♯          black to black
>
> pointing finger on E, thumb down or left a half step to black note, then to white note D
> E - D          white to white
>
> pointing finger on E♭—3rd finger up half step to E, then up half step to F
> black to white

## Aural Discrimination of Half and Whole Steps

A few remarks regarding ear practice on whole and half steps might be apropos here. In such a lesson as these just described, it is not uncommon for some teachers to try to drill the students on recognizing whole and half steps as they are *sounded.* They ask, "Do you hear it?" Students may or may not answer yes, but how can the teacher possibly know whether the students can or cannot distinguish the difference? *AT THIS STAGE* of development such an activity is not useful. It isn't that students cannot eventually do it. But students who are only at the stage of development which these lessons imply usually cannot; some because of lack of ability, others because of lack of experience. Although it is important to keep sounding these intervals as we measure them, we must recognize that at best it is a kind of casual "aural readiness" experience and that some students cannot even distinguish *difference* in the sounds, or *direction,* (up or down) let alone *distance* (half and whole). Knowing what a sharp is and does, is quite different from distinguishing how it sounds. There is a time later on when the student has experienced and learned more, when the teacher can hope for more success in such a drill, and when it is more meaningful. We should remember that one of the worst faults of teachers has been to expect or require more from a student than he is able to produce, or more than he has been prepared for. Instead of the series of small successes which motivate students to move ahead, such misplaced drills only teach a student that he is stupid and un"able." We have all met adults or older children who tell us this about themselves. They have learned it from their teachers.

However here are activities and experiences which the teacher can provide for his students which will build that very aural readiness just mentioned and make it more likely that he will be able to distinguish by ear the difference between half and whole steps.

### Writing Drills

1. Draw a sharp before each of these notes. Make sure the correct line or space goes through the little box.

2. Use your keyboard to measure out the note a whole step higher than the note written on the staff. Do it by measuring two half steps. Write the note and name it as in the sample.

C

Answers:

G♯          B          F♯

**Playing Experiences**

3.  Use a planned mistake.

*Flutes or xylophones*

Teacher places before the students a song which they know well, and which is simple enough that they can play it on their instruments, either at sight or with very little practice. The song can be written in various languages, whichever is familiar to them; numbers, letters, or musical notation. If musical notes are used, there should be no key signature and the few necessary sharps should be omitted. (Teacher can use a chart, the chalk board, an opaque projector, etc.) He starts the class matter-of-factly and waits for them to make the mistake—the mistake he has written into the score. Usually flutes are pulled out of mouths as if they had suddenly bitten the player. Bell players jump and wince. Everybody enjoys the joke on themselves. *But nobody misses the point.* Something sounds WRONG. They know because they know how the song should sound. First they must locate where there is something wrong. This may necessitate a slow re-play. **What's the matter? What makes it wrong?** The students may not know, but whenever possible they should try their own suggestions. Since this activity is done at a time when sharps and flats are being studied, someone will surely suggest sharping or flatting the offending note.

And here comes a very tangible concrete part of the lesson. On the xylophone which is similar to the keyboard, the player must go a half step to the right to sharp, or left to flat the note correctly, and the corrected bell will be appropriately labelled. A flute player must change his fingering—maybe even learn a new fingering. A change must be made. It is physical, tactile, visual, labelled, as well as aural.

It is a very good idea to save until this time the introduction to flute players of how to play a certain sharp or flat. It could be done this way:

Teacher places on the board or chart the song "America" (fl., Her: 72) with no key signature (which at this point wouldn't be used or referred to or understood anyway) and leaving out the important F♯. Teacher gives a good introduction at the piano and off the players go, only to crash to a jarring laughing halt after playing the offending F. Everybody knows how "America" goes! You put the wrong note there, the students accuse. **What note should it be?** Sooner or later F♯ is suggested. But how do we play F♯? Teacher shows—two holes and half the third covered on the melody flute; three holes and half the fourth on the flutophone and other such flutes; on the recorder:       The students try it—play F, Play G, F♯.

Some may not be able to hear that F♯ is between the pitches F and G, but they will hear that it is the right tone when inserted into "America." They now play the new note at the proper place in the song. Teacher should fix the score. A sharp will have to be placed before every F. Now the song sounds right. Two important things happen in an experience like this:

1. What we are learning about sharps is reinforced and applied to an actual musical situation.
2. The fingering of a new note is learned under circumstances of the highest motivation. No one needs to wonder WHY. This note is needed to make the song sound right.

It is just as dramatic if students are using resonator bells. An exchange has to be made. This bell sounds wrong, sounds sour. The name on it says F. Here, trade it for a different bell which has F♯ written right on it. Try it out in the song. It sounds right. Here is a good physical and tactile, as well as aural and visual experience.

Instruments are usually much more effective in a situation like this dealing with pitch, than the singing voice, which is so intangible. We cannot see or touch what we do to change pitches with our voice, or always know if we are correct.

However, if students can use syllables with some skill, (see Chapter 9) teacher should choose a song within the limits of their syllable skills, which has one or several sharp accidentals and deal with the problem of *what to call it.* If the tune is unfamiliar, teacher shouldn't expect the students to be able to sing the correct pitch without the help of an instrument. The learning point here is a new name resulting from the sharp sign. If the tune is familiar the situation is the same except there is no problem in singing the correct pitch unassisted. What is learned is that Fa sharped is Fi, Re sharped is Ri, and so on. (See Chapter 11) Here are some examples:

*O Little Town of Bethlehem*: This should be a song the students know well but have never played on their flutes. The song encompasses an octave plus one so it is suitable for most of the blowing instruments. (Range of flutophone is octave plus one, melody flute is almost two octaves, recorder is two octaves.)

**Let's play the song through slowly. Read either the notes or numbers, whichever you prefer.**

After a few notes, flutes pop out and faces are full of outrage and complaint. Teacher has written the wrong note! **What word sounds wrong?** TOWN. **What do you think is the matter?** Because we have been discussing sharps and because some few students may be able to hear what is needed, some will suggest placing a ♯ before the G. With the flannel board this is easy and quick. Practice the fingering.

Now play the song. Now it sounds right.

*I Heard the Bells on Christmas Day.* Teacher uses the same approach. What words don't sound right? THE and THEIR. Try sharping each of these notes. Fingerings:

Now it sounds correct.

*Optional*—if students know syllables. **What is the syllable name of D?** RE. **When it is sharped what is its name?** RI. **And F?** FA. **Sharped?** FI.

Other songs which can be used are:

*White Christmas*: mi — — fa mi RI mi fa — — FI so

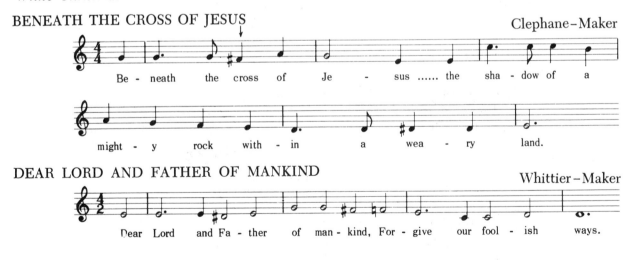

## BENEATH THE CROSS OF JESUS
                                                                Clephane–Maker

## DEAR LORD AND FATHER OF MANKIND
                                                                Whittier–Maker

## GOD OF OUR FATHERS
                                                                Roberts–Warren

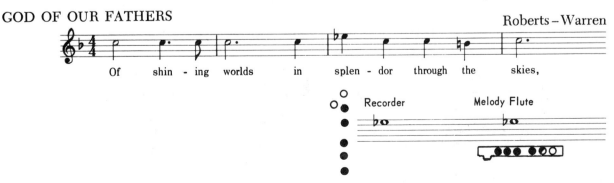

*Sweet and Low* (fl., Her: 142). Music on board or chart. **Who can find the signs we have been discussing?** F♯ and A♭. **What is the syllable name for each?** FI and LE. **Practice the fingering on your instrument. Play the song through.** Try singing syllable names to the song (already a familiar tune, so this is not for reading purposes). **Try playing the phrase, leaving out the sharp or flat. Doesn't sound correct, does it?**

SWEET AND LOW                                                                                 Barnby

Here is a sample lesson on half and whole steps. This tune is wonderful for beginners on eight-bell diatonic xylophones. It could be taught by rote.

    G A G A G A G
    E F E F E F E
    D E D E D E D E
    D C D C D C

1. **Point with your fingers to the notes on your xylo as I say the letters of the first line.**
2. **You say the letters and point again.**
3. **Now take your mallets and play first line.**
4. Do the same with the other three lines.

    Or read it from musical notation:

1. **Practice once with your fingers, pointing silently.**
2. **Now play.**

**Who could tell us a way in which all the four lines are similar?** They are all very repetitious. Each line uses only two letters. Each line moves only by step. **Can you tell by LISTENING whether the steps are whole steps or half steps?** This is hard. It could be done if a student can assign by ear the proper syllable or number to the music, and if he knows that half steps occur between 3 and 4, mi and fa.

| PUT | A | NOTHER | NICKEL | IN | | |
|-----|-----|-----|-----|-----|-----|-----|
| 5 | 6 | 5 | 6 | 5 | 6 | 5 |
| so | la | so | la | so | la | so |

| IN | THE | NI | CKEL | O | DI | AN |
|-----|-----|-----|-----|-----|-----|-----|
| 3 | 4 | 3 | 4 | 3 | 4 | 3 |
| mi | fa | mi | fa | mi | fa | mi |

| ALL | I | WANT | IS | LO | VIN' | YOU | AND |
|-----|-----|-----|-----|-----|-----|-----|-----|
| 2 | 3 | 2 | 3 | 2 | 3 | 2 | 3 |
| re | mi | re | mi | re | mi | re | mi |

| MUSIC | MU | SIC | MU | SIC | |
|-----|-----|-----|-----|-----|-----|
| 2 | 1 | 2 | 1 | 2 | 1 |
| re | do | re | do | re | do |

Music! Music! Music! Words and music by Stephan Weiss and Bernie Baum. TRO Copyright 1949 and 1950, Cromwell Music, Inc., New York. Used by permission.

**How can you tell if you can LOOK?** If the student is playing on chromatic bells or the piano, which indicate as we have shown the whole and half steps, we can see that the second phrase is made up of half steps. Try singing this way as you play:

| 5 | 6 | 5 | 6 | 5 | 6 | 5 |
|---|---|---|---|---|---|---|
| WHOLE | STEP | WHOLE | STEP | WHOLE | STEP | WHOLE |
| G | A | G | A | G | A | G |

| 3 | 4 | 3 | 4 | 3 | 4 | 3 |
|---|---|---|---|---|---|---|
| HALF | STEP | HALF | STEP | HALF | STEP | HALF |
| E | F | E | F | E | F | E |

| 2 | 3 | 2 | 3 | 2 | 3 | 2 | 3 |
|---|---|---|---|---|---|---|---|
| WHOLE | STEP | WHOLE | STEP | WHOLE | STEP | WHOLE | STEP |
| D | E | D | E | D | E | D | E |

| 2 | 1 | 2 | 1 | 2 | 1 |
|---|---|---|---|---|---|
| WHOLE | STEP | WHOLE | STEP | WHOLE | STEP |
| D | C | D | C | D | C |

(Keyboard diagram showing D E F G with arrows over E and F)

Try echo playing and dictation, using one phrase of the song. For example: **What words am I playing?** "All I want is loving you and —." **Can you play that line back? Can you write the music on the board or flannel board? You are allowed to look at the music of the song.** Etc.

Here are other kinds of ear game-drills:

1. **Sing the scale from Do to Do.** (Use numbers or letters if syllables are unfamiliar.)
2. **Sing do-re; sing ti-do. Which sounds more like a finish—like "The End"?** Ti do.
3. **See if you can distinguish between do-re and ti-do, remembering that Ti-Do sounds like "The End."** Teacher plays several of these patterns.
4. **Using your keyboard to help you, which is the half step?** Ti-Do.
5. Then teacher and pupils can play to each other, whole and half steps, playing on xylos or piano, and identifying them by the syllable name, or letter, or number.

*Echo playing a la Orff*

1. Students each have their own 8-tone diatonic xylophone. Teacher also. Teacher plays 1-2 or 7-8 as students listen and *watch*. They take turns echoing teacher, playing the interval and naming it by number or letter or syllable or name of interval; also singing it. In this procedure the eye is of great assistance to the ear. For example:

   Teacher plays: 7-8. Student echoes on his xylo and sings 7-8, or ti-do. He says, half step.

   Teacher plays: 1-2. Student echoes on his xylo and sings C-D; he says whole step. Etc.

2. Do the same thing without watching. It is now pure ear: Teacher plays 3-4. Student plays 6-7. No, he realizes this is wrong. He may lightly tap each bell till he arrives at 3, which sounds right to him, then plays 3-4 and sings E-F and says, half step. Another student taps C lightly, then goes immediately to 3 and plays 3-4. He is using C or Do as his reference point. Another student can go immediately to 3 without any intermediate steps.

All are training their ear; building their knowledge of number relationships, the letters of the musical alphabet, the visual and aural "picture" of steps and half steps, their sense of direction, high and low, their ability to vocalize and verbalize this knowledge.

*Songs to illustrate sharps*
I've Been Workin' on the Railroad (Her: 38)
Erie Canal—Amer. Folk Song (Her: 256)
Beautiful Dreamer—Stephen Foster

*Songs to illustrate flats*
Tit Willow—The Mikado—Sir Arthur Sullivan
Sweet and Low—Barnby (Her: 142)
I'm in the Mood for Love

White Christmas ⎱—Irving Berlin
Easter Parade  ⎰
Poor Little Buttercup—Sir Arthur Sullivan
Water Boy
Minuet in G
Me and My Shadow

My Hero—The Chocolate Soldier

*Songs which illustrate both sharps and flats*
Stout-Hearted Men—Romberg
Fly Me to the Moon
Tit Willow
Song to the Evening Star—Tannhauser-Wagner

Swing the Shining Sickle (Her: 248)
God of Our Fathers
Fling Out the Banner

*Songs to illustrate half and whole steps*
Humoresque—Dvorak
Les Preludes—Liszt
Never on Sunday
Music, Music, Music

Alley Cat
One of Those Songs That You Hear Now and Then
Hello My Baby

*Songs for Scales, half and whole steps*
Taffy Was a Welshman
I Know a Little Pussy
Anywhere I wander
The First Noel (Her: 86)
Joy to the World (Her: 51)
Do, Re, Mi (The Sound of Music)
I'm in Love with a Wonderful Guy (South Pacific)
Just the Way You Look Tonight
Fly Me to the Moon
My Romance
The Bells of St. Mary
Billy Boy (Her: 44)
Beautiful Dreamer
I'm in the Mood for Love
All of a Sudden My Heart Sings
Love Me Tender (Auralee)
Caro Nome—from "Rigoletto" by Verdi

Theme from "Petroushka" by Stravinsky
Long, Long Ago (Her: 204)
Alouette (Her: 63)
Danny Boy (Londonderry Air)
Bring a Torch, Jeannette Isabella (Her: 70)
Lady of Spain
All Creatures of Our God and King (Her: 56)
Away in a Manger (Her: 32)
Streets of Laredo (Her: 83)
Deck the Halls (Her: 127)
Good King Wencelaus (Her: 180)
Partner Come and Dance With Me (Her: 226)
Over the River and Through the Wood (Her: 113)
Tell Me Why (Her: 268)
We Wish You a Merry Christmas (Her: 95)
White Coral Bells (Her: 257)
Yankee Doodle (Her: 91)

## SUMMARY

Teachers often make the mistake of presenting scales as a purely visual concept. When it is done that way the student really has nothing very familiar to cling to. The signs and symbols which are so significant to musicians are likely to be a strange meaningless jumble interspersed with a few slightly familiar symbols to the student. The best approach is through the ear and eye together, using the sound of a familiar tune.

Part of the teacher's job will be to "unteach" some common misconceptions:

1. *THE* scale goes from C to C. Therefore the only half steps occur between E − F, and B − C. Not true: *ONE* scale goes from C − C. Scales can start on any other letter name also. There are many other half steps also.

2. Half steps occur only between white and black keys. Not true. Half steps can occur between two white keys.
3. The black keys are the sharps and flats—*ONLY* the black keys. Not true. White notes can be sharps and flats too.

And to clarify a few new conceptions:

1. Every key on the keyboard has more than one name. We call this condition ENHARMONIC.
2. Sharps can be sharped. They are called double sharps. Flats can be flatted. They are called double flats.

# Chapter 7

# The Major Scale

## WHAT YOU NEED TO KNOW

The material in Chapter 6.
Sharps, flats.
Whole and half steps.
Enharmonic.
The Look and Sound of the Scale.

## FREQUENTLY RAISED QUESTIONS WHICH WILL BE ANSWERED

1. Why do scales need sharps or flats?
2. Why do some scales have so many sharps or flats, and others just a few?
3. Why would a scale have sharps rather than flats?

## BASIC FACTS YOU WILL LEARN

1. A scale is built to an exact formula or blueprint which requires that there be a whole step between each note and the next, except between the third and fourth notes, and the seventh and eighth notes, where there is a half step.
2. The four tones comprising either the bottom or top half of a scale are called a Tetrachord.
3. The Circle of Fifths refers to the relationship of scales to each other through common tetrachords. Such scales are five steps apart from each other, hence the term Fifths.

## WHAT THIS LESSON LEADS TO

This lesson literally opens the door to a huge vista of knowledge:
1. It is the raison d'être for key signatures—it shows where they come from.
2. It provides the foundation for chords, chord structure, chord relationships; the whole magic area of harmony.
3. It provides the door-way to the realm of minor and the relationship of minor to major; also church modes.
4. It leads to Latin syllables, or provides the theoretical and visual explanation for syllables which students may already have been singing and reading.

---

Here is a slight variation in procedure. Teacher follows the procedure previously outlined in Chapter 6, p. 66 to the point where we amass a list of characteristics of the scale. Then the lesson continues this way.

When we play or sing from C to C all of these characteristics seem to fit and the notes do sound like a scale, or Joy to the World. If that is so, let's try playing from D to D using all the white notes in between. Use a longer xylo or the piano. Let's check the list: eight notes in one direction, starting and ending on D, using every letter of the musical alphabet, using every line and space, no repeats, no skips. Now, in the rhythm of Joy to the World, teacher plays the scale descending from D to D. **Does it sound like the song?** No. **Then there must be something else that helps to make a scale. Where does our song on D sound wrong? Play it slowly and sing lightly, and see if we can tell which notes don't agree with the song.** By trial and error, F and C can be singled out. **Try nearby notes to see what sounds better.** By trial and error we should be able to determine that F♯ and C♯ should replace F and C. This way can circumvent the possible confusion over whether the note should be called F♯ or G♭, C♯ or D♭, since it replaces a form of F and C already there according to requirements. Then the question to ask and solve is why did the scale need an F♯ and C♯ in order to sound correct—like Joy to the World?

## THE STRUCTURE OF A SCALE

**What does make a scale? How can we start Joy to the World on any note and make it sound correct?** This is the point at which the teacher must make sure that all the preliminary facts have been learned or reviewed. Every student should have his own keyboard and close access to the staves. In what follows, teacher will insist that each student touch and feel each key and that they measure the intervals with their fingers. It is important for the teacher to remember that effective as these teaching tools are, many students are totally unfamiliar with the keyboard, do not know the names of the keys, and may even be very uncertain of the names of the degrees of the staff. So he must use every teaching aid he can. A large lettered staff and also a lettered keyboard should be placed in plain view.

The teacher should establish a strict routine and not deviate from it. In this way he can impress on the student a comprehension of WHAT he is doing and WHY, and keep him from getting lost. **Since it has been suggested that the steps have something to do with a scale, let us now measure the intervals between each note. Everybody finger his own keyboard and stay with us. If you get lost or don't understand, stop us and we'll go over it for you.**

It is important that as many students as possible understand this procedure and are made to feel that they *can* understand, that teacher wants them to and that he will help each individual to understand. This is a very important step. It is the culmination of all the previous points, and the stepping-off phase to many other concepts. It is the WHY, the explanation of many facts people sometimes learn by rote without any understanding of what it really means or how to use it. If this step is done carefully and considerately, it is gratifying to hear the exclamations of "oh," from many students as insight suddenly makes clear to them many little pieces of information they have gathered in their schooling (good or bad) and which now fall into place. This whole lesson and succeeding ones on scale structure can do this if teacher will move slowly, carefully and considerately. It is difficult, but students will work hard on it because they can themselves see the possibility of their own comprehension and revelation.

Teacher must give directions clearly and word his questions carefully. It helps to cover the lower half of the keyboard and work on the upper half. The scale from C to C is on the chalk or flannel board.

1. **Put your thumb on a C.**
2. **Now what is the next note in the scale on the board?** D.

3. **Place your pointing finger on D. What is the distance between C and D on the keyboard in terms of steps?** A whole step. **Prove it.** Teacher can do this, or the student, or both. **Move the pointing finger from C to C♯. That's one half step. Then from C♯ to D. That's another half step. Two half steps make a WHOLE STEP.** The students will see this better if they slide their fingers up the key to its narrow upper half. Resume the routine.

4. **Put your thumb on D. What is the next note in the scale on the board?** E.

5. **Place your pointing finger on E. What is the distance between D and E? Measure it in half steps.** (This helps greatly to cut confusion and getting lost.) A whole step. Indicate it on the scale on the board. Perhaps use a dash. **So the interval between the first and second notes of the scale is a whole step. There is also a whole step between the second and third notes.** Mark it. Teacher can use any system he likes but shouldn't let it clutter or confuse.

6. **Place your thumb on E. What is the next note on the board?** F

7. **Place your pointing finger on F on the keyboard. Measure the distance.** A half step. There is sometimes a hue and cry at this point. Those two adjacent white notes look like the others. Why a half step? But is there a key between them? Nothing but a crack. Remember you will see this better if the lower part of the keyboard remains covered. Recalling the definition, the smallest distance between two notes is a half step, this is then a half step. Indicate it, perhaps a caret.

8. **Place your finger on F. What is the next note in the scale before us?** G. **Find G on the keyboard. What kind of step?** Whole. **Mark it.**

9. **Finger on G. What is the next note?** A. **Finger on A. What kind of step?** Two half steps—a whole step. **Mark it.**

10. **Finger on A. What is the next note?** B. **What kind of step?** Whole. **Mark it.**

11. **Finger on B. What kind of step to the last note of the scale, C?** Half step. **Mark it.**

Now the students can begin to see that not all the notes of a scale are the same distance apart. Although the *ear* may not detect this and the *staff* does not show it and at first glance all the white notes on the piano keyboard look like a row of evenly-spaced gleaming teeth, closer examination of the keyboard, especially fingering the upper part of the keys, indicates clearly the varying distance between keys.

All continue the routine, leaving no step or question out and stopping to clear up all confusion, until the entire scale has been measured out. The scale indeed is built according to a formula or pattern.

### The Formula

**What have we discovered? The scale consists neither of a series of whole steps or half steps as some have suggested. It is a combination; but mostly whole steps. In fact every interval is a whole step except for two half steps between the third and fourth scale members, and between the seventh and eighth members.**

Here let us stop a moment to discuss how to state this formula. It is often stated this way: WHOLE, WHOLE, HALF, WHOLE, WHOLE, WHOLE, HALF. Or, ONE ONE ONE-HALF, ONE ONE ONE ONE-HALF. This terminology can cause great confusion. These words all involve two notes, referring to the relationship between them, such as whole step between D and E. What with remembering which note to measure *from*, which note to measure *to* and which kind of step is being measured, many a student bogs down. It is the silent thinking of *numbers* which seems to cause the confusion: one step between one and two, one step between two and three, one-half step between three and four, now-where-am-I?

Why not avoid all the confusing definitions and formulae and just say: A SCALE CONSISTS OF A SERIES OF WHOLE STEPS EXCEPT FOR HALF STEPS BETWEEN THE THIRD AND FOURTH NOTES, AND BETWEEN THE SEVENTH AND EIGHTH NOTES. What a relief! It all seems simpler. Just two special places to remember. Try it. Now we can define a scale more completely: A SCALE CONSISTS OF A SUCCESSION OF EIGHT NOTES IN ONE DIRECTION FROM ANY LETTER TO ITS NEXT RECURRENCE, INCLUDING ALL LETTERS IN BETWEEN. NO LETTER OR STAFF DEGREES ARE REPEATED OR OMITTED: THE NOTES PROCEED BY THE FORMULA JUST STATED.

Some authorities define the scale as having seven notes, rather than eight. This is more consistent with the definitions of other scales in which the recurrence of the starting note is *not* included. The reader is free to make his choice.

A strong argument for eight notes can be advanced however:

It seems necessary for the complete formula.

When considering tetrachords (later in the chapter) the eighth note is needed.

It is the way the scale is practiced on instruments and sung.

When considering syllables, Do, and the Tonic Chord (next chapter) the eighth note is necessary.

Some teachers use the tetrachord approach. This will be dealt with in detail later. Even though it is fingered easily at the piano with two hands, the theory of it is an advanced rather than a simple approach. Some folks can never remember what kind of step goes between the tetrachords for instance, and the WHY of tetrachords is complex. The subject of tetrachords will not be mentioned further at this point. It is appreciated later on when the student knows more, but tends to confuse at this stage. Also, it is suggested that the teacher avoid using the upper tetrachord of one scale to become the lower tetrachord of the next scale in order. This is a very interesting and pertinent fact but it is not basic to the *understanding* of scale *structure* and tends to confuse the concept rather than clarify.

Now we have discovered that the scale is built according to a formula. We come to an important question. What significance does this have for us? What good does it do to know this formula? The answers ought to be:

1. With this formula we can build a scale starting on any note. It could be compared to a blueprint for a building or a pattern for a dress.
2. That's why some scales have a few sharps and flats, and others many; why some scales have sharps and others flats. We'll prove this.
3. That is why The First Noel or Joy to the World will always sound right no matter where we start it on the keyboard.

Students who have been shown the various scales by their teachers instead of being encouraged to figure them out themselves will understand for the first time why those scales contain the notes they do. Other students will discover these facts as they continue to prove out the formula.

### Apply the Formula

The next step is to apply the knowledge about the formula by spelling out other scales. The questions to be answered right now, the answers to which are beginning to glimmer in some minds, are: Why do some scales have so many sharps or flats and others few; and why do they need them?

The answer to the question of course is the formula we've just discovered. You may want to use the word BLUEPRINT or PATTERN.

The scales chosen next should be selected carefully. They should prove out the formula dramatically and unequivocally. For this reason teacher should *not* choose a scale related by tetrachord to C, or one with few sharps or flats. Many inexperienced teachers just naturally choose the next scale in order of difficulty or according to the circle of 5ths (see p. 88); that is, the G or F scale. But many seasoned teachers feel that a better choice would be a scale that is vastly different from the "all-white-key" C. If we are going to make a point, make it dramatically. It will make a greater impact on the students, and bring to teacher's ears the sweetest sound a teacher ever heard—the "oh" of insight. What scale should it be? If teacher chooses B or B♭ or A or A♭ there will be the problem of leger lines which are a major obstacle to a novice student. The scale of E or E♭ is good; all the notes remain on the staff yet there are some dramatic differences from C.

Teacher must insist that everyone finger the keyboards. There will be some surprises. He must word his directions and questions carefully. It helps to have someone write in the notes on a staff on the chalkboard or flannel board as they are named.

1. **Thumb on E. This is the first note. What kind of step do we take?** Whole. **Measure two half steps. What color note do you land on?** Black. **What is its name?** F♯. **Why?** Because it is going up. **No.** This is the common answer, but of course it is not right. **The notes of a scale have the same names coming down as going up. Why is it F♯ and not G♭?** In some cases it *could* be called G♭. **Why not here?** Because scales which have sharps in them don't have flats too. **No. This is mostly true (except for certain minor scales) but it is not the reason. Check the definition.** (p. 82). **Every letter of the musical alphabet in order, skipping none. If we went from E to G♭, there would be no form of F. The second note must be some kind of F: in this case F♯. Write it in. The second note must be some kind of F because of the conditions of the formula which says we never skip a letter.** The meaning of "ENHARMONIC" and the fact that *relationship* determines the name begins to clarify. In this relationship, that black note must be called and notated as F♯. Write it. (The scale that we build next ought to have flats to disprove the idea of "going up.")

2. **Finger on second note F♯. What kind of step between the second and third note?** A whole. **Measure it from F♯—two half steps. Another black note. Its name? It must be some kind of G—therefore G♯. Write it in.**

3. **Finger on G♯. What kind of step between third and fourth note?** This is where the formula calls for a half step. **Measure it. Color?** White. **Name?** A. Write it.

4. **Finger on A. Fourth note. What kind of step?** Whole. **Color?** White? **Name?** B. **Write it.**

5. **Finger on B. Fifth note. Kind of Step?** Whole. **Color?** Black. **Name?** C♯. **Why?** Must be some form of letter following B — C. **Write it.**

6. **Finger on C♯. Sixth note. Kind of step?** Whole. **Color?** Black. **Name?** D♯ **Write.**

7. **Finger on D♯. Seventh note. Step?** Half. **Color?** White. **Name?** E. **Let's hope so! A scale that begins on E should end on E.**

We discover that a scale on E needs four different sharps. **Why does this scale have so many sharps?** The formula requires it. E is a good choice—it provides a strong contrast to C. It uses no leger lines to confuse. Test the completed scale. Does it sound like Joy to the World? Does it sound like The First Noel? These are safer questions to ask than Does it sound like a scale? Not everybody can tell. But more can recognize a song they know well. **Suppose I left out one of the sharps —would it matter?** Yes, almost everybody can tell when they hear it that it would.

Students can usually tell immediately that it no longer sounds like the song—something is "sour." This whole procedure of measuring out and spelling one scale may take ten or fifteen minutes, but the students understand what they are doing, they work intently and it is worth it.

## NAMING THE SCALE

Since there can be questions about flats in an ascending scale, let's do a scale with flats. **Start on Db. Incidentally, we've been talking about starting a scale *on* E, *on* Db. What do you suppose the scale on E is named?** The E scale. **It could be called the scale *of* E. A SCALE IS NAMED BY ITS FIRST NOTE, WHICH IS ALSO ITS LAST. So the scale we are going to build now can be called the scale of Db.**

1. **Finger on Db. First note. Step?** Whole. **Color?** Black. **Name?** It must be some kind of E . . . Eb. **Even though it's going up.**
2. **Finger on Eb. Second note. Step?** Whole. **Color?** White. **Name?** F.
3. **Finger on third note, F. Step?** Half. **Color?** Black. **Name?** Gb. (Not F♯. There already is an F.)
4. **Finger on fourth note Gb. Step?** Whole. **Color?** Black. **Name?** Ab.
5. **Finger on fifth note, Ab. Step?** Whole. **Color?** Black. **Name?** Bb.
6. **Finger on sixth note Bb. Step?** Whole. **Color?** White. **Name?** C.
7. **The last note doesn't really need to be measured. It should be the same as the first.**

Teacher might want you to do a quite hard scale now, or try an easy one by yourself. Then the next problem to take up should be a scale like the scale of F♯. The problem occurs at this point in the procedure: **Finger on D♯, 6th note. What kind of step?** Whole. **Color?** White. **Name? NOT F!** The students are elated as here they see an example of *enharmonic* and of how the relationship determines

name. This *must* be some kind of E. It will be a "white sharp." The name is E♯.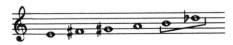

Now the students should try to build a scale without help. Teacher should choose carefully, avoiding complications like leger lines, or "white sharps." Some students prefer to write out all the notes first and then place in the sharps or flats as they figure them out.

No harm in this. It helps to avoid silly mistakes like

Next build a scale like A, A♭, B or B♭ because of leger lines, then G♭ or C♯ or C♭ because of so many sharps and flats, and "white sharps" or "white flats." By then the students ought to be able to spell any scale. They understand better many concepts like enharmonic, leger lines, half and whole steps; even transposition, although they may not yet know that they know.

### Leger Lines

A scale on A or B will bring up the question of leger lines. Incidentally, this word appears with the spelling LEDGER sometimes, but we will spell it LEGER. Sometimes students will write the B♭ scale like this:

Teacher might write something like this and ask, **Who can tell what these notes are?** There's no sure way to tell. **What do we need?** More lines which will divide up the space—mark off the space. Leger lines are like an extension ladder or a rope ladder hanging out the window. After all the treble staff is just a piece of the Grand Staff about which you have already learned. The solution is to add lines as needed.

The A scale could then be begun below the staff  or ended above the staff.

### Apply the New Knowledge

This knowledge has been hard won. Teacher should make it worth the while of his students by constantly applying this knowledge.

1.  Single out by ear passages of complete scales from the songs you sing.
2.  Do the same by eye. Measure the intervals to confirm the formula. (If it is noticed that flats and sharps are not in their acustomed place before the notes, good. It will set the stage for key signatures.)
3.  In unfamiliar songs, single out the scale passage and sight sing or play by sight.
4.  Do simple dictation using portions of a complete scale. This needs to be done carefully as follows.

    Flannel boards will be much more effective than having students attempt to write music at a chalk board. Teacher places a scale on the board, say E♭. He plays it to give pitch feeling (and key feeling too although students may not know yet what this is).

    **I'm going to play pieces of the scale. If this is E♭ (teacher plays it) what is this?**

One student sings back on neutral syllable; another plays it back on his xylo; someone else names the letters: Eb F G Ab Bb; another sings the letters. Teacher says, **If you can name them, you can put them on the flannel board or write them down on your own music paper. If you need to, copy the notes you want from the scale on the board.** He uses other patterns such as:

**In the following, does the music go only in one direction? If not, the important thing is to find the turning point. On what note does the music change its direction?**

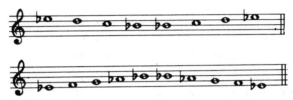

If the music starts on some tone other than DO, teacher should either name the note, or have the students play or sing up to the starting tone:

5. Various students can take over the role of giving the dictation on their xylos. Teacher sets limits—start on Eb, only on Bb, etc. Later on all these restrictions won't be necessary. Once students get over their first disbelief that they can do this sort of thing, many make quite good progress.

6. Do echo playing à la Orff, as mentioned earlier in the chapter. Teacher plays portions of scales on his xylo or other instrument and encourages echo playing by the students. They are allowed to watch what is being played if necessary at first. Hints are allowed. The object is to help the student achieve and succeed without actually giving him the answer. Sometimes holding the xylo vertically and having the students do likewise reinforces the concept of high and low, up and down. Step bells are effective here.

7. Sight sing on letters, syllables, numbers or neutral syllable. Use scale passages similar to those suggested for dictation.

8. Build scales by trial and error, using resonator bells and selecting those which "sound right." Check the bells selected by ear: does it sound like one of our familiar scale songs? Or write out the names of the bells selected, or the note pictures and check them according to the formula. For instance: **Jerry, go to the set of resonator bells, start on Eb and build a scale.** Jerry takes Eb out of the set, taps F, decides that is correct, taps Gb, no, G, yes, takes that. He plays all three before trying A, no, Ab, yes, and takes that. And so on till he reaches the next Eb. Now he starts at the top note and going down in order, plays Joy to the World. Yes, it sounds right. In the meantime, as he has selected each note, Jean is at the flannel board, putting up the proper notes. The rest of the students are using their keyboards to measure the distance between each note and sometimes they know before Jerry which note should come next. Jerry is doing it by ear and trial and error, the others by the formula.

9. Use pieces of colored tape (easily removed) to press on the proper keys of a keyboard facsimile when building scales. For instance: Teacher says: **Let's start a scale on D. Jim, you take the D resonator**

bell and play it and keep it. Mary, you go to the flannel board and put D on the staff. Greta, you put the red square of tape on a D of the keyboard. Larry, you measure on the other keyboard what the next note should be, while Shirley sees if she can tell which bell should come next, by playing the bells near D. Shirley chooses E and plays it and takes it. Larry checks it and says it is a whole step from D, therefore correct. Greta puts a red square of tape on E, and Mary puts the note E on the flannel board, **John, you go next to choose a bell. It should be some form of . . .?** F. John takes F and plays it. Most of the other students call out No. He tries F♯ and nods. Greta puts up the tape, Mary puts the note on the flannel board and Larry checks it by measuring. Etc. When the entire scale has been built, they sing a song in the key of D which contains scale passages (see p. 77) and each resonator bell player plays his bell at the proper time on the proper tone. Teacher may help by pointing and cuing or they may be able to do it all by themselves.

10. Make a human scale. Each student represents one note; he can carry or wear a sign with the name of the note and space himself with the others to indicate the whole and half steps:

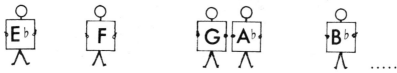

If the sign is made so he can hang it around his neck or pin it to his clothing, then he has a free hand to hold the proper resonator bell and play it as the scale is built and when it is completed. This builds an "aural readiness." If possible, use varying heights to approximate the steps. If necessary, use furniture in the room; chairs, stools, desks, platforms, to assist in making the proper heights of the "human" scale. Again the step bells are very effective.

## TETRACHORDS

Using a human scale carefully placed, teacher can ask, **can you notice any other pattern the scale makes in addition to the formula?** Someone notices that the scale can be divided into halves which are exactly alike. **How many people in each half?** Four. **How do the steps go?** Two whole steps and then a half. There is a Greek word for these four notes: TETRACHORD. (These four notes could be arranged so that the steps are different and still be called a tetrachord.) We will see that later—(see Chapter 12 on Minor). We could say this scale consists of two tetrachords, exactly alike. There is something highly interesting about these tetrachords. For this next step it would help to have all the scales before the eye—in a book, on a board or chart. Best would be a separate chart for each scale with the chart able to be separated in two to show the tetrachords. (see p. 91)

**Who can find a tetrachord from another scale which is exactly like the top or upper tetrachord of the C scale?** They will find that the upper tetrachord of the C scale is identical to the lower tetrachord of the G scale; the upper tetrachord of the G scale is identical to the lower tetrachord of the D scale and so on. **What facts can we deduce from this?**

1. Even though all the scales are different from each other, they are enough alike that a whole tetrachord can belong to more than one scale.
2. Every tetrachord can be the lower tetrachord of one scale, the upper tetrachord of another. (When we get to minor scales we will find that there are even more scales to which the same tetrachord can belong.)
3. When we compare the two scales to which one tetrachord can belong, we find that there is only one note in the one scale different from the other scale.
4. The scales in such a relationship always seem to be 5 letters or 5 scale degrees away from each other.

These are all interesting facts about scale structure and relationship, but the tetrachord is not the way to *introduce* scales. The tetrachord relationship is not the WHY or HOW scales are built; it is the

RESULT of the formula. The whole concept of scale structure is tough enough to learn and understand without the further unnecessary confusion caused by tetrachords.

Reversing the process, we can take the lower tetrachord of the C scale and discover it is the upper tetrachord of the F scale and so on. The scales in this relationship are again 5 letters or scale degrees away from each other; in this case down. This relationship is often referred to as the CIRCLE OF FIFTHS and is indicated this way:

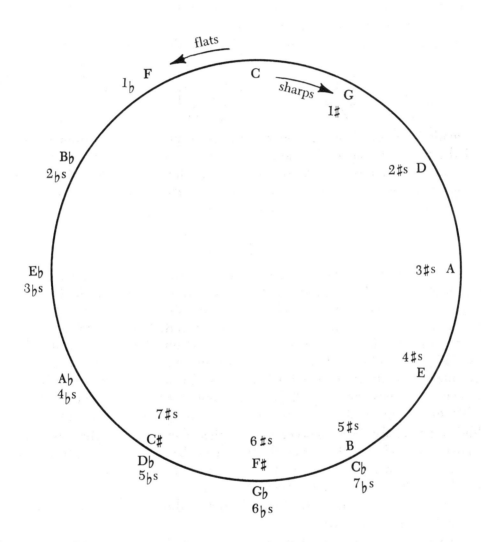

## CIRCLE OF FIFTHS

This is a widely taught fact, the significance of which could be questioned. It certainly is not necessary for the knowledge of scale structure, and is in fact quite an advanced concept. Piano teachers may be likely to use the method of the tetrachords, but they use it to aid the student in the fingering and spelling of a scale when playing it, rather than as a means of explaining the WHY and WHAT and HOW of scale structure. The Circle of Fifths really refers to a number of other relationships besides that of scales through tetrachords. The same circle shows us:

1. The order of sharps in the signature.
2. The order of flats in the signature.
3. The order of the sharp scales or keys from no sharps to all seven.
4. The order of the flat scales or keys from no flats to all seven.
5. The relationship of keys as it affects modulation, in that the most common modulations are those to the most closely related keys.
6. The relationship of chords. One of the most natural progressions of chords to other chords is by fifths: the chord on 6 of the scale, to the chord on 2, the chord on 2 to the chord on 5, the chord on 5 to the chord on 1, and so on.

$$\left.\begin{matrix} 6 \\ 5 \\ 4 \\ 3 \\ 2 \end{matrix}\right] \text{5 degrees} \qquad \left.\begin{matrix} 2 \\ 1 \\ 7 \\ 6 \\ 5 \end{matrix}\right] \text{5 degrees} \qquad \left.\begin{matrix} 5 \\ 4 \\ 3 \\ 2 \\ 1 \end{matrix}\right] \text{5 degrees}$$

## RECAPITULATION

A short review of some of the points made in this chapter might be helpful.

The formula of the scale can be presented a number of ways:

1. Tetrachords: two groupings of notes exactly the same, one whole step apart.

   Objections: tetrachords are not necessary to the basic concept of scales; they are irrelevant and confusing. There is always the problem of remembering what the distance is between the two tetrachords. Besides its very name is a mouthful.

2. 1  1 ½  1  1  1 ½

3. W W H W W W H

   Whole, whole, half, etc.

   Problems: The student figuring the steps by means of these formulae gets lost. In reality, he must first count or identify the scale *member* (1, 2, 5, 7) and then the kind of interval—1 or ½. So in his mind he is saying 1 between 1 and 2, 1 between 2 and 3, ½ between 3 and 4, etc. leading to a confusion of numbers.

4. The ladder. Let us hope this ineffective device is discarded forever. In its effort to give a visualization of intervals, it too runs into all the complications of 2 and 3, plus some others. When we think of a ladder we think of a series of rungs on which we climb from one to the other. We do *not* step on the spaces in between. On the staff of course we do use the spaces. In addition, the rungs on a ladder are evenly spaced, but on the ladder used to show the steps of the scale, they are not. Of course there are similarities between the ladder and the musical staff; we even used this analogy when illustrating leger lines. But in that case we are not attempting to illustrate intervalic relationships, merely an extention of the lines of the staff.

5. The analogy of steps only places before the eye all the confusions of methods 2 and 3.

Why do we not use as a tool the object which most of us have around us in our musical environment, and which best presents a picture of scale structure because it is incorporated into its design—the *piano?* Or any keyboard instrument. Or, of course, keyboard facsimiles. No teacher should attempt to teach scale structure and all the related topics without placing before *each* student a keyboard, preferably lettered, which he can not only look at and hear, but touch. Distance (intervals) is something to be seen, measured, heard and felt—*experienced.*

To gather around the piano is useful occasionally, but should not be the only way used. To point at one cardboard facsimile at the front of the room is not enough—most persons will not be able to see clearly enough. The letters will be unreadable, the distances from piano key to key unreal.

Each student should have a keyboard before him. A cardboard facsimile is the least; a roomful of pianos, organs, or small keyboard instruments which sound is more than most of us can at present hope for. Classes which play the Melodica should certainly use them here. Good enough equipment would be either the Diller Keyboards from Schirmer or the plastic interlocking keyboards from Vandre. Don't forget games such as "Take a Giant Step," as illustrated and described in Madeleine Carabo-Cone's books.

*Suggested Assignments:*
1. Spell out scales in whole notes using a keyboard.
2. Take each note of a scale and list the enharmonic names for each note

| D | E | F♯ etc. |
|---|---|---|
| C double sharp | D double sharp | |
| E double flat | F flat | |

3. Spell out a scale, and then spell the scale which evolves from the upper tetrachord of the first scale; also the scale which uses the lower tetrachord of that first scale.

The student who has come this far is no longer a musical novice. He will have mastered difficult concepts and procedures. He is ready for greater complexities. He may find what follows in the next chapters to be pleasantly simple after the struggle just completed. In mastering the work of this chapter however, he will have attained an important pivotal position regarding what is to follow. Perhaps we could compare it to the summit of a mountain; and now the descent down the gentle slopes of the other side is his reward.

# TETRACHORDS

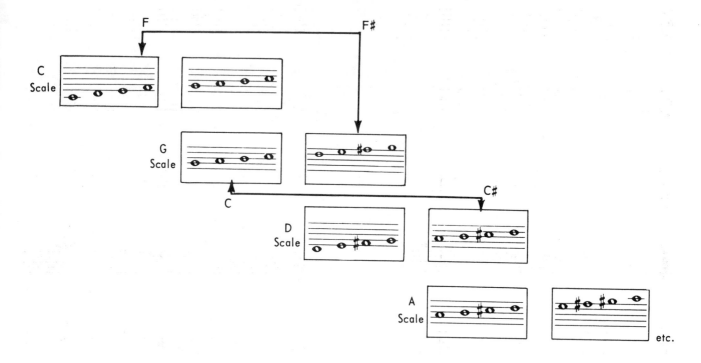

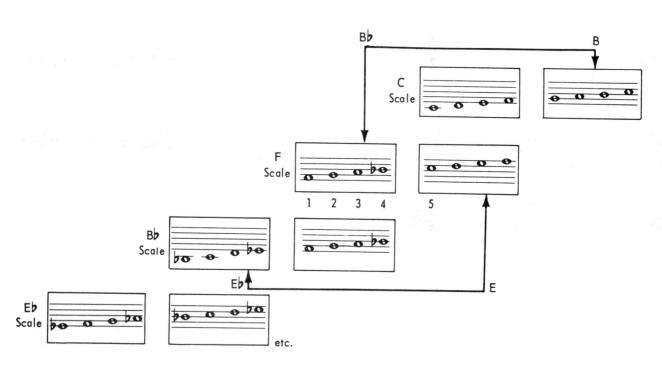

# MAJOR SCALES

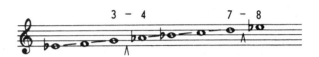

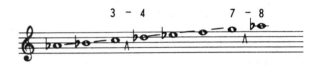

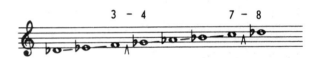

# Chapter 8

# Key Signatures

## WHAT YOU NEED TO KNOW

1. Steps and half steps.
2. What flats are and what they do.
3. What sharps are and what they do.
4. Scale structure.

## BASIC FACTS YOU WILL LEARN: THE ANSWERS TO THESE QUESTIONS

1. What is a key signature? A sign which tells all the notes in a scale, particularly the sharps or flats.
2. How can we know whether a key has sharps or flats? The name of the key tells this.
3. Why are flats or sharps written in that arrangement? The order of the sharps or flats in the key signature is determined by the order in which they appear in scales.
4. How can we tell which flats or sharps are in a certain key?
5. Do we just have to remember whether or not a note in a scale is flatted or sharped? Yes.
6. Is there a way to look at the flats or sharps at the beginning of a piece and know the key? When there are flats in the key signature, the next-to-last flat will be the same as the key. Otherwise, count down four degrees from the last flat. When there are sharps in the key signature, go up one degree from the last sharp; that is the key.

## WHAT THIS LESSON CAN LEAD TO

1. The understanding and use of key signatures.
2. Reading and dictation skill—the use of Latin syllables.
3. The Tonic Tone and Tonic Chord.
4. The understanding of chords and their use.

---

## KEY

Let's take a song we know and have played and sung, but write it out using different notes. In other words, using a different scale. Usually, when a composer decides to write some music, he selects one of the scales like those we have worked with (see Chapter 7) and uses those notes in the scale for his composition. Oh, maybe not *only* those notes—there are ways to add to them—and probably not just that one scale for the whole composition, but at least mainly that scale as a sort of home base. Only, no one is likely to refer to the composer's composition as being in the SCALE of, say, G. We will say it is in the what? The KEY of G. What then is a key, and is it different from a scale? A composition in the *key* of G is using the notes in the *scale* of G, the home-tone (first tone) will be G, it will sound really finished only if it ends on the tonic tone (last tone) G. (The terms, "home-tone" and "tonic" will be thoroughly dealt with a bit later in this chapter.)

This turns into a really interesting question. Here is an analogy which might help. When the eleven members of a football team pose for a team picture, they take a formal pose with the guards in a certain position, the tackles in a certain place, the fullback a certain way and so on. But when they scrimmage on the field and practice certain plays, the same eleven men are all scrambled up on the field as they execute the play, constantly moving and changing their position in relation to each other. Same eleven men, same names and titles, but not in the static formal order. The parallel would be the eight notes formally arranged in a *scale* from 1 to 8, (DO to DO); but when the same eight notes are used in a musical composition they are all scrambled up, and the composition is said to be in a key. The key uses the notes of the scale but does not have to confine itself to the order of the notes in the scale. The captain is the leader of the football team; Do or the tonic (first-tone) is the leader of the scale.

These two very good definitions were given by two Elementary Education sophomores. One said, "A SCALE IS A WRITTEN OUT KEY." The other said, "A KEY IS A SCALE IN ACTION." See if these help you.

**Now, back to the song. Suppose we have played and sung Three Blind Mice many times this way:**

**But now we want to start the song on C and we have found, by trial and error, using xylos or resonator bells or the piano, that the notes will be:**

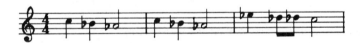

**Is this the way the music would really appear in printed music—the way we have written it here? Compare it to songs in any of your song books. No, the music won't look like this. It would look this way:**

**All the flats, instead of appearing before each note to be flatted, are gathered together in a bunch and placed at the beginning of the song:** Immediately there comes a flood of questions.
1. When you come to each note how can you remember whether or not it has a flat if it isn't there with the note? Do we just have to remember?
2. Why did you put the flats in that arrangement?
3. How do you know which flats to write there? How can you know which flats belong to which scale? How can you know whether a scale contains sharps or flats?
4. Is there some way these flats can tell you what scale or key they represent?

## Key Signature

In addition, teacher should have a question of his own. **What is an arrangement of flats like this called? Well, first of all, they comprise a kind of sign. Secondly, what is it they are indicating? They** are showing which notes of the scale will be flatted. And in reality they are telling us all the other notes of the scale—those that are NOT flatted. And all the notes of the scale together tell us the KEY. So, this is a KEY SIGN, or KEY SIGNATURE.

Really, then, at the beginning of every musical selection are three important signs which too often we ignore:

|  |  |  |
|---|---|---|
| The clef which names the lines and spaces of the staff. | The key signature which tells all about the key and scale. | The measure signature which tells how to count the music. |

Now, answering the other questions each in turn.

### Question One: Do We Have to Remember?

Yes, we just have to remember. For instance in Three Blind Mice, A is flatted, so is B, but **C** is not, etc. In the long run it is more efficient, makes for a neater manuscript, easier and clearer to read; but yes, you do just have to remember. That's why lots of us prefer certain keys to others and groan when we have to remember the keys which have many flats.

### Question Two: The Order of Flats in the Key Signature

The answer to this is interesting and if you try to figure out the answer you soon discover two answers which are NOT correct: No, the arrangement of the flats at the beginning does not come from the order of the flats in that particular scale. If so, it would be ♭♭♭. No, it does not come from the order in which the flats appeared in Three Blind Mice. That would be ♭♭♭. If either of these were the correct answers, the "picture" of those flats at the beginning of a piece would differ with each song, or with each scale. An interesting fact about this order of the flats in the key signature is that it is always the same. If there are three flats in a piece they are always ♭♭♭. If there are five flats in a piece, they are always ♭♭♭♭♭.

Unless someone were to remember the pages on tetrachords (Chapter 7), this answer is not usually known, even among many music majors. We will need to use our knowledge of scales—their spelling and structure. Let's try to discover the answer together. Teacher can use the same charts of scales that were suggested for the study of tetrachords (see Chapter 7) or at least have some way of displaying all the scales for all to see.

**What is the scale which has no sharps or flats?** Everybody knows. The scale of C. "The refuge of the destitute" a former music professor used to call it. **What scale has only one flat—What is the flat and the scale?** Refer freely to the charts.

F Scale

Let's write down that flat. ♭
B♭

**What is the scale that has two flats and what are the flats?**

Scale of B♭)
B♭        E♭                                                    B♭E♭

Notice that this scale doesn't have just *any* two flats. One of the flats, B♭ appeared in the previous scale. It goes first in the key signature, then the other flat.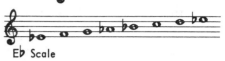

What scale has three flats? What are the flats?

E♭ Scale

Notice again that the B♭ reappears in the scale. Also the E♭ recurs. Evidently, once a flat has appeared in one scale it reappears in all the subsequent scales, which contain a greater number of flats. The new flat is A♭ . Now you are beginning to understand where the order of flats comes from. It may not be necessary to illustrate further, but just in case, here is one more. The scale with four flats? Which flats?

A♭  B♭      D♭  E♭            A♭

new flat

B♭ E♭ A♭ D♭

Notice the B♭ is there, also E♭ and A♭. The new flat is D♭, so that goes next in order. The order of the flats in the key signature is determined by the order in which they appear in the scales—or are added into the scales. That order, then, of course, is fixed, so if a scale has two flats, it will always be and if it has six flats it will be . Since there are only seven different letters of the musical alphabet there will then be only seven flats. Here is the complete order of the flats of the key signature . While I point to them, you say the letter names: B E A D G C F. This, as you can see, spells a word which will help you remember the order. (Well, at least, there is the word BEAD, and then GCF.) There is another way to help you remember this order and you really *should* remember it. The flats make a symmetrical picture: . Even if the staff is not there, if you know the order, you should be able to identify the flats. For instance, what is the name of the fourth flat? And so on. Tradition has it that the flats must make this picture, so even this

BEAD...D

would be wrong:

This traditional arrangement of the flats in the key signature may be derived from the location of the flat as it first appears, when the scale is written out on the staff.

Let's prove out the importance of the key signature. Let's play on our xylos (or recorders) a song we like, Brother Come and Dance With Me from Hansel and Gretel. The music is here on the flannel board (or chart). Study it quietly and practice pointing to each bell with your fingers (silent practice—no noise) or practice fingering it on your recorder without placing the instrument in your mouth.

Now let's play it.  etc.

Ready, play. Something certainly is not right. What is the matter? The KEY SIGNATURE. We've forgotten the key signature. Teacher places four flats after the G clef (it could be three sharps). Now let's play it. Now the song is correct.

etc.

### The Order of Sharps

With the sharps of course you should now understand the reason for the order, but here is an illustration anyway: (It can be done exactly as with the flats; however here is a slightly different approach.)

**The scale with one sharp? G scale.**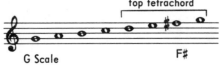

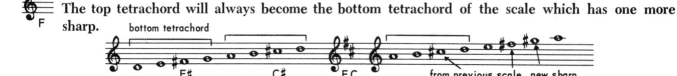

**The scale with two sharps? Instead of using the charts, use the tetrachord method if you wish. The top tetrachord will always become the bottom tetrachord of the scale which has one more sharp.**

The conclusions are similar. Once a sharp appears in a scale, it will reappear in all subsequent scales which contain a greater number of sharps. The order of the sharps in the key signature is determined by the order in which they are added into scales—or appear in scales.

**The complete key signature of sharps looks like this:** 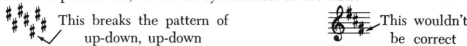 **Say the letter names as I point: Try as we might, I guess we can't make a word out** of **these letters! However** here are some helps for your memory.

**If you point to the sharps in reverse order, you will discover:** F C G D A E B    B E A D G C F **that the order of the sharps is the exact reverse of the order of the flats.**

Make up a silly saying for the order of the sharps. One student came up with *Frank Can Go Down And Eat Beans.*

The sharps make a picture too, almost as symmetrical as the flats:

This breaks the pattern of up-down, up-down              This wouldn't be correct

If we were to write out every scale, you would see that the location of each sharp or flat, when it *first* appears, in a scale, is its location in the signature. For example:

For further illustration, F♯ appears first in the scale of G, and probably in the location ⬐. Later, in the scale of D, it appears here ▭ but the *first* time it occurred, it was on the fifth line. And that is where it is placed in the key signature.

Here is a picture a student drew to help him remember. He called it a pyramid of sharps.

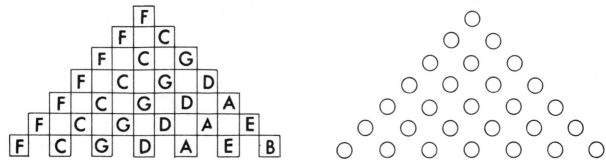

Why don't you build your own pyramid of flats?

Another student used this picture:

Sharps:      6  7  1  2  3  4  5
             F  C  G  D  A  E  B

The numbers over the row of letters tell the number of sharps in that scale or key. The letters tell the order of sharps in the key signature.

If you start the row of letters with the second letter, C, you have the order of sharp scales from no sharps to all seven.

Flats:       B  E  A  D  G  C  F
             2  3  4  5  6  7  1

The numbers beneath this row of letters tell the number of flats in that scale or key. The letters tell the order of flats in the key signature.

If you start this row of letters with the next-to-last letter, F, and then go from the F to the beginning, you have the order of flat scales from no flats to all seven.

## DETERMINING THE KEY

Question Four: Is there some way these flats can tell you what scale or key they represent. **The flats or sharps in the signature tell several things. First, obviously they tell us which notes must be flatted or sharped. The signature acts as a short hand. We don't have to spell out the scale. It tells us all the notes of the scale and particularly those to be sharped or flatted.**

It is particularly at a stage like this that the students as well as the teacher find the study of an instrument so valuable. Teacher can use the planned mistake again. Suppose it is a recorder group. He should direct the students to turn to a song with the signature of one sharp. Usually teacher doesn't have to structure anything else—chances are the students will blithely ignore the key signature and play F *natural*. Here again, because the song is familiar, the players know they have made a mistake and where.

CARELESS LOVE—American Folk Song

SUMER IS ICUMEN IN—Old English (Her: 65)

**What did we forget to notice?** The key signature. **There is an F♯ in it. What is the fingering? Now play the song.** The meaning, function, and need of the sharp is very clear under such circumstances. We need it because this familiar song sounds wrong without it. Because we understand how a scale is built we know the sharp is demanded by the formula. Because we know the origins of the key signature (it is a short-cut for spelling out the scale) and we know that it represents the spelled-out scale, we understand its meaning; and because we know that a sharp is one half step higher than a tone without the sharp and causes the tone to sound higher we know the function.

Or of course teacher could just do it "straight": **What do you see after the G clef? An F sharp. What does it mean?** Every F in the piece must be F♯ and fingered **Practice playing four F sharps—ready, one two, play. Now let's play the piece.**

High F♯

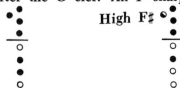

The second fact the key signature tells us is the key. We've said it tells us all the notes in the scale—Bb, Eb, Ab, and Db (see p. 94 top) and the remaining letters are C, F and G; but this doesn't indicate the starting note of the scale, sometimes called the home tone. There is a very easy way to ascertain the key just by looking at the key signature, but first a question. Why do we need to know the key? Is it always necessary? Some teachers religiously drill this into students even when the information is not necessary or pertinent.

For instance, when we play a piece on bells or flutes or recorders, do we need to know the key? No—the notes are all there—just play them. When we sing a song by memory or from the music with words, do we need to know the key? No—we can sing the song without knowing the key. When we strum an accompaniment on a guitar or uke or autoharp, do we need to know the key? No, not if the chords are indicated. But yes, if the chords are not indicated we must know the key in order to select the appropriate chord. When else do we need to know the key? If it is a song we never saw before and we are going to sight read it using numbers or syllables then we must certainly know the key so that we can determine which note is 1 or DO, and all the other syllable names. If we want to change a song from one key to another—to transpose the song, then we would certainly need to know the key. So the important thing is to learn how to find the key from the key signature at a time when the knowledge is needed.

## TELLING THE KEY FROM THE SIGNATURE

Look at these key signatures and see if you can detect a relationship between the flats and the name of the key:

The name of the key always seems to be the same as the name of the flat next to the last. **Yes, it's as easy as that.** When there are flats in the key signature, the key is the same as the next-to-last flat. **Prove it. What are these keys? Remember that next-to-last means the flat next furthest away from the clef.**

This will always work except in this case: There is no next-to-last flat! For this key there are other ways. For one thing, you might just remember the scale with one flat, Bb, is F. Another way involves a count-down like that for our astronauts. Call that flat, Bb, number four, and count down each line and space to number one. Number one names the key. It is the key of F. This system will work with all the key signatures containing flats—merely count down four from the LAST flat.

Call the last ⌈Flat or ⌈Fa. The Ab, which is number one, turns out to be the
           ⌊our     ⌊
next-to-last flat, which is the first way we did it, and surely the first is an *easier* way.

### Problems

This is such a simple procedure, you wonder why students find it so confusing, or forget it so quickly, or why teachers have so much trouble teaching it. One reason is failure to make it clear.

Sometimes it is taught this way: count down to four from the last flat:

This can give rise to confusion about where to start counting, where one ends, is the degree numbered four the key, or the degree below it . . . ? Calling the last flat four—a backwards count—eliminates that confusion. Another cause of confusion is a signature like this: When we count down from the last flat in this signature, there is no flat there! How is the beginner to know that the Db up on the fourth line names *all* Ds Db?

Another reason is failure to apply this knowledge. For instance, in order to sing an unfamiliar song, we might use syllables, so that we can find out how it sounds. For this we must know the key. The key tells what note to call one or DO. (More on this in Chapter 9 on syllables—p. 106.)

Or consider an autoharp player. He knows that to determine the home chord of a song he must know the key. And he knows that the second chord for most two chord songs will be five scale notes up from the home tone. Hence, at the beginning of a song means the key of B♭. The home chord will be on B♭ and five steps up will be the F chord. (The larger autoharps even have F7.) Now, because he has figured out the key, he can accompany the song using B♭ and F, having to decide only when to use each chord.

## The Home Tone

There is something else the flats (or sharps) in a key signature can tell us. It is almost the same as the name of the key—that is, the key-tone or first tone—the home-tone, or DO. Sometimes students are taught how to "find DO." (Some may wonder why they need to "find DO" or how it got lost.) It is for the reason just stated; so as to know what syllables to assign to each note. The first note of the scale, the starting note is the most important one. Its syllable name is DO. It starts and *ends* a scale and names the scale, and says "THE END" at the end of almost all music. Because it does all these things, we sometimes say that DO gives us the "key feeling." Everything seems to circulate around DO. It is the "tone-center." So to "find DO" is to arrive at all these things. DO is usually what the teacher will play on a pitch pipe and what you may hum before starting to sing a song, familiar or not. The key signature will indicate all that.

Have you noticed that every flat key has the name FLAT in the key: E♭, D♭, G♭, etc. Except F. You can see why—there is always a flat at the end of the count down 4 - 3 - 2 - 1. Just to remind you: To determine the key from flat signatures, 1. IT IS THE SAME AS THE NEXT-TO-LAST FLAT; 2. COUNT DOWN FOUR FROM THE *LAST* FLAT.

Do you know why the key is always the same as the next-to-last flat? Because the newest flat to be added into the scale is always the fourth note of the scale, or FA. Hence, DO is always four scale notes down.

## SHARP SIGNATURES

With sharp signatures, there is a different "gimmick" but similar. See if you can detect it. These first examples should be chosen very carefully, to avoid "exceptions" and difficulties with leger lines. The name of the key or DO seems to

Key of D      Key of E

be one degree higher than the last sharp. Test it: These are the three signatures teacher should use first.

(Or the next letter in the musical alphabet after the last sharp.)

When there are sharps in the key signature the key is found one degree (line or space) higher than the last sharp—the sharp furthest from the clef. This interval is a half step.

The next signatures pose the problem of leger lines or almost leger lines. Because of this it is better not to use them first and even when using them later to *prove out* the rule. Students may need help.

The space G is sometimes a challenge. Just count up to it.

F♯ Key of G

This is a hard one, and requires counting carefully up the leger lines.

G♯ Key of A

Now here comes a tricky one. What is the key? Go up one degree from the last sharp, E♯, F? Not quite! No one warned you, but if you check the signature you will see a sharp on line F.

E♯

Therefore the key is F♯. Now how many keys are going to have a sneaky trick like that? Only two. The key of F♯ and one other: up one degree from the last sharp. Some people say up to eight. But why would anyone teach *Count* Key of C Sharp. To recapitulate, count "call the last Sharp Seven and go *down seven degrees?* Seven chances to make a mistake! Because the sharp signatures present these few complications, it seems preferable to teach the flat signatures first and in the order described. Here again, as in other instances, some teachers just take the signatures "in order" of their increasing numbers of sharps or flats. This is not the simplest presentation. And why is the key to be found up one degree from the last sharp? Because the new sharp is always the next-to-last note or TI; going up one takes us to DO.

## Question Three: Sharps or Flats?

Another question often arises at this point. IS there a way to know which a certain key contains, sharps or flats? Yes, there is. You've already noticed that every key with a flat signature has *flat* in its name: B♭, A♭, D♭, etc. with the exception of F. Just this information alone is the answer to the question. But going further: all the keys with sharps in the signature are plain letters: G, D, E, B, etc. with two exceptions, F♯ and C♯. One other little fact to help your memory. C is an "all or nothing" letter. The key of C has *no* sharps or flats, the key of C♯ has *all* the sharps and the key of C♭ has all the flats.

## Determining the Signature of a Key

Is there a time when you really need to know these facts? Yes. You now know how to examine a key signature and determine the key it represents. But what about the reverse? Referring to the question on p. 94, suppose we wanted to know about a certain key, say D♭. Does the key of D♭ have sharps or flats in it (I hope you are grinning) and exactly which notes are flatted, and what are all the other notes in this key? And when would we need to know this information? To answer the last question first: not often, really. It is the more advanced musician who needs to know this—to know what notes to play on his instrument without the help of printed music; to know what notes to write down if he wishes to notate music. There will be some examples of this soon.

Do you know a way to determine every note in a key? Yes, you do. You know how to measure out a scale on a keyboard by interval and formula. Trouble is it takes so long. Here is a way to do it in two seconds.

Back to the first part of the question. The key of D♭ has *flats* in it—its name tells us that. Next, how did we determine the key D♭ in the first place? Like this:

<table>
<tr><td>Given information<br>the key signature</td><td>The information we are seeking<br>The name of the key?</td></tr>
<tr><td></td><td>D♭—SAME AS THE NEXT-TO-LAST FLAT</td></tr>
</table>

Now suppose we reversed the captions to these columns:

*Information we are seeking*
the key signature?

*Given information*
the name of the key—D♭. Now what do you know about D♭ in relation to the whole key signature? IT IS THE NEXT-TO-LAST FLAT. Well, if you know the order of the flats — our famous word BEADGCF — can you not write out the flats of the signature in order until you get to D♭ which you will know to be the NEXT-TO-LAST FLAT. Then write one more flat. That will be the last flat in the signature and the complete key signature.

Now you can really do this more quickly than it takes to read these remarks. Try another: What is the key signature for the key of A♭? Start saying or writing the flats in order B♭-E♭-A♭ and when you get to the flat which is the same as the name of the key, you know that is the NEXT-TO-LAST FLAT, so write or say one more flat and you have the key signature, B♭-E♭-A♭-D♭.

What is the key signature for G♭? B♭-E♭-A♭-D♭-G♭-C♭. You now know every note in the scale: from its name you know it begins and ends on G♭ and all the notes just listed are flat, the remaining ones are not: G♭-A♭-B♭-C♭-D♭-E♭-F-G♭

| To determine the key signature for any key containing flats, merely say the flats in order, going one flat beyond the name of the key. | Easy, isn't it? Takes two seconds compared with the effort of several minutes to measure out a scale. You won't have to do that anymore. But at least you know where the short-cut comes from and what it represents.

It's not even necessary to use the staff. Just *say* the flats in order:

Signature for the key of E♭? B♭ E♭ A♭

Signature for the key of C♭? B♭ E♭ A♭ D♭ G♭ C♭ F♭

Signature for the key of D♭? B♭ E♭ A♭ D♭ G♭ (Say the flats in order, go one beyond.)

Or refer again to the picture: B E A D G C F
                                2 3 4 5 6 7 1

How many flats in the key of D♭? The number 5 is under D so the answer is 5 flats. Which are they? The letters in the picture give the order: BEADG.

Suppose you wanted to know the key signature for the key of E. First, does it have sharps or flats? Since it doesn't have FLAT in its name, it must have sharps. Following the same procedure as in the former illustration, start from the reverse.

| *Given information* | *The information you are seeking* |
| The key signature | The name of the key      ? |
| | GO UP ONE DEGREE FROM THE LAST SHARP, E. THAT IS THE NAME OF THE KEY. |

Now, reversing the captions, and reversing the procedure:

*Given information*

key of E—contains sharps

D♯, last♯ – one degree
below E

*The information you are seeking*

The key signature. E is one degree above the last sharp; therefore to find the last sharp, back up one alphabet letter to D—D♯ is the last sharp of the signature. Say or write in the sharps in order: F♯-C♯-G♯-D♯- and you have the signature.

Some students prefer to work at a staff, others just to say the letters. Here it is both ways: Suppose you wanted to know the key signature for the key of B.

A plain letter, so contains sharps. Using the staff, go one degree down (the reverse) from B to find the last sharp of the key signature—A♯. Fill in the sharps in order, making the A♯ the last.

Or go one alphabet letter back from B—A. Now say the sharps in order, making A the last: F♯ C♯ G♯ D♯ A♯.

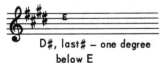

A♯ Key of B

Signature for F♯? It has sharps in its name, so contains sharps. One alphabet letter before F♯ is E.

E♯ is the last sharp. Key signature:

F♯ C♯ G♯ D♯ A♯ E♯

Signature for key of F. BE CAREFUL. F is the only plain lettered key containing flats, and let's hope you just decided to remember that the key of F contains one flat, B♭. To determine the key signature when there are sharps in the key, back up to the alphabet letter preceding the key name. That will be the last sharp of the signature. Fill in the sharps of the signature in order stopping at the designated "last sharp."

Refer to the picture:  6  7  1  2  3  4  5
                       F  C  G  D  A  E  B

How many sharps in the key of A? The number 3 is over the letter A so the answer is 3 sharps. Which are they? The letters in the picture give the order = F C G.

**Review**

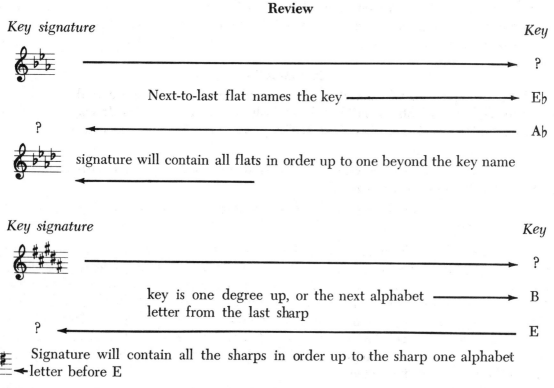

The occasions when it would be necessary to use this information are not so numerous. One would be if you were to compose a piece and want to write it down without benefit of piano or other instrument. For this, and also, just to develop better musicianship, simple melodic dictation is an excellent game-drill. After all, when we compose, what we do is to dictate to ourselves in our inner ear what we wish to write down. A little bit later on composing will be discussed in greater detail.

**Tonal Dictation**

**I am going to play a melody in the key of E♭. Figure out the signature and write it down.** At the piano, teacher plays E♭ and then the complete scale ascending and descending. **Hum the HOME-TONE (first tone). Hum or sing on "duh" what I play.** Could you write it? Most can. **Put it on the board. Now try this. Hum, sing, then write:** Here are others. Notice the level of difficulty—mainly scale.

Someone almost always asks, why do we have to have all these keys? Why can't everything be in a nice easy key like C? The answers are several:

1. For variety—everything in one key would become very monotonous. Would you be satisfied with only one style of furniture, or one color of clothing?

2. For range and convenience. Some songs have a very great range which would make the key of C uncomfortable if not impossible. Some songs remain in a low range, others in a high. Since our voices vary, we need a variety of keys to accommodate everybody.

   As for instruments, some are better suited for certain keys and their ranges affect this as well as other considerations. Some instruments sound better in certain parts of their ranges; sometimes players are more comfortable in particular keys.

3. For color—some claim that different keys have a different color—create a different emotional climate. Composers have preferences. One key will be referred to as noble, another as bright, another dark or sombre, etc.

## SUMMARY

Some teachers may question whether it is necessary to teach scale structure so thoroughly, whether it is necessary to require students to build so laboriously a number of scales. It may not be necessary and could be omitted if teacher wishes. The spelling of scales is recommended for the following reasons:

1. If it is made clear, and if teacher will help the students, they will work with a will and really master this difficult piece of knowledge.

2. It is good for students to submit to the discipline of this exercise, although this is hardly the justifying reason.

3. Working with these materials, immersed in them, handling and naming them really teaches students to be familiar with these basic tools of music: white and black keys—their look, their names, steps, and half steps, flats, sharps, enharmonic, the formula, or blueprint for the structure of a scale. The next reason (4) is really the most important, but even if it (4) didn't exist, this reason (3) would be enough to justify the procedure of spelling scales. We don't really learn something until we use it. A teacher need just watch and listen to his pupils as they work with their keyboards and speak and write the language of music. It is clear they understand what they are doing, and they will be intent and interested.

4. Scale structure is really the foundation for much of our basic knowledge of music—key signature (major and minor), how to tell keys from the signature; how to determine the signature of a key; what key signatures do; what they tell us, the relationship of scales to each other—major to major and major to minor; the circle of 5ths, key, etc. All of these facts are more clearly understood if scale structure is understood; many of them are determined by this knowledge. That is the strongest reason for spelling out scales.

# Tonal Concepts

## WHAT YOU NEED TO KNOW

Scale structure
Keys and key signatures

## BASIC FACTS YOU WILL LEARN

The music language of Latin syllables enables us to recreate in sound the music on the printed page, or to recreate in written symbol the music in our ears.

The first note of the scale has many names and many functions. Among its names, it is known as the Tonic, and is also referred to as the Home-tone, or Tone-Center, the tone about which all the other tones of the scale revolve.

A three-note chord called a triad can be built on the Tonic. Much of many melodies is based upon the Tonic Triad, and when the tones are sounded together, they harmonize much of music.

## WHAT THIS LESSON CAN LEAD TO

1. The understanding of minor.
2. The relationship of minor to major.
3. The accessories or decorating tones.
4. Other scales.
5. Reading.

## SYLLABLES

By now we can expect the students to be familiar with the sound and look of the scale (see Chapter 6 on scales—the look and sound). We hope he will have done months and months of singing and playing songs which contain complete scales. He should have looked at them, pointed them out and heard them. Also, we hope he has done drills in which the scale is sung or played routinely as part of the drills of the music lesson.

Experience shows us there is a good chance the students will have made the acquaintance casually of the syllable names by means of these techniques. There are songs containing passages in syllables, which is another way. Most basal song books have songs for just such purposes. The syllables may have been explained as nonsense words, or that this is a music language and those are the actual names of those notes. Or that they are Latin in origin and that we sing in Latin when we sing them.

Perhaps whole songs will have been translated into the Latin music language. On this basis students can accept such procedures, although they do not understand why and how the syllables are used, and do not know by memory the syllable names.

Since the advent of "DO, RE, MI" from "The Sound of Music" we may often have wondered what we did before that delightful song. The whole scene from Rodgers and Hammerstein's charming show is a perfect explanation of why syllables are, and what they do. It wouldn't hurt to hear that whole scene so often we could sing and recite it by memory. It is the perfect stepping-off place.

After such building of familiarity with the scale and the syllable names the teacher is ready to concentrate on reading skill. This can be begun at any age. It is the beginning stage, no matter what the age. Even so, teachers encounter many college students who never have had such experience with syllables. Many times they must embark on this adventure without these preliminaries.

Teacher begins: **Suppose we wanted to refer to scales in general. How can we refer to them?** Letters won't do, because there is a different set for each scale. Numbers will work: every scale goes 1 2 3 4 5 6 7 8. The need for another set of names was felt some centuries ago. There was a Latin hymn in which each new little phrase began on a succeeding note of the ascending scale, and it is from this chant that we got the famous names for the scale: DO RE MI FA SO LA TI DO.
Solmization:

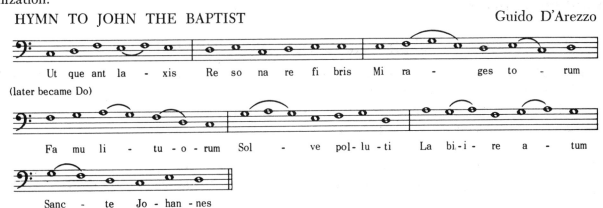

HYMN TO JOHN THE BAPTIST                                    Guido D'Arezzo

Ut was later changed to Do and Sol later became So.

**Sing the scale with me as I point to the notes.** Everybody needs moral support here. **It doesn't matter how you sound, I'll sing with you. Try it anyway.** There are some to whom what we do will not make much sense. If you can't carry a tune, syllables don't mean much to you. There are others who are wanderers, and others who can sing but don't like to. The best that can be offered here is some clarification of what syllables are and can do.

Teacher should choose a scale with all the notes on the staff. It will be easier to read and in the most comfortable singing range. He should label each note with its syllable name.

**Sing the scale up and down.** Then, teacher should follow with very simple changes in direction of the

scale-line:

Some will probably sing the right names but on the wrong pitches: teacher can expect all kinds of errors and giggles and laughter. Let him join in. Students may change the pitch correctly but sing the wrong names. Or flub both. **If the notes go down, what must your voice do?** Go down too. Try again. It helps for teacher to warn of a coming change in direction. They should do a number of these

changes in direction, always in scale line. Students' mistakes make them AWARE. Syllables will help you do this right. And they are motivated to try again and do it right. When students can do this well they are ready, and only then, for the next step.

Slowly, and with deliberation, teacher should start a scale drill like those just mentioned, and then, from one tonic note (DO-MI or SO), skip back to another tonic note. More break-downs into gales of laughter. But it is laughter like that of people who like to be tickled or caught in a game, and who will try next time not to be caught. Teacher should laugh too, and all try again. The errors will be either a wrong name, or the right name but an adjacent pitch, rather than the pitch of the note a skip away.

**How can you sing the right tone when there is a skip?** The answers are very important.
1. You have to REMEMBER the sound of the note when it was sung several notes ago.

2. Or just go back down or up the scale till you get to the note which was skipped to.

3. Or sing very softly or even silently those notes in between the skip.

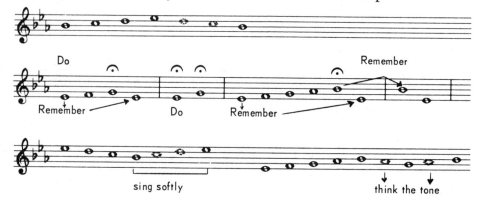

**Now that we have a way to do this, let's try again.** With these helps it proves easier, and the students become more AWARE of how a skip looks; how to make it sound right. The skips must be carefully chosen (see good and bad examples). There should be short fun drills of this kind until most can

Good examples:

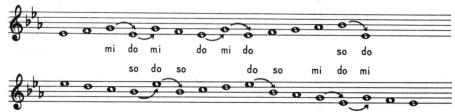

Poor examples:

do it. Students usually like this game as long as they have been shown ways to do it. Teacher must remember continually, that to the student who cannot carry a tune, or who is a "leaner" or "wanderer," a drill like this has very little meaning, and so do syllables. Unless his ear can be improved, he shouldn't be made to submit to such drills. It is highly frustrating and meaningless to him.

Now since the students can play "follow the pointer" on simple drills which both follow the scale and skip from one member of the tonic chord to another, they and teacher can play this game. Let the notes that teacher points to, seemingly at random, be, in fact, a song that everyone knows, so all can enjoy the joke as they hear themselves sing this song on syllables. There is usually delighted laughter and buzzing—and more dawning INSIGHT. A number of songs should be done this way—by pointing to the notes in the scale. They are written out here, but should not be used that way.

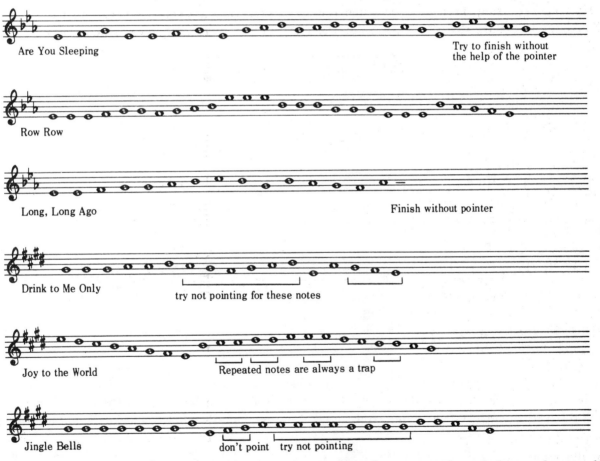

Use several of the current "pop" songs. Of course choose those that are mostly scale line and tonic chord. This always delights the students and is a revelation to them.

Here is a 20th century symphonic piece, and an operatic aria consisting mostly of scale.

Petrushka                                   Stravinsky (simplified)

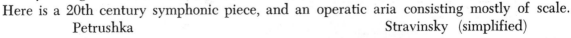

ti  do  re    mi  re  do  ti    la

CARO NOME (Rigoletto)                                                    Verdi

Songs like the following are particularly suitable for this activity:

Looby Loo (Her: 233)

The Bells of St. Mary

Farmer in the Dell (Her: 165, fl.)

Alouette (Her: 63)

Twinkle Twinkle (Her: 41)

Battle Hymn of the Republic (Her: 26)

Long, Long Ago (Her: 204)

Swanee River (Her: 237, fl.)

Mary Had a Little Lamb (Her: 103, fl.)

The First Noel (Her: 86, fl.)

Yankee Doodle (Her: 91, fl.)

Ach, du Leiber Augustin (Her: 159)

Joy to the World (Her: 51, fl.)

Marine's Hymn (Her: 30, fl.)

Jingle Bells (Her: 149)

Billy Boy (Her: 44)

Danny Boy

Jacob's Ladder (Her: 119, fl.)

You Are My Sunshine

Lucky Old Sun

Love Me Tender (Auralee) (Her: 3)

Clementine (Her: 176)

Good Christian Men

Bring a Torch (Her: 70)

Taps (Her: 183, fl.)

Found a Peanut

My Bonnie Lies Over the Ocean (Her: 134, fl.)

All of a Sudden My Heart Sings

I'm in Love with a Wonderful Guy

Anywhere I Wander

My Romance

Just the Way You Look Tonight

Lady of Spain

Fly Me to the Moon

Because

Old Man River

Beautiful Dreamer

When the Saints Come Marchin' In

Songs that don't start on DO need to be prepared:

1. sing **DO**    2. sing **DO RE MI**    3. **Sing MI—this is your starting tone.**

These kinds of game-drills can be done many times. They are fun. **Notice how these songs move. Mostly they go up and down the scale. Some songs have a complete scale in them. Most songs really do not skip much. But when they do there is something very interesting and helpful about the way they do skip. Let us turn our attention to that.**

## Home-Tone

A scale has other characteristics besides all those we have listed about it. For instance, what note in the scale would you say is the most important and why? Yes, the first note—DO, or the last. WHY?

1. The starting note names the scale, and therefore the key.

2. The whole formula is measured from the starting note, which starts the scale.

3. The last note ends the scale.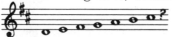

If we played a scale without its last note, what would be the effect? It doesn't sound ended. We haven't arrived at the end, or "home." In fact, that finished feeling is so important that the first (and last) note is often referred to as the "tone center" and called the "home tone." When you really stop to think about it, no matter how complicated the music, or how varied one selection is from another, the only way to say "THE END" in music is to end on the home-tone. Almost all our music does. The other notes in the scale seem to gravitate to it. They revolve about it. I'll play this and you end it.

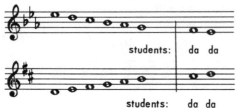

### "The End"—Last Note

Leaf through many songs in your song book (or flute book or instrument book). Identify the key from the key signature and then check the last note. Almost always the last note of the song will be the same as the key—that is, if E♭ is the last note, it is the key of E♭; if D is the last note, the key is D. (Important message—avoid all minor songs.) It happens so much that we can make it a rule and it is one of the best and quickest ways to tell the key. There are exceptions which students will delight in pointing out.

THE FIRST NOEL

Born is the King___ of Is - ra - el.

Teacher can encourage it—they are learning and interested. Songs like Because. The First Noel, Black is the Color, I Know Where I'm Going, You'll Never Walk Alone, do not end on Do. But usually the effect of not ending on the key-tone is a deliberately vague, modal or unfinished effect which the composer specifically desired. As wonderfully varied as music is, there are really very few ways for the music to say "THE END" and almost always the last note will be the key-tone or "home-tone."

| | Home Tone | | | | | | Home Tone |
|---|---|---|---|---|---|---|---|
| 1 | 2 | 3 | 4 | 5 | 6 | 7 | 8 |
| F | G | A | B♭ | C | D | E | F |
| Do | Re | Mi | Fa | So | La | Ti | Do |

---

**TO TELL THE KEY OF A PIECE, LOOK AT THE LAST NOTE. THAT IS THE KEY.**

To illustrate this another way, sing by ear through many familiar songs with teacher stopping for the last few final notes and letting the students finish, noting the feeling of finality and "at-homeness." Or the song can be projected on a screen, or song books can be examined and the students will indeed see this.

Yet another name is used for the home tone. And in case you're beginning to sigh because of all these names to remember, you really know and can use most of the names already.

## TONIC

The name is TONIC—you can see how it is related to the word *TONE*. We already know a great deal about the Tonic.

1. First and last note of a scale.
2. The "home-tone," key-tone, tone center.
3. It names the scale.
4. It names the key.
5. It is also known as "DO."
6. Its number name is 1 or 8; it is 1 of the scale, or 8 of the scale.
7. Most music ends on the TONIC.

Now, go back to singing the songs on syllable and notice that these songs go mostly by scale, or that when they skip, they skip a certain way. **Let us look more closely at the skips in the songs we have been singing on syllable. Do you notice how often the skip is from Do to Mi or So, or from any one of these three notes to the other two? Almost always.** Teacher writes them first horizontally as they come from the scale so students can notice that they are every other note—numbers 1, 3 and 5.

### Tonic Triad

Then teacher writes them vertically one on top of the other so that you can notice that they make something many of us recognize: a chord. Several notes sounding together make a CHORD. This is a special kind of CHORD—consisting of three notes, every other one from the scale. **Do you know what it is called? Think of other words having to do with three—trio, triplex, tripod, tricycle, etc. The chord is called a TRIAD. And because this TRIAD is built on the first note of the scale it takes the name of the first note—TONIC TRIAD. In other words, these skips we have been noting in our songs go from one member of the TONIC TRIAD to another: DO MI SO.**

Practice singing the Tonic triad. Here is one way: sing DO RE MI FA SO. Now sing aloud just the tonic triad, and sing very softly to yourselves the other notes: DO re MI fa SO.

As you follow the pointer and sing songs like those in the list, teacher points out the skips from one member of the tonic triad to another, and the few skips which are not from that chord. Sometimes when a passage is very easy and obvious, teacher stops pointing and some students will be amazed and

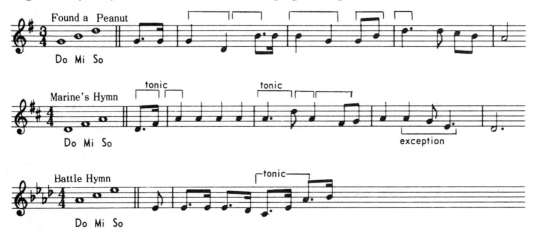

delighted to find that they can finish with the correct syllables even when they are not pointed to. This is a skill they didn't know they had.

It is very revealing to try this syllabalizing of a familiar song, even though not everybody can do it. The student gains a clearer concept of how notes arrange themselves in patterns and how many patterns are used over and over again. He begins to have an EXPECTATION as to how music "goes," which will help his "ear" for music and his ability to sight read. What teacher specifically wants him to notice in addition, is how much of music is composed of portions of a scale and the tonic triad.

There are some very good drills for developing facility with syllables. They are like the scales and arpeggios practiced by every music student on his own instrument and the warm-up exercises of athletes. Some people know them as *sequentials*. Syllables and sight reading may not be for every student, but if these skills are going to be taught the sequentials are of enormous help. Teacher can make games out of them, use teams and contests and competitions. Just a very short time should be spent

# DRILLS FOR SYLLABLES

1.
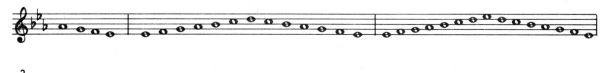

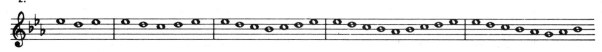

2.

3.
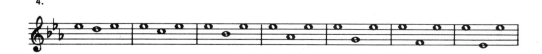

4.
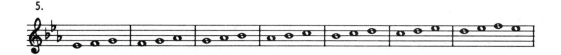

5.

6.
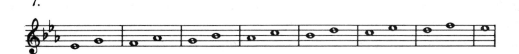

7.

8.

on them at one time, but teacher should make sure the students know WHY they are doing them, and WHAT sort of help the sequentials give. They help us

1. to articulate the musical language quickly
2. to create a familiar vocabulary of common melodic patterns found over and over again in the music we read
3. in training the ear to hear these patterns, the eye to see them, the tongue and lips to speak them. The sequentials are given here in a good order, but change it if you like. Make up your own.

It is important to reassure those students who can't do this; otherwise they regard it as further evidence of their lack of musical ability. At least, they can understand the concept of the frequent occurrence in music of scale and tonic triad. They will know the theory and this helps their understanding of how music is put together, even if they can't sing it. The teacher should be very matter-of-fact. Some people can't throw a ball very well. Others are poor spellers. It doesn't have to interfere with learning.

It sometimes is useful to sing familiar songs on syllable another way. Instead of pointing to the notes written out in the scale, write out just the syllable names vertically and point to them. This helps the vertical high-low concept of the scale, but removes the musical notes. For some this is a help and for others it is more difficult. Places that are best to stop pointing and put the students on their own would be:

| Do |
| Ti |
| La |
| So |
| Fa |
| Mi |
| Re |
| Do |

    1. repeated notes
    2. scale passage
    3. a repeated passage
    4. an obvious ending.

From this step we can move into singing songs on syllable by ear completely. **Let's take some of the same songs and see if you can sing these on syllable without having the notes or the syllable names pointed to. It is not even necessary to look at the notes or syllable names, but you can if you want to.** Teacher can have them on the board. Sometimes he may have to help with a note or two, or occasionally to indicate pitch pictures with the hand. Sometimes it helps to have the students indicate hand levels themselves, giving the general direction of the pitches; other times teacher might do it. When they get stuck, teacher helps them or supplies the missing name. If necessary he gives them the starting note. **For instance, try Yankee Doodle. I'll start you on DO. Move your hands to show pitch pictures.**

What purpose, you might ask, is there to singing songs we already know on syllable language? The answers:

    1. it builds familiarity and facility with the syllable language
    2. it requires and develops the ability to visualize or in some way sense tonal direction and distance—size of intervals, etc.
    3. it develops the inner ear—the ability to hear inside one's head
    4. it is the reverse of the process of dictation —the ability to sing at sight.

This ability is a major goal of all our study of the fundamentals of music. It is dictation—the ability to take pitch out of the air and identify it enough to give it its proper name. If you can name it, you can then write it. And just as in Chapter 1 on RHYTHMS, when the dictation should precede the reading, even though for many people it is harder than reading, so should tonal or melodic dictation precede the reading, and then the two should constantly be combined or interchanged, the one process with the other.

Teacher should try to help his students reach the point where they can do whole songs by ear on syllable without his help. If he keeps it light, this is really great fun and usually a revelation to students. An activity like this together with a light relaxed fun attitude from teacher will prevent one of the worst sins we music teachers commit—teaching our students that syllables are hard and hateful and beyond their understanding or skill. The frequent quizzical looks of the students warn teachers that we must explain WHY we do this, and offer the promise of what this skill will enable us to do.

The hardest part of this is getting the starting note, and here is where you can tie together many of the facts dealing with DO. Teacher and students can leaf through some songs to notice that although music always *ends* on DO, it does not always *start* on DO. The *scale* starts on DO but not necessarily the *song*. However, it does seem that if a song does not start on DO, it is quite likely to start on some member of the tonic triad—DO, MI or SO.

So here is another EXPECTATION. Students like nothing better than to present an exception (Danny Boy is one) but instead of regarding this as deliberate opposition, teacher should encourage his students to find exceptions. They learn much from the search and the preceding steps are positively reinforced.

Now how can you use all your knowledge about music to find out on what syllable a song begins, if you can't look at the music and if you don't seem able just to "tell" by listening in your inner ear? Some people can do this, others can't—just "tell." You can use the fact that you expect the song to end on DO. Just compare the first note to the last. If they are the same, the song begins on DO. If they are different, try MI or SO. This is not easy. It involves remembering in your inner ear the first and last notes, and the ability to reproduce both accurately out loud. If that is too tough, do it this way: **Judy, you and all the persons on your row keep humming DO. Jim, you and your row start the song— Way Down Upon the Swanee River and then sing "Way" again and hold it. The rest of you, are the two notes the same? No. Then the song doesn't start on DO. Keep humming DO and "Way." John, you and your row sing DO—MI—SO. The others, is "Way" either MI or SO? Yes, it sounds the same as MI. Then Way Down Upon the Swanee River must start on MI. Let's try it:**

Mi    re    do    mi    re        do    do    la    do        so    mi    do    re

| all scale line |      | teacher helps here |    | all tonic chord |

Even if a student can't do this, he learns something from just trying and observing others do it. The teacher by his matter-of-fact attitude, can keep him from feeling serious failure.

The tonic triad not only occurs frequently as the notes making up a piece of melody, but when played as a chord, can harmonize much of some songs, all of others. They may not have much harmonic variety, but there are some songs which can manage all right when harmonized only by the Tonic Triad. Such songs are:

1. most rounds   Are You Sleeping, Three Blind Mice, Hey Ho, By the Singing Water, Oh How Lovely is the Evening
2. most pentatonic songs   (see Chapter 15)
3. other songs like Grandma Grunts, Whistle Daughter, Hanging Out the Clothes

## INSTRUMENTS

In addition to syllabalizing by ear, Orff's technique of echo playing is very effective also in building tonal concepts. In this procedure the students have bells or flutes or recorders. On his instrument, the teacher plays a very short simple passage of the same nature as those described here—all scale, or including simple tonic triad skips—and the student then echoes on his instrument. The student may look if he wishes as his teacher plays. At first he should be encouraged to, so that his visual picture of up and down (as it goes on his instrument) helps his ear to identify what he hears and then to duplicate it on his instrument. Sometimes those students who can't sing accurately enough to play this game-drill with the singing voice are successful when doing it on an instrument. Teacher should encourage the proficient student not to look, but to rely completely on his ear AND HIS KNOWLEDGE OF HOW MOST MUSIC IS BUILT. It should be pointed out constantly to the students how their ability is increasing.

## Dictation Proves Tonal Concepts

Although you are discovering how useful syllables can be for you, they have a characteristic which isn't easy to master. DO keeps moving around! That means that all the notes keep changing their names. Although this takes a bit of getting used to, who can see some advantages to this?

1. No matter how DO moves around, DO-MI-SO always sounds relatively the same.
2. DO will always be the beginning sound, and the ending sound.
3. The first note of any scale will always be DO.

**Let's try a different scale from those we have worked with recently. Make it the scale of D♭. What will be the key signature? B♭-E♭-A♭-D♭-G♭. Point out to yourself where DO is and sing it** (teacher gives pitch). **Sing DO-MI-SO. Now listen to what I play.**

Do   re   mi   mi   re   do   do   mi   so   do

**Sing it back on DUH. Who can sing the syllables? If you can name it, you can write it. Write it on your own music paper, and John, you write it here for us on the board. Now I'll sing one on LUH:**

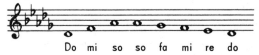

Do   mi   so   so   fa   mi   re   do

Students echo on duh. **Who will sing the syllables? Yes, do mi so so fa mi re do. If you can sing it, you can write it.** What you are doing is a very important skill. It is dictation. You really have to understand musical symbols and language to be able to do it. And yet most of you are able to do this. You are taking out of the air the music you hear, and without the benefit of seeing anything, you are able to write down the exact sounds you heard.

## Reading Applies Tonal Concepts

**Now let's do something else with the music you have written on the board. June, look at the first one. It begins on what syllable? MI. Here is the pitch DO, and MI. Try to sing it on syllables.** June does. **George, look at the third one. What syllable does it begin on? SO. Here is DO. Can you sing up to SO and give yourself the pitch? Good. Now try singing the music. Good. Now you are doing an even more important thing. What was it? Reading. Yes, you are reading music. That didn't seem so difficult,**

Sample Selection of Sight Reading Patterns

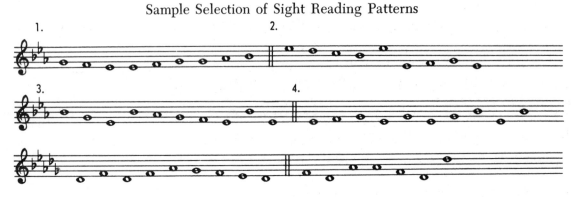

did it? And what helped you to read the music? Yes, the syllables. This is what syllables can do for you. Just to prove it, let's sing these little patterns backwards. Good. Now sing whatever I write on the board, as I write it:

**Do it backwards.** No trouble.

Notice that here as in the chapter on rhythms, we do dictation before we do reading. It certainly is not the only way to approach reading, but it is highly effective, and not enough used. Again, one is the reverse of the other.

There seems very little reason for ever speaking the syllable names instead of singing them on their pitch. There may be special circumstances occasionally, but syllables are the names of pitches, and to speak them is not only useless but negates the whole purpose of using them. Incidentally, you don't have to use syllables to use these techniques. Adapt the procedures to whatever language you prefer.

### The Power of the Home-Tone

An interesting question sometimes arises, and if it doesn't, the teacher should bring it up. Here is a group of flute players who know about key signatures, how to find the home-tone, DO, and who can read the music they are playing on their flutes. We are playing Farmer in the Dell (fl., Her: 165) in the key of G on our song flutes when someone raises this question: Why is there an F♯ in the key signature when there is no F♯ in the song? This excellent and important question and the answer provide a good illustration of the importance and power of the home-tone. Let's look at the song:

THE FARMER IN THE DELL                                                        England

1. What is the last note of the song? G. **Does it sound like "THE END"? Yes. It sounds finished. The song comes to rest on that tone.**
2. **Are there many Gs in the song?.** Notice almost every note of the song belongs to the tonic triad. **Very few notes are not G, B, or D.**
3. **It does seem then that G is the *tone center* of this song, and that the key is G. Even though every note in a key or scale is not used in the song, F♯ must be placed in the key signature not only to say all Fs must be sharped, but to say that the scale is organized around G as the tone-center or Tonic.**
4. **We could go a step further and see that in the piano accompaniment, which uses more notes than the flute, there are indeed F♯s.**

Here are some other songs, which, when in certain keys, illustrate the same point: (all are in the flute book.)

Key of G:  Auld Lang Syne, Drink to Me Only, O How Lovely is the Evening, Schubert Waltz in G, Joyful, Joyful We Adore Thee from Ode to Joy by Beethoven

Key of F:  Liza Jane, (Her: (D) 272) Swing Low, (Her: 96) Playing to Pierrot (Au Claire de la Lune) Auld Lang Syne (Her: 60)

Key of B:  Drink to Me Only

## WHAT THIS KNOWLEDGE CAN LEAD TO

You are now ready to tackle head on the business of reading music. It won't be easy, but the previous pages have given you the knowledge. Now it is up to you to practice.

## SUGGESTED ASSIGNMENTS

1. Sing the sequentials.
2. Write the sequentials down in various keys.
3. Try to sing on syllable music you know well.
4. Write down as much of this music as possible.

# Chapter 10

# Reading Music

### WHAT YOU NEED TO KNOW

All the material in the book to this point.

### BASIC FACTS YOU WILL LEARN

Further skill in writing and reading music.

### WHAT THIS LESSON CAN LEAD TO

The world of music. Start to read it.

### MELODIC AND RHYTHMIC DICTATION COMBINED

You have been doing quite well with the dictation. Try this. The key is F. What is the key signature?

One flat. B♭. This is **DO**. (Teacher plays.) You sing the tonic triad: Good. Now
Do Mi So Mi Do

listen to this and sing it back to me Students sing back on duh,
or hum. Put in syllables wherever you think you know what they are. DO -MI DO -MI duh duh duh
duh DO. Count backward up the scale to find where the "Duhs" start.

Duh Duh Duh Duh Duh Do      Do - do  re  mi  fa  so - so - so  fa  mi  re  do

Students sing: DO - MI - DO - MI - SO FA MI RE DO **Write it.**

Very good. Sing it to me again. Walk with your fingers as you sing. Are the notes all the same length?
No, your fingers go walk, walk, walk, walk, run run run run walk. Write the music again and this time give

the pitches rhythm: Listen for the accent this time, so you know where to

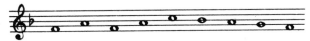

put a bar. Yes, there is an accent on the 5th note, C. How does it count? What would be the measure signature? This is the beat, the quarter note: Beat Beat . . . .

The music counts in fours. **Then the measure signature is 4. Put it in your music. Add a**

**double bar. Is it now correct?** No, the last meaure has only three

beats. **Suppose you count and conduct and listen carefully on the very last tone. Count to see what happens.** One - two - three - four - Teacher plays. . . . The last note is a two-count note—a half note.

**Right. Change it. Now your music is completely correct.** Let's

**try another. Same key. Sing DO. Sing the tonic triad:** Does it start on DO? Teach-

Do mi so mi do

er plays . . . No. **On what syllable?** Some humming and singing of the tonic triad.

etc.

MI. Yes. **Now be ready to sing back:**

Students sing back on duh. Not all can remember beyond the first or second measure. **That's all right. Don't worry about what you forgot. Keep singing what you do remember. Do you notice something easy about the first part?** It repeats. **If you have it once, you have it twice. Try changing to syllables.**

Some sing Teacher says: **Sing just the first two notes. Are they different? No—then**

mi re do ti

**both are MI.**

mi mi re do mi mi re do

**Write it. Walk that much. What are the rhythms?** Listen for the accent. **Conduct**

**it.** Teacher plays just the first part. It goes in threes. **Write it.**

**Listen carefully. After the first quarter note, are** *all* **the other notes eighths? Walk it with your fingers. Do your fingers keep walking?** No. Last note is a quarter. **Yes.**

Let's review the ways you can check yourself to see if your note values are right.

1. Listen to confirm what you've written.
2. Walk it with your fingers.
3. Count and conduct: How many notes go to each beat? Or if it is a long note, How many beats go to the note?
4. Use mathematics and check each measure: Not enough beats.

1    ½  ½  ½ = 2½

**Now let's go on and complete this. You sing the first part on syllables, and then I'll play the rest. Then you sing the second part on Duh. One-two-three . . .** Students echo duh duh . . . Some students start the

third measure on SO. **Check to see where you end. Write that part first if you want. Then work back-wards. Or listen to the whole last half as you sing it again to yourself. What is it?** A whole scale. Some-times the rhythm starts to come with the pitches. All the notes are eighths until the very end. Then they

are long notes. The second half materializes:

Soon two more join the first melodies on the board:

The steps again for taking this kind of dictation:

1. Sing back—get it down on the "tape recorder" in your head—get it in your memory.
2. Determine the starting syllable.
3. Begin the transition to syllables—one might say, the *translation* into syllables as soon as the melody is secure. This doesn't have to be done in any order—wherever in the melody you are able to determine what the syllables are.
4. Walk, count, conduct to determine the note values and measure signature.
5. Write it down.

Students often develop the habit of wanting to write too soon. How can you write anything till you know what it is? When this happens, teacher should cut out the last step of writing down, talking it through instead. After the routine is firmly established, teacher can allow a little more flexibility. If some stu-dents prefer to get the rhythm first, that's fine. The important thing is to have some procedure to fol-low. A fair proportion of students can get this far. For them it is a rewarding achievement. Many stu-dents cannot. The significance of this fact is that teachers should not regard skills such as these as a means by which to evaluate students.

## READING MUSIC

**Try to sing the melodies. Everybody together. Here is DO. Sing the first melody. One, two . . . . . Ready sing. . . . . . Good. Who will try the second melody by himself?** All are sung well. **What is it you are doing here?** *Reading.* **Just to show how well you can do it, let's read them backwards.** Now you could turn to any simple music and read it. Leaf through the song books for lower grades. Carefully select songs of similar simplicity and READ them.

A useful game-drill is the Mystery Melody. The student must read the music, then identify what song it is. For example:

A good number of students can get this far. It gets to be beyond the reading capacity of many when there are dotted notes, anacruses, skips outside of the tonic triad and so on. Then, unfortunately, we do what most teachers resort to: we teach by rote whatever passages have been too difficult for the students to read.

There are several concluding thoughts on this.
1. The greater the skill we build, the less we need to be helped by rote procedures.
2. However, rote is not necessarily bad. It enables many persons to participate in the making and experiencing of music far beyond their capacity to read it. Therefore it follows that it is not necessary that the *reading* of music be the main or only goal of music in school.
3. One of the most effective approaches to reading is through Dictation.

All of this book has to do with some aspect of reading music, but here let us consider particularly the process of looking at a song or a melodic and rhythmic line of music and converting it into the complete musical sound it represents. How do we read music and more specifically, how can we teach it?

From what has been said by a cross section of people of all ages and backgrounds, nothing in their school music experiences was more frustrating, confusing and defeating than the attempts of their teachers to teach them music reading. Their most unpleasant memories are of bouts with the "syllables." Embarrassment, humiliation and complete lack of comprehension were their common predicament. The experiences left bitter scars. Next to "I can't sing," the most common complaint is "I could never learn to read music." This is the legacy left by many a well-meaning music teacher, or class-room teacher who meant only to teach the reverse. Music reading is very difficult, but such broad failures can be attributed only to one factor: poor teaching.

Until recently, the approach to music reading most commonly taught in the schools was the so-fa system, probably the legacy of the Singing-School philosophy of our pioneer forebears. And even now, when the social or recreational instruments figure so prominently in the music curriculum of present-day music teaching, their significance as tools for the teaching of music reading is often largely overlooked. The more honest and objective music teacher will recognize that those children who know and understand the most about music reading are those who play in the orchestra or band, or who "take piano lessons" or study some other instrument PRIVATELY. Although the school music teacher can take no credit for this child's knowledge, he far too often relies on such children in his classes to carry the music lesson, and deceives himself that because those children know the answers, all of his class has learned them. Who in his desperation or self-deception has not turned to such children to save the lesson from complete collapse? We blame everything but the real cause—our own methods of teaching these highly difficult skills. Speaking to you now as one teacher to another:

We ought first to admit to ourselves several probable truths about the skill of music reading.
1. It is a very difficult skill.
2. It needs constant drill and practice and a careful, developmental, step-wise presentation by a skilled teacher.
3. Maybe the ability to read music cannot be learned by all of our students.
4. Maybe it is not even necessary that all students should learn to read music as part of their musical education.
5. Maybe it should not even be one of the most important goals of music education in public school music. (Private instruction and conservatory education are another matter.)
6. It is not necessary to be able to read music in order to have a great many wonderful musical experiences: singing in all kinds of ensembles, dancing, listening, creating, correlated experiences with other arts, playing social instruments, etc. This is quite a startling revelation when we first admit this to ourselves, because as music educators, most of us suffer from a fervor to TEACH MUSIC, which really means to "teach music *reading*." Much of this probably stems from the fact that when we ourselves first started to study music, the first thing our teachers taught us was to "read notes." The

fact that we can indeed read notes may be merely that we were the ones who survived, who stuck while many others fell by the wayside. Consider the acute disappointment of a youngster who arrives full of excited expectation for his first lessons on the piano or clarinet, and who instead never gets to touch the instrument for several lessons because his teacher is teaching him about notes, and "time," etc., or hand position and finger placement. That is why, of course, many contemporary "methods" start the student out with rote experiences on his instrument, get him making music right away, and defer till a bit later the difficult business of getting down to notes and time and finger technique. This is surely the philosophy of present-day music education in public schools, and one of the main reasons behind the many-faceted spectrum of musical experiences comprising the music curriculum.

7. Music reading has for some a very narrow connotation. It does not necessarily have to be just "syllables," or just learning to play an instrument. There are several techniques and approaches which could teach large proportions of students to read music. They are:

1. Social or Recreational Instruments
2. Rhythms
3. Intervals
4. Syllables

## Social Instruments

Social or Recreational instruments have been considered in this book usually as teaching tools. This of course, is not the only way these instruments are useful, as any text or course on music education will make abundantly clear. They are highly effective as enrichment tools, and in all sorts of casual rote experiences where reading and playing technique is not at all necessary. Because this aspect is most thoroughly covered in many other texts and is not really germane to the topic of this book we will not go into detail about this.

There is another use which can be made of these instruments which has not been nearly so fully exploited in our schools, although the texts do discuss this, and that is giving instruction to an entire class of students on these instruments. The magic and beauty of this particular teaching technique has yet to be fully realized. The author does not hesitate to make several unqualified statements about mass lessons on all the bell and flute-like instruments such as xylophones, resonator bells, recorders, melody flutes, melodicas, tonettes, and song flutes.

Almost every student will achieve—will successfully learn to play these instruments. This statement has tremendous significance, because one of the main concerns of music educators has been a rate of attrition unreconcilable with our concept of music as a joyful enrichment experience for all. Gone will be the non-participants. Gone will be the failures and the feeling of non-achievement and defeat which follows such a person his whole life. Gone will be many discipline problems, the apathy, the sheepish embarrassment, the strange reaction of some boys that music is unmasculine. These instruments perform magic. You do not have to be talented. You do not have to be smart. You do not have to practice (although most students want to). You do not have to spend lots of money to buy the instrument or to take private lessons. It isn't hard. In fact it is awfully hard to fail on these instruments. Students are amazed and delighted to find themselves actually playing a musical instrument and getting from it sounds they themselves enjoy and accept.

Playing such instruments builds true "music appreciation" far better than sessions where the class sits with hands folded listening to a recording while the teacher has a soulful expression on his face. We are more apt to like what we are involved in, and to remember it. What we play, we remember and like. Students who have played arrangements of great musical works on their flutes or bells love and remember them.

There are many other wonderful results of experiences in mass lessons on such instruments, but let us get to the reason why these instruments are mentioned here. They are probably THE MOST EFFEC-

TIVE AND SUCCESSFUL WAY to teach the reading of music. Whole masses of students can easily and pleasantly learn to read music, to PLAY IT AT SIGHT, with few if any failures. At the end of this chapter some specifics for doing this will be given, but at this point it can be stated that any instruction book which comes with the instrument can show you how to do this. Some methods introduce the instrument and music reading simultaneously; some defer music reading for a short while. Either way works, but the second approach is preferable because it probably loses fewer students. Consider that even with these very simple instruments, there are a number of skills to be mastered, even though they are of minimal difficulty.

1. Holding and fingering the instrument, which requires physical dexterity and coordination.
2. Blowing and tongueing technique (or striking technique). Usually learned in a few minutes or a few lessons.
3. Keeping together with other players; following some kind of direction.
4. Being able to play the instrument while following some kind of written score. It may not be notes at all, but may consist of numbers, colors, letters or other symbols.

Then comes the written score, the musical symbols, the sort of thing this book is all about.

1. Counting time and understanding the symbol language of time and meter.
2. Reading notes—their rhythmic value and their pitch indication.
3. Understanding the why of all of this—music theory, actually.

The teacher, who is so used to knowing and being able to do all of this, has to remember that all these separate processes must be coordinated to bring about successful music reading, and a good teaching approach will help the learner master one at a time and then combine several, rather than demanding he do all simultaneously. Therefore it is wise to defer briefly the second list until the first list of four skills is acquired. This is usually done quickly and easily, and success breeds success as well as high motivation. Teachers will have their students begging them to teach them to read music, so then teacher begins the second list. That is why a number of instruction books will suggest helping students master the physical aspects of playing these instruments while reading numbers or letters or some other familiar symbols. Then they illustrate how to introduce musical symbols in combination with the simpler language, and then how to gradually eliminate the substitutional symbol, until all that remains is music pure and simple, which students read with grace, ease and joy. All of this can happen within a few weeks, with ten lessons, to state a round figure in a bold prediction.

## Rhythms

Reading rhythms is reading music. It may not be all of it, but fully one half of it if it is singing, and maybe three quarters of it if reading is done with recreational instruments. There are some instances when rhythms are the sum total of reading music, as with percussionists or in the case of the rhythm band. Although many of these instances are mentioned more fully in the section which deals with rhythms, they are dealt with now in their relationship to reading notes.

First experiences, no matter what the age of the student, should be physical and listening activities to build concepts of fast-slow, even-uneven, long-short, accented-unaccented. Students should

1. Respond physically: walk, run, gallop, etc.
2. Play percussion instruments.
3. Say words—the action words: gal——lop.
4. Do echo clapping or playing.
5. Engage in varied physical actions as in Orff—clap, tap, patsch, etc.
6. Do chanting: names, words, expressions.
7. Dance.

These procedures are rote and do not involve looking at the musical symbols by which these rhythms would be represented. They develop more acute listening powers, the physical "feel" of rhythms, the ability to combine and coordinate rhythms, and they build a vocabulary of most of the rhythmic patterns to be encountered in all of music. It also encourages creating and improvising, which aside from the very obvious value of developing creativity, are another means of building familiarity with and mastery of the rhythmic vocabulary of music. To create a dance to music develops the ability to select slow from fast, steady from jerky, loud from soft, etc. To create a rhythmic pattern which is going to be echoed demands the student examine closely his vocabulary of rhythms and then apply his physical co-ordination. Much of what is mentioned here really comes under the title of ear-training and dictation.

The minute the teacher introduces some symbol (a substitutional one that may be more familiar, or the genuine musical symbol) then reading and reading readiness is involved. As a rule, the ability of the student to perform, produce or echo will be far ahead of his ability to symbolize what he hears, or to interpret symbols into the proper sound (dictation and reading)—a principle in the teaching of all language arts with which we are familiar. The procedure then goes like this:

1. teacher or student presents simple rhythm pattern.
2. the pattern is duplicated by echo, physical response, chant, etc.
3. a symbol is utilized to represent each member of the pattern. It can be worn or carried in some way (à la Madeleine Carabo-Cone) or used in a game (Bingo, spelling—a la Montessori), written down on chalk board or placed on flannel board. When it is selected and written down, this is Dictation. When it is then re-examined and played, or recreated WHILE LOOKING AT THE SYMBOL, this is Reading.
4. Continual experiences like this, with all the above activities in combination, is READING. As students become more proficient, we begin to eliminate some of the "experiences" and move directly from the sound to the symbol and vice versa.

So secondly comes a symbol—perhaps a simple substitute symbol which all can understand like the dashes and circles mentioned in the section on rhythms. And then finally, or perhaps immediately, the actual technical musical symbol—quarter, half notes, etc.

We must constantly use these symbols to identify what we hear, as in the dictation game-drills mentioned in detail in the section on rhythms in which the student selects the proper symbol which represents what his teacher or another student is playing for him.

Then comes the reverse of this procedure—the other side of the coin. In the dictation procedure, the listener picks out of the air so-to-speak, certain sounds which he can identify to the point of selecting the proper representative symbol which he then names and writes down or places on a flannel board, etc. If a student can do this, he ought then to be able to look at the symbols he selected and re-create their sound—in this case to beat out the rhythm as he looks at the symbols. And this is READING. In reading, we look at the symbol which is clearly before us and we transform this into a sound which goes out into the air—the reverse of DICTATION.

Now it is very important to use and apply this skill of reading rhythms. There are many ways to do it. We can look at any music—songs, music for the flute or bells, etc. and wherever possible beat out the rhythm. In this process we extract from the music one of its elements—rhythm. But why not use music in which the rhythm is the total of it? That is, music written for percussion ensembles—rhythm bands. Rhythm bands have been much maligned; are often relegated to Kindergarten and first grade only, or generally abandoned in disgrace. There may have been reasons for this, but with the new enlightened and enriched philosophy, they are a much neglected but potentially effective teaching tool. What better way to use our new skill of reading rhythms, than to use them to read rhythm band scores? We can hope that in previous rote experiences which comprise part of the broad foundation laid in the early music education of students, that they have many times played rhythm instruments: to enrich or punctuate singing, dramatizing, to accompany the playing of pitched instruments, etc. These have been rote experiences and creative activities, in which the largely meaningless musical symbols were not specifically referred to. But now these symbols mean something to the student and like anyone who has a new skill, he should look eagerly for ways to use and prove this skill. Reading scores for rhythm bands is a valid way. Now the students are like a genuine orchestra, playing from music. Teacher can combine rhythmic and pitched instruments in arrangements which include them both. Orff does this. So does Slind in his book "Rhythm, Melody and Harmony" published by Mills. Also Golding and Landers in "Melody Makers," Frederick Beckman in the Ginn song series, and Burakoff and Wheeler in "Music Making." If the teacher can't find enough, he or the students can write their own. What better creative project than one which requires the student to use all his newly learned knowledge and skill in an undertaking which will give pleasure to the participants and those who listen and witness? How do you write a rhythm band score? Well, play enough of them so that you know what they look like and what is to be found in them. Then take an instrument at a time and experiment by playing it to the melody you wish to "orchestrate" till you find a pattern you like. To write it down you must use your dictation skills. Walk it out if you must, or use your fingers. And to play it you must use your reading skills. A marvelous application of all that we have learned, and in no way an infantile activity. This can be a highly meaningful activity to growing and grown students. It is usually so successful that it ought to be a much more common part of the curriculum. (See final chapter: Creativity.)

## Intervals

A good teacher can teach his students anything, but some regard the intervalic approach to reading as among the more difficult methods and best suited to those people with marked talent. Among the methods used to develop the ability to recognize and sing the intervals at sight are

1. Plenty of repetition via drill (games) at recognizing by ear the various intervals, emphasizing contrast in size or distance and the subjective effect of the sound (hollow, sweet, close, far apart, etc.).
2. Using snatches of familiar songs to identify various intervals.
3. Using fixed DO syllables, where C is always DO. This builds a strong sense of intervals and pitch.
4. Using games which require stepping off intervals, or measuring them off on a giant staff, a la Madeleine Carabo-Cone.

## Syllables

A very effective approach with syllables is to interchange constantly simple dictation with reading of the same complexity, as described earlier in this chapter. The dictation experiences should precede the reading. If a student stumbles while reading, we are not always able to diagnose his difficulty; but dictation clearly pinpoints areas of confusion, enabling the teacher to deal with the specific problem.

## A PROCEDURE FOR LEARNING TO READ MUSIC THROUGH SOCIAL INSTRUMENTS

The most successful approach to reading notes goes like this:

Recorders or Flutophones will be used in this example.

1. Let's sing **Hot Cross Buns.**
2. Pretend you are playing the recorder and sing the song on "too" (or "doo" if you prefer).
3. This time whisper it on "too" as if we wanted to keep it a secret, or not disturb others around us.
4. Now whisper "too" on one pitch like this:

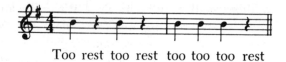

Too rest too rest too too too rest

Melody flutes will be used in this example.

1. Let's sing **Hot Cross Buns.**
2. Pretend you are playing the flute and sing the song on "too" (or "doo" if you prefer).
3. This time whisper it on "too" as if we wanted to keep it a secret, or not disturb others around us.
4. Now whisper "too" on one pitch like this:

Too rest too rest too too too rest

5. Hold the recorder in your left hand between the thumb and pointing finger—thumb on thumb hole, pointing finger on top hole.

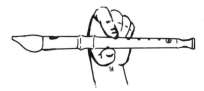

6. Now place the mouthpiece between your lips and whisper the same "too, rest, too, rest," etc.

7. Good, our first sound. Be sure to whisper—hardly blow at all or even breathe. Do it again.

8. Now place your third finger on the second hole, and covering both holes, play the same pattern.

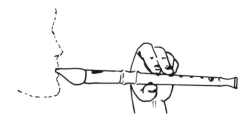

9. What did you hear? The sound is different. How? Lower. We'll call the second sound 2 because we used 2 fingers to cover 2 holes. The first sound we'll call 1 because we use only 1 finger to cover 1 hole.

10. Now play whatever number I say using the same rhythm pattern.

11. Now cover the next hole with your fourth finger, so that three fingers are covering three holes. Play the same pattern. The pitch is different from the other two. What number shall we give it? Three. Why? Because 3 fingers are covering 3 holes. *Not,* for instance, because the third finger is covering the third hole as might be done on the piano.

5. Hold your flute in your right hand like this:

6. Now just turn the flute so that the mouthpiece is at your lips:

7. Now place the mouthpiece between your lips and whisper the same "Too, rest, too, rest," etc.

8. Good, our first sound. Be sure to whisper—hardly blow at all or even breathe. Do it again.

9. Now take your left pointing finger, point it at me; now bring it up to cover the hole nearest the mouthpiece and play the same pattern.

10. What did you hear? The sound is different. How? Lower. We'll call that one because we use one finger to cover one hole. The first note we played we'll call none (0) because we didn't use any fingers or cover any holes.

11. Now play whatever number I say using the same rhythm pattern.

12. Now use your left pointing finger *and* the third finger to cover the *two* holes nearest the mouthpiece, and play the same pattern. The pitch is different from the other two. What number shall we give it? Two. Why? Because two fingers are covering two holes. *Not,* for instance, because the second finger is covering the second hole as might be done on the piano.

12. **Play whatever number I point to: 1, 2 or 3.**

First just step-wise, then the skip.

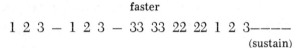

13. **Now forget the pattern we've been using and follow the bouncing ball. Play as I point:**

faster

1 2 3 — 1 2 3 — 33 33 22 22 1 2 3————
                                                (sustain)

**What have you played? Our song, Hot Cross Buns.**

13. **Play whatever number I point to: 0 1 or 2.**

First just step-wise, then the skip.

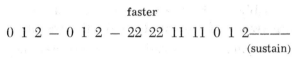

14. **Now forget the pattern we've been using and follow the bouncing ball.** Play as I point:

faster

0 1 2 — 0 1 2 — 22 22 11 11 0 1 2————
                                                (sustain)

**What have you played? Our song, Hot Cross Buns.**

This whole procedure takes five or ten minutes. Then there is no stopping them. They can play an instrument! If it is a teacher who is learning this for the first time, it will take longer! They are stiffer, more frightened, more sure they will fail. More is at stake in terms of self-esteem and what others will think. They've had more time to suffer, blunder and fail. Teacher should treat them gently. They can learn to play the flute too. Younger children (in primary grades) will need to move a bit more slowly too.

All fingerings can be learned this way, a new note or two each lesson. The instruction books show how. In no time the students can play lovely music even in several parts all by numbers and rote. The advantages of this approach are

1. Immediate achievement and success.
2. Numbers, no notes.
3. Playing skill—muscular coordination—is established before confronting the student with the musical language.
4. Familiar songs are used at first so there is no rhythmic or memory problem.
5. The student moves from no fingers to all six; from the easiest sound to the slightly more difficult. The instinct of the average person when first picking up the flute is to cover each hole with a finger, thereby tackling first the most difficult note with the greatest amount of potential errors. This procedure starts instead with the easiest note—*no* fingers.
6. The student makes music immediately, from his first lesson. He is able to play his instrument before he knows anything about music or theory or rhythm or notation, etc. Then he begins the transition to musical notation.

The disadvantages (which are quite minor) are
1. The order of the numbering is the opposite to the most logical:

| 1 | | 7 | | 0 | | 6 |
|---|---|---|---|---|---|---|
| 2 | on the | 6 | | 1 | on the melody | 5 |
| 3 | recorder | 5 | | 2 | flute | 4 |
| 4 | rather | 4 | | 3 | rather than | 3 |
| 5 | than | 3 | | 4 | | 2 |
| 6 | | 2 | | 5 | | 1 |
| 7 | | 1 | | 6 | | 0 |

Bells or piano or singing might well employ the ascending numbering. The teacher should certainly never use the two numbering systems at the same time.

2. Some teachers prefer to introduce musical notation immediately. It can be done very successfully. They claim that the transition from numbers to notes becomes very difficult and some players never do successfully make the switch. They are right about this. One can only counter by wondering if the players who can't switch to musical notation could ever have mastered it by the immediate introduction to it, or would even have learned to play at all. As marvelously simple as these flutes are, there are still three separate processes to be mastered:
    1. Tongueing and blowing
    2. Fingering
    3. Reading the musical language.

As believers in simplification to make learning easy, some choose not to confront the student with all three of these problems at once. Hence numbers instead of musical notation.

The transition to musical notation *is* the most difficult step to confront the new player. Some will probably fall by the wayside and not be able to learn to read "real" music, but more students than otherwise *will* be able to make the transition because they are fortified with

1. Playing skill already acquired—even advanced.
2. A foundation of successful achievement.
3. Experience with rhythm if only by rote.
4. The motivation provided by these factors to go on.

The presentation of musical notation is quite similar to the number procedure. It could be used immediately instead of the numbers, or used as here presented, following some experience playing from numbers. When the teacher chooses to make the transition is best determined by him. Some wait until the students have learned all the notes in the C scale, have a repertoire of over ten songs, have played in parts and have learned to overblow to get the octave. Also it is highly effective to coordinate the introduction of musical notation on the flute with the study of scales, intervals, key signatures, etc. The flute serves as the proof of the pudding.

| **For Recorder or Flutophone** | **For Melody Flute** |
|---|---|
| 1. **When you play 1, the pitch is B, and is written on the line B.** | 1. **When you play 0, the pitch you play is called B and is written on the line B.** |
| 2. **When you play 2, the pitch is A.** | 2. **When you play 1, the pitch is A.** |
| 3. **When you play 3, the pitch is G.** | 3. **When you play 2, the pitch is G.** |

4. **See if you can play whatever note I point to. Then I am going to erase the numbers and leave just the notes.**
5. **As I point, play the correct note. We'll play Merrily We Roll Along or Mary Had a Little Lamb.**
6. In each lesson, the notes already learned are reviewed and one or two new notes are introduced without the numbers. Because this is always hard it helps to continue to play music from numbers as well.

This procedure really isn't much different from a typical choir or orchestra rehearsal, or lesson on another kind of instrument. And the whole procedure would be similar for piano, bells, melodica or any keyboard instrument, all of which are just as effective in teaching the ability to read music.

To sum up the main theme of this chapter:

Music reading is hard.

When it is poorly taught it discourages students and sours them on music.

Not every student *needs* to learn to read music; not every student wants to.

There are a number of ways to learn music reading. The easiest, most successful and enjoyable is by means of social instruments. A concentration on a Rhythmic approach is also effective. Harder methods are by intervals or syllables.

## Developing Note Reading

1. **Sing the first three words of Hot Cross Buns.**
2. **Does the song start low and go high, skip a lot? Show me with your hands as we sing. Hands start high, go lower, then lower.**
3. **How many different notes?** Three.
4. **We divided the air space in front of us into high, middle, and low. Let's do the same on the chalkboard.**
5. **We'll draw a line across the middle. Above it is high, below it is low. Where will Hot go? Cross? On the line. Buns?** Below the line.

6. **Suppose this time we use two lines. Top line for high, space between for middle, etc.**

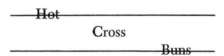

7. **Listen to the "talking drum." What kind of notes is it playing?** Teacher beats: WALK, WALK, WALK-HOLD. Students answer, WALK, etc. then QUARTER, QUARTER, HALF NOTE.
8. Teacher places the notes next to the words:

9. **Now you've used your ears to write a musical picture of the song.**

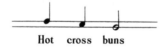

10. **The top line is the B we referred to earlier, the bottom line is G, and the space is A.**

11. **This is how it fits into the complete staff.**

12. Follow the same procedure with the middle part of the song:

13. Follow the same procedure with other 3-note songs: Au Claire de La Lune
$$\text{Ding, Dong, Bell}$$
$$\text{Trampin'}$$

## Play Measure Hunt

1. Teacher has several charts easily taped on to the chalkboard. On each is one measure of a familiar song, but the measures are mixed up.
2. A student selects one measure. All play it on recorders, or other pitched instrument.
3. Each measure is played. The idea is to place them in the correct order to make the familiar song. This game calls upon three skills: reading, playing and ear.
4. Obvious helps are the measure which contains the clef (first measure), and the measure which has a double bar (last measure).

## A Good Routine for Developing Ability to Play at Sight an Unfamiliar Piece

1. Walk-talk the rhythm: walk walk walk-hold.
2. Chant the letter names in rhythm: B A G-hold.
3. Chant the numbers in rhythm, while fingering the instrument: 1,2,3-hold.
4. Play.

# Chapter 11

# The Chromatic Scale
# and the Twelve-Tone Row

## WHAT YOU NEED TO KNOW

1. Key signatures (not absolutely necessary)
2. Sharps
3. Flats

## BASIC FACTS YOU WILL LEARN

1. There is a sign in music called a NATURAL (♮). It cancels out the effect of a previous pitch modifying sign, either in the key signature or appearing as an accidental in the same measure. Such a pitch modifying sign which appears in the music rather than in the key signature is called an ACCIDENTAL.
2. An accidental could be either a sharp, flat, or natural. It has to be written in before the note.
3. Sometimes the effect of the natural sign is to restore a note to its natural state, before it was affected by an accidental sharp or flat. That is why it is sometimes called a natural sign. The sign then acts to cancel out or restore. That is why it sometimes is called a CANCEL sign.
4. The cancel or natural sign sometimes acts as a sharp or flat:

   To sharp a flat, use the ♮.
   To flat a sharp, use the ♮.
5. A pitch modifying sign lasts only for the measure in which it occurs. The barline nullifies its effect in all succeeding measures.
6. The chromatic scale consists of all twelve notes between a given note and its first recurrence.
7. A twelve-tone row consists of these twelve tones arranged in a chosen order by the composer.

## WHAT THIS LESSON CAN LEAD TO

1. Improved reading skill
2. Minor scales
3. New kinds of music

## THE NATURAL OR CANCEL SIGN

Teacher distributes the following resonator bells, one to each player. **Play your note as I point to it in rhythm and you will be playing the first phrase of the Star-Spangled Banner (fl., Her: 156). Since** we often forget to look at the key signature, or to remember what it tells us, I am placing reminders next to the notes.

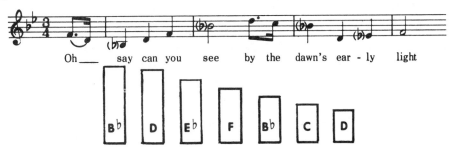

Oh___   say  can you    see     by the  dawn's ear - ly   light

B♭    D    E♭    F    B♭    C    D

Something doesn't sound right. Let's try everyone playing on xylophones. Practice once with your fingers as your mallets, and when you think you can play it accurately, sit with your mallet in your hand so I know you are ready. All ready? Begin.

The students wince as they play the last notes and there is much "doodling" on the bells as they try to seek out what went wrong. **Is that the way the Star-Spangled Banner should sound?** No, there was a mistake at the end. **See if you can experiment with your bells to find the error. On what word did it occur? Sing the phrase with me as I play it at the piano.** The answer soon comes. Something is wrong on the word "ear-ly." The next-to-last note should not be an E♭, but just E. **Let's all play it that way. Now it sounds the way we know it. The student who was playing E♭—trade your bell for an E bell. Let's have all the resonator bells play the phrase again. Now it sounds right.**

**John, will you go to the board and erase the flat in front of the E we changed. Is it now written correctly on the board?** No! The key signature at the beginning still tells us to flat all Bs and Es. It is not enough that we *erased* the flat in front of the offending E. Music requires us to use a *sign* to show that we have in fact *erased* the flat, a sort of musical eraser. Because the sign *cancels* out the effect of the flat in the key signature it is sometimes called a CANCEL. It looks like this: ♮. Two Ls, one upside down, L ⌐ or perhaps you would rather think of them as two sevens 7 L. Notice that like sharps and flats, they cover many degrees of the staff: How then, can we tell which degree the cancel sign is on? By seeing which line or space goes through the box made by the sign ◄♮-. The cancel sign as we used it in

"The Star-Spangled Banner" is sometimes referred to by another name. Because it occurs only once or occasionally throughout the piece, and the rest of the time the flats of the key signature do prevail, such a sign as the cancel is called an ACCIDENTAL. The composer decided that although he wanted B♭ as the tone center of this song and B and E to be flatted, in this particular case almost *incidentally,* he would prefer the plain E. So maybe it is a kind of *ACCIDENT* which occurs in the song only once or twice.

Take the example of the aria, Habanera, from Carmen by Bizet. Notice first the sharp and then the cancel sign ♮ on G. Here again the ♮ sign is cancelling out the effect of the sharp, but there is a

Love ___  is ___ a  re - bel  bird,___  Love is  free___as a way-ward  breeze

difference from the previous example, The Star-Spangled Banner. In The Star-Spangled Banner, the E♭ was part of the key signature, it *belonged to the key.* In this case, the key does not have G♯ in its signature, so G♯ is functioning as an . . . ? ACCIDENTAL. So not only is the ♮ sign cancelling out the effect of the accidental G♯, we could say it is *restoring* the G to its *natural state* as it appears in this key. So often, the sign ♮ is called a NATURAL. The notes would be called G♯ and then G NA-TURAL. Notice that actually naming this particular key is avoided. It is D minor and it may well be you haven't learned minor keys yet. In this case it really doesn't prove necessary to name the key, but just to note that the key signature does not include a G sharp.

In the Cesar Franck example the ♮ is functioning as a sharp, similar to the way it is used in "The Star-Spangled Banner." It is cancelling out the effect of a flat in the key signature. How does it function in "Sweet Genevieve?" The same.

In "Song to the Evening Star," the ♮ is acting as a FLAT and it is restoring the C to its natural state after having been sharped by an accidental. How does it function in "Song of India?" The same.

But note what happens if we change the key of some of these songs. Now that "Sweet Gene-vieve" is in the key of B instead of B♭, the natural sign is acting as a flat, cancelling out the effect of the D♯ in the key signature, and later the C♯ in the signature. If we put Song of India in F instead of G, the ♮ sign now acts as a sharp, and in order to restore the B to its flatted state of the key of F, a flat must be placed before the following B.

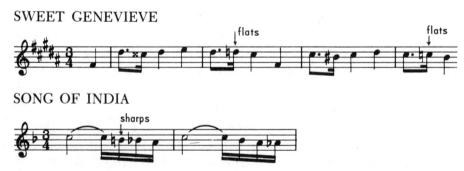

Going back to "The Star-Spangled Banner," the effect of this sign ♮ is to cancel the effect of the flat. How else could we describe the effect of the ♮ in this case? What happened to the E♭? How was it changed? It was raised a half step, or sharped. So in this case we could say the sign ♮ sharped the E♭! Strange and confusing as it may sound. TO SHARP A FLAT, USE THE NATURAL.

And notice what the natural sign did in Habanera. G first appeared as G♯, then followed by G natural [music] How was the G sharp changed? Its pitch was *lowered* one half step, or flatted. The G was restored to its natural state. In this case the natural sign acted as a flat. TO FLAT A SHARP, USE A NATURAL. Both of these statements can get pretty confusing. It is easier just to remember that the natural sign nullifies the effect of any pitch-modifying sign whether it is in the key signature or occurs as an accidental. It gives to the note a plain letter name. You might say the ♮ is the musical eraser.

I have several themes placed on the board. I am going to send a whole group of students to the board and each of you is to take one pitch modifying sign and label it—give it an appropriate name—several if they fit—and describe how it is functioning.

Now I am going to question you further about the music. (Song of India).

1. **How does the sharp in the key signature affect the music?** All Fs are to be sharped throughout the piece.

2. **How about the C♯ in measure one? How long does it last?** Only that note. It is immediately CANCELLED. **What about the B♭ in measure two? Is the B in measure four a B♭?** No, there is no flat before that note. The flat lasts only for the measure in which it occurs. **Notice that the B♭ in measure five has to be flatted again in measure six.** We can say that the BAR which indicates the end and beginning of measures also has the effect of nullifying any accidental occuring in the measure. Imagine the chemical foot bath at the entrance to a pool, or magical rays which detect metal at a doorway as a person enters. The bar purges or purifies the next measure of the influence of accidentals in the previous measure.

In the lessons on RHYTHMS we said the bar had only one function: It is a picture of the ACCENT or DOWNBEAT. Now we can add two other facts about the bar: A bar delineates or marks off measures. It nullifies the effect of accidentals. Therefore, accidentals last only for the measure in which they occur.

## The Syllable Names of Chromatics

Look again at "Sweet Genevieve" in the key of B♭. Let's name each note by syllable. Skip the accidentals at first. SO MI  MI FA MI  RE SO RE  RE MI RE  DO. If C had no sharp before it, what would be its name? RE. But now it has a different pitch so a different name seems necessary. **Can you guess? Its name is RI. In fact all sharp chromatics will use the vowel I (pronounced EE). In the third measure instead of DO it will be . . . ? DI.**

Look at the D♭ in the second measure. Without the flat it is . . . ? MI. With the flat? MOO? MOH? The answer is ME (pronounced AY). Most flat chromatics use the AY vowel sound. But the last measure of the excerpt presents a problem. C is already RE. So the flat of RE (AY) is RA (AH).

We'll send a group to the board to label all the accidentals in the theme from "Song of India."
SO FI FA MI | SO FA MI ME | SO FI FA | MI
MI ME RE DO | ME RE DO | MI ME RE RA | DO

A reminder about something which confuses many students. "Sweet Genevieve" illustrates the problem. Looking at the third note of the excerpt, C♯, answer these questions:

1. What does the sharp do to the C? It makes it higher.
2. Higher than what? Than C without the sharp.
3. But, where is C♯ in relation to the second note, D? Lower. Yes, some students want to sing it higher than D. After all, a sharp makes a note higher, they reason. What they forget is that C, any C, is lower than D. The sharp just makes it less lower, but it is not the D which the sharp affects, it is the C.

## Which Sign to Use

There is still another rule about these sharps and flats which is not universally observed, but will help you understand what follows. First, what can you say about these two notes: ♯♮ ♭♮ They are ENHARMONIC (see Chapter 6). They are two different names, two different symbols for the same sound. Do you remember what we said determined which name or symbol we used? The *relationship*. An example was the major scale and the formula of intervals.

In actual compositions where the music moves about and doesn't remain in the formal line-up of the scale, there is another relationship which controls how the accidental is written and named. Can you tell by looking at "Sweet Genevieve"? It is decided by how the accidental moves to the next note. If the note with the accidental moves up, the accidental is written as a sharp. If the note with the accidental moves down, the accidental is written as a flat. You will see this checks every time in "Sweet Genevieve," no matter what the key. "Sweet Genevieve" would really look quite strange and be harder to read if it were written this way:

## THE CHROMATIC SCALE

Now you know a name for every single possible note within an octave. How many notes are there, not counting the repeated top note of the octave? Use a keyboard to count them. Twelve. Twelve is an easy number to remember—it is an important number in our lives. Think of the twelve months in the year, or twelve hours in a day, or twelve inches in a foot. Describe how each note moves to the next. There is something the same about them all. They are all a half step apart. This comprises another kind of scale, called the CHROMATIC SCALE. How would you define it? A scale which moves by half step, within an octave, from any letter to its reoccurrence is called a chromatic scale. How the notes are written and named will be determined by the rule we mentioned earlier—the direction *from* each note. The name CHROMATIC is often applied to notes preceded by an accidental. For instance, if the key signature is two sharps ♯♯ a C♯ would belong to the major scale, so although it is called C♯, it is not an accidental and not a chromatic. In the same key signature, A-sharp or F natural would be called chromatics or accidentals.

You can see this is quite complicated. What is one of the first things you noticed?

1.  The descending form is quite different from the ascending form. Why is this? Because of the rules regarding how the chromatic moves to the next note. What else do you notice?
2.  The same scale can have sharps and flats and naturals in it all at the same time!
3.  Sometimes the rule regarding direction from the chromatic is broken—see G♯ in the descending scale.

The question you must be thinking is how do we keep this all straight? One answer is that this way of writing the scale is not always rigidly observed. There are ways to vary it. More important than knowing all the ramifications of the CHROMATIC SCALE at this stage is to know

1.  That there is such a scale.
2.  How it sounds and looks.
3.  How it is used.

There is one help you can give yourself. Use the major scale as a frame around which to build the chromatic scale. That will help you with some of the problems concerning where to put a sharp or flat. Notice that in the chromatic scale written out for you, the notes of the major scale are filled in. Use this scale plus syllables to build a chromatic scale.

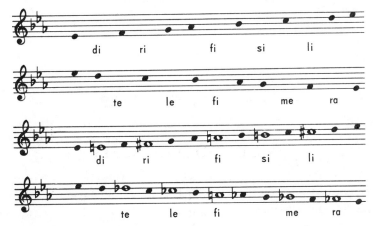

A definition used earlier for Major scale seems even more appropriate here: A SCALE IS A WRIT-TEN-OUT KEY. It is all the tools lined up in order, waiting for the composer to select from them. We are not quite so likely to find compositions using a whole chromatic scale. It is more common to find pieces of the chromatic scale in a composition. Here are some examples:

1.  Song of India      Rimsky-Korsakoff  (Her: 177)
2.  Flight of the Bumble Bee      Rimsky-Korsakoff  (Her: 179)
3.  My Heart at Thy Sweet Voice from Samson and Delilah      Saint-Säens
4.  Song to the Evening Star from Tannhäuser      Wagner  (Her: 176)
5.  My Hero from the Chocolate Soldier      Oscar Strauss
6.  Theme from Symphony in D minor—Franck  (Her: 175)

Chopin uses portions frequently as embellishments. But the chromatic scale is more like a spice rack containing an assortment of special "seasonings" to be used with care—a little bit here, a little bit there.

Try playing on your xylophones some of the examples given here, and on the previous pages.

MY HEART AT THY SWEET VOICE            Saint-Säens

NOCTURNE, Op. 9, No. 3            Chopin

Songs like "Sweet and Low" and the Children's Prayer from *Hansel and Gretel* by Humperdinck (in the flute book) contain occasional sharp and flat chromatics.

## THE TWELVE-TONE ROW

The chromatic scale offers the composer a whole new array of interesting tones. Why don't we assume the role of composers for an experiment? We've written our own songs and poems before and our own rhythm band scores. But probably you never composed a song like this. I'm going to give twelve of you numbers from 1 to 12 to wear in your paper hats. One at a time go to the box of resonator bells and without looking, take one bell. I've placed only the twelve bells of the chromatic scale in the box, but not in chromatic scale formation—just in any order.

Now play the bells in the order of your numbers, 1 to 12. As each bell is played, Sue, you check the name on the bell and place the corresponding note on the flannel board; and you four students place the corresponding bars on our Orff xylophones, metallophones and glockenspiels, in the order they appear on the flannel board.

Play the resonator bells again, but this time sustain some with a tremolo to change the rhythm. Now we'll have each player at an Orff instrument play your row of twelve tones, one at a time, and do it in a rhythm different from those who played before you. You can even go backwards! Jerry, you try that. Arch, try repeating one or two of your bells before moving to the next note, but you can't return to a bell already played once.

What do you notice about such a melody-line? You can't tell where you are. Where's DO? The jumps are hard; they are very big jumps. Yes, the composer does this to eradicate the home-tone feeling—he doesn't want a tone center. This is just how some composers have elected to write their music, by using the twelve tones of the chromatic scale and lining them up in a row called the TWELVE-TONE ROW.

Bill, you start in the middle of your row on the metallophone, go to the end, then start at the beginning and play till you reach the bell you started on. John, you do the same thing, but give it a different rhythm. In a steady rhythm this time, Alice you play your glockenspiel from left to right; at the same time Sue you play your xylophone from right to left. Interesting effect, isn't it? These are some of the things composers of twelve-tone row music allow themselves to do. Note that if a D♯ is used, its enharmonic partner E♭ is not used. That would be the same note.

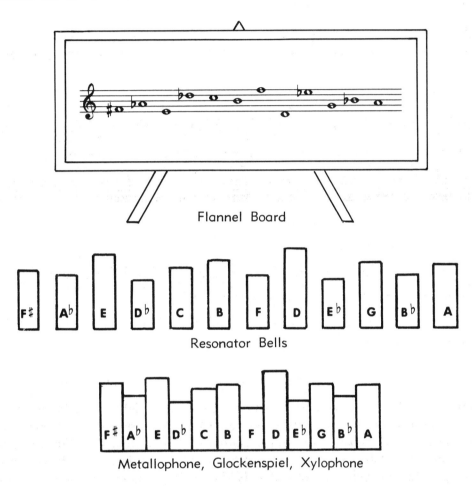

Flannel Board

Resonator Bells

Metallophone, Glockenspiel, Xylophone

This time each Orff player select one bar to replace with the same letter bar but an octave higher or lower. Play your row now. This kind of replacement is also allowed in the twelve-tone row.

The composer, Arnold Schoenberg, who lived from 1874 to 1951, was one of the leading exponents of this kind of composing, in fact he is credited with devising this method. An example of this kind of

### SUITE FOR PIANO OP. 25

Arnold Schoenberg

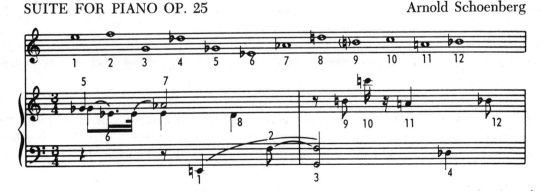

writing would be his Suite for Piano, Opus 25; also his String Quartet No. 4. The third movement contains a unison statement of a twelve-tone row. The critic and composer, Virgil Thomson, wrote a charming composition called, "The Alligator and the Coon." One of the themes is based on a twelve-tone row. It occurs briefly in the composition. **I want you to play it on your instruments, so find where your bells should play and be ready when I point to the note. Now listen for it in the music.** Notice at the end he combines some of the notes from the row into a "chord." Teacher can point to the theme when it occurs in the music, or see if the students can recognize it on their own.

THE ALLIGATOR AND THE COON                                          Virgil Thomson

The Music Educators National Conference has published a report entitled, "Experiments in Musical Creativity" as part of a Contemporary Music Project. (MENC Washington, D.C. 1966) This report describes work in the modern idioms with children. They list several other compositions which are examples of twelve-tone row composition:

Igor Stravinsky, Agon
Webern, Symphony, Op. 21, 2nd movement     The opening theme is a twelve-tone row

They also mention the following Columbia Records:

"Berg, Schoenberg, Krenek," Piano Music
"Berg, Schoenberg, Webern," Orchestra Works
Webern, The Complete Music

In the last movement of Five Piano Pieces, Op 23 by Schoenberg, every note is derived from the following tone row. Try this on your xylophone, and let it serve as a reminder that composers use other scales besides the one to which we have paid so much attention earlier in the book. This interesting new scale requires you to understand clearly about sharps, flats, naturals and half steps; and opens the way to a quite different kind of music.

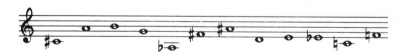

## SUGGESTED ASSIGNMENTS

1. Spell chromatic scales up and down.
2. Compose a 12-tone row and write it down.
3. Make up spelling puzzles.

For instance:
1. Think of the ascending chromatic scale on D.
2. Take the 4th note (E♯).
3. Use its enharmonic name (F).
4. Consider that note the eighth note of an ascending chromatic scale (use syllables—SO; the scale would then be B♭).
5. Name the 4th note of that ascending chromatic scale (C♯).

## Chapter 12

# The Minor Mood and Mode

### WHAT YOU NEED TO KNOW

1. A thorough grounding in Major—scales, keys, signatures, syllables.
2. The tonic chord in major.

### WHAT YOU WILL LEARN

1. The realm of minor is a whole new area: it has a completely different sound and structure.
2. There are three variations of the minor scale.
3. No two major scales contain the same notes or have the same key signature; but for every key signature indicating a major key, there is also a minor scale called RELATIVE minor.
4. The minor scale which begins on the same note as a major scale is referred to as its PARALLEL minor or TONIC minor.
5. The tonic chord in minor sounds different, its structure is different and it is named either LA -DO- MI or DO- ME- SO.

### WHAT THIS LESSON CAN LEAD TO

1. Better reading and performing skills.
2. The ability to listen with greater understanding.
3. The acquisition of more tools and resources with which to express ourselves.

---

### THE MINOR MOOD

We are going to do quite a bit of listening today, but you won't be sitting still. Push back your chairs so you have plenty of room to move. Remove your shoes so that you can move around comfortably in your stocking feet.

*Anitra's Dance from Peer Gynt Suite by Grieg.* Teacher plays the recording but does not mention the name of the composition or composer.

1. **Find some empty space and show us what you think the music is expressing.** The girls (adults) seem to feel more comfortable with this music and there is much whirling, undulating and light quick movement. **Sit down and catch your breath.**
2. **What words would be good to describe this music?**

| | |
|---|---|
| light | swirling |
| fast | whirling |
| seductive | haunting |
| poignant | bittersweet |

*In the Hall of the Mountain King from Peer Gynt*

1. **Remember the game of Statues in which you are swung around and freeze in the position in which you are released? Try now to show by your face and body position the mood of this music.**

2. **What words would suit this music?**

|                 |            |
|-----------------|------------|
| lugubrious      | whirling   |
| grotesque       | misshapen  |
| lumbering       |            |

3. Try to paint something which fits this music. Later teacher could show several paintings which seem best to suit the music.

*Ase's Death from Peer Gynt*

1. **Let's try to have a group of you act this out together.** The group crouches or kneels. Slowly they raise heads, bodies, rise. Some raise arms in supplication, some fold hands in prayer, others bend in great grief, sway or bury their faces in their hands. With bodies bent they form a mournful procession. **Yes, the aura of death and despair seems very evident here.** Many conclude that this is a funeral dirge.

2. This could also be done as a tableau.

The strong emotional content of these selections seems to be clearly conveyed to the listeners, who are encouraged to express themselves in a variety of ways: painting, dramatization, dance, discussion. There is a great deal of music well suited to the purpose of this particular learning experience, such as

In Deepest Grief   closing chorus from St. Matthew Passion by Bach
Allegretto (2nd movt.) from 7th Symphony by Beethoven
Prelude in C Minor Op. 28, No. 20 by Chopin
Prelude in B Minor Op. 28 No. 6 by Chopin
Funeral Dirge from 3rd Symphony (Eroica) by Beethoven

**Not only do all these selections we've listened to have in common a strong emotion, but they are all − − − ? MINOR. What makes music minor?**

**You probably know more about minor than you realize. You probably can recognize minor music when you hear it, even if you didn't know you could. Listen.** It helps if teacher can improvise at the piano no matter how meagerly.

1. Teacher improvises a slow dignified processional, but MAJOR. Appropriate recorded music could be

O Praise the Lord from Athalia, by Mendelssohn
Pomp and Circumstance, by Elgar
Largo from Xerxes, by Handel

Or music of a quiet serene pastoral quality like

Largo from Fifth Symphony (From the New World), by Dvorak
Sheep May Safely Graze, by Bach
Jesu, Joy of Man's Desiring, by Bach

Is this music minor or not? Even if opinion is well divided, the point is made more dramatic if the teacher can play his own improvisation now in minor, or improvise at the piano a minor version of the recorded music. Now more students see. It is not how slow, dignified, or heavy the music is which makes it minor.

2. Teacher improvises light, gay, airy, fast music, but MINOR. "Anitra's Dance" is very suitable here. Even light fast music can be minor and it is certainly not sad. Whimsical, piquant, seductive may-

be, but not sad. If the whole composition is played through, there is even a section where the theme does turn to major and the sound and its effect can be compared.

3. Teacher improvises something tragic sounding in minor, then the same thing in major. Any of the music listed at the beginning of the chapter is appropriate here. Most of you are able to tell when the music is or is not minor, but even if you cannot, you are realizing that minor is not created by tempo, weight, or volume. It is something else. Words which are sometimes suggested to describe minor, like lower, slow, flat, sour, off-key, and which are highly personal opinions, really won't do. Besides being subjective words, they are wrong! As confirmation, listen to *America* played in minor, or *Yankee Doodle*. And let us explore further into the realm of MINOR.

To make "America" minor, actually add or picture in your mind's eye two flats in the key signature:

## SIGNS OF MINOR

**I want you to look at a certain group of songs and have you notice something you may not have noticed before.** These songs can be ones already known to the students—some should be—or unfamiliar songs to be listened to or sight read, or learned by rote. The list that follows is long and varied purposely, but it is not necessary to use them all.

1. *I'm Just a Poor Wayfaring Stranger.* (Her: 5). **Sing it. Play it on your flutes. Do you think the music fits the mood?** Yes. **What words describe the mood?** It expresses loneliness, tribulation, longing. (*There is always the risk of someone saying no. This a very subjective thing and that is their privilege.*) **What is the key signature?** One flat. **The key?** F. **DO?** F. **Does it end on DO?** No! **What syllable does it end on?** LA. **That's unusual, isn't it? Are there many LAs in the music? Count them.** 20. **We don't usually find so many, do we?**

2. *Ghost of Tom.* **Let's sing this using the wood block, gong and ratchet where you feel it is appropriate. Does it suit Hallowe'en?** Yes. **What words describe it?** It's spooky, stealthy, sneaky, scary. **What key?** G. **Does it end on DO?** No, LA. **Count the LAs.** Seven.

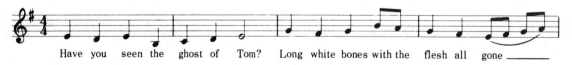

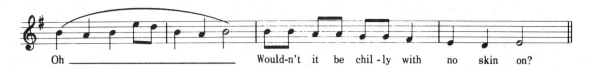

Oh _____ Would-n't it be chil -ly with no skin on?

3. *Hallowe'en.* **Does it fit gypsies and Hallowe'en? What words could we use to describe it?** Wild, gay. **Does it end on DO?** No. LA. **How many LAs?** Five. **Anything else we might make special note of?** There are some sharp accidentals. **What syllables?** FA sharped, and SO sharped.

Gyp - sy girls there a fai -ry queen, Clowns and elves dart -ing in be - tween. Here a dash -ing

cow - boy There a hand -some plow boy, Such a jol -ly scene, This is Hal -lo - we'en.

From MERRY MUSIC, copyright © 1939 by Summy-Birchard Company, Evanston, Illinois. Copyright renewed. All rights reserved. Used by permission.

4. *Russian Sailor's Dance.*

Gliere

5. *Minka.* Russian dance. If we play either of these selections from our flute books, using auto-harps and guitars to acompany our flute playing, we could agree again that the music is lively and gay, that the music ends on LA and contains an unusual number of LAs. Here again are sharp acci-dentals—ten G sharps. What syllable is that? SO sharped.

6. *Hatikva.* Hebrew anthem. From our flute books, play it and some sing. The key is F, but it ends on LA and contains many LAs. It expresses an appropriate sad dignity and steadfastness.

7. *Go Down Moses.* (Her: 254) The mood? Long-suffering. The key? A♭. Ten LAs and it ends on LA. And six SOs are sharped.

When Is - rael was in E - gypt's land, Let my peo - ple go;
Op - pressed so hard they could not stand, Let my peo - ple go;

Go down, Mo - ses, way down in E - gypt's land, __ Tell __ ol' Pha - roah, Let . .

8. *Coventry Carol* Its mood? Serene, quiet, infinite. Some verses end on DO sharped, others end on LA. It also has several sharped SOs.

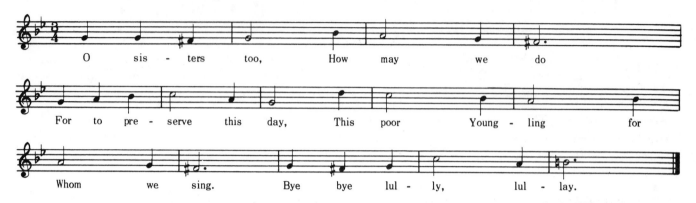

9. *Greensleeves* (Her: 10) Sing it or play it or listen to a recording. Its mood? Sort of bittersweet, haunting. There is a feeling of distance, of longing. When we look at the music we see that in the key of A it ends on LA, and both SO and FA are sharped; sometimes SO appears alone sharped, sometimes FA and SO right next to each other, both sharped.

(This song could be identified as being in the Dorian mode, but it suits the purpose of this lesson.)*

Of course, the answers giving the keys to these songs aren't right—except they are correct within the scope of knowledge now possessed by the students. This is one of those times to exercise the prerogative of the teacher: exaggerations to make a point, oversimplification, omission of the complete truth as in this case.

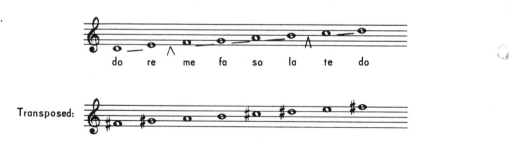

*The Dorian mode is a scale which can be found on all the white notes from D—D.

Also, whatever music teacher chooses to make the coming point, he should make sure he chooses music which expresses a variety of moods, *not just sadness.* Calling music in the major mode happy, and music in the minor mode sad, is a sin of gross oversimplification and misinformation committed too long in the name of music education. As just illustrated, all minor music is NOT sad. It is probably true that most *sad* music is *minor,* but minor music does not have to be sad. The next example does illustrate the classic sad mood.

10. **Listen again to  Ase's Death.**  Other good examples to make this point would be  In Deepest Grief  by Bach or  Elegy in E minor  by Massenet. **After you have heard this I would like you to comment. Feel free to say you liked or disliked it, but I'll be interested in why you did, and also in what you think the music is expressing. This is not abstract music; the composer meant to depict a particular happening.** Typical answers about Grieg: "it's too slow," "it's very monotonous." **Yes. Can you say why it's monotonous?** "It's the same theme over and over again." Yes, it certainly is. This five minute selection is amazing in that there are really only two themes repeated over and over, and the second is really almost like the first—the rhythm is the same and the melody is almost the reverse of the first. The first

theme consists of three ascending tones                                                         and then a sort

of expansion of them. The second theme is mainly descending:

Why do you suppose the composer deliberately created this monotony? He wanted the one mood—emotional tone—to prevail. Does he provide any variation at all? Yes, the theme keeps going up higher for the first half and steadily down for the second half. It also gets louder and fuller going up and decreases going down. A picture of it's general direction would make a triangle or peak like this. What does the mood seem to be? Great sadness, grief, loneliness. Someone has died. There is a funeral procession.

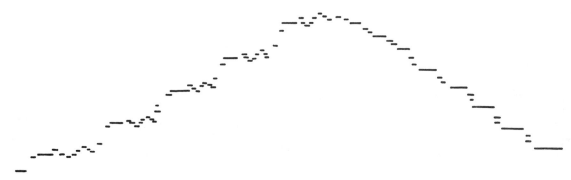

**The emotional tone of this music is unmistakable. The aura of death is always detected—deep grief, despair. It is five minutes of unmitigated grief! How does the composer make this music so sad? We've already seen it is not the tempo or weight, or volume, or rhythm or range or instruments which create this effect. What *is* it? It is the notes, the chords. Yes. If you could see the Grieg music, you would see it ends on LA and has many LAs in it and the chords have some SOs sharped. We have noticed this about all the music we have sung, played and listened to today. These selections don't end on DO but LA, they have many LAs in them rather than a great deal of the Tonic chord, and often SO is sharped, sometimes FA and SO together are sharped. The moods expressed by this music vary but it is almost always a mood strongly and clearly enough expressed that we have little trouble determining it. What were some of the characteristics or moods expressed?**

despair, grief, death                                  Gypsy, Slavic, wild, gay
longing, haunting, distant, lonely                     stealthy, sneaky, spooky, scary
grotesque, piquant

**And what does all this music have in common? It is all MINOR. Not minor meaning *lesser,* just different. It is MINOR as opposed to MAJOR, which most of the music we've studied up to now has been.**

MAJOR is a word which this book has assiduously avoided until now, exercising the teachers' prerogative to exaggerate, over-simplify or omit some of the truth—for the sake of the student and the learning situation. Not the whole truth has been told. The reference has been to "scale," not to MAJOR scale. The truth is, almost all the facts presented thus far regarding scale, key, signature has pertained only to *Major* scale, not all scales. Students have a hard enough time mastering what there is to know about scale and key. The knowledge that this scale is only *one* of *several* might be the crowning blow. They might give up before starting. But, now that you have come this far and have the confidence in yourselves that such progress deserves, you have a strong enough foundation to tackle a new area.

MINOR is another language, another world. Almost everything you have learned to this point has to do with Major. Minor will be different—but NOT harder.

**We've heard minor music and sung and played it but not examined it so closely before. And what makes music minor? Do you remember what we discovered makes Joy to the World sound always the same no matter where we start to play it? The SCALE. Could it be the scale which makes music minor?**

## THE MINOR SCALE

In this minor music, what seems to be the most important note? LA. You remember how important DO has always been. Could it be that in minor, it is LA which is the central note? Students sometimes say that LA is the DO in minor. To put it this way can lead to complications. Better just to note that LA does appear to be the tone-center. This seems to be borne out as we examine music which is minor. **Here is the song  We Three Kings of Orient Are.  (Her: 92)**

**What does the key appear to be? G. Then what is DO? G. And yet, how does the song end? On E. What syllable? LA. Notice that the song ends with an almost complete scale concluding on LA.**

**Assume for the moment that LA *is* the note which starts and ends the scale. Let's extract the scale from**

the song. We have from the song:  or the same scale in

its more familiar ascending form: Compare this scale

to the scale we would have ordinarily spelled from the key signature of one sharp:

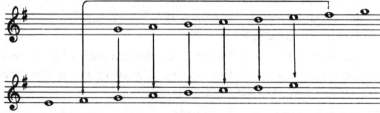

**Are any of the notes in one scale different from the notes in the other scale?** No, every note is the same. **Are they in a different order?** No, the order is exactly the same. **Here is truly a little miracle.** Here are all the same notes in exactly the same order, with no notes added or left out. The one difference is that instead of going from DO to DO, it starts on LA and ends on LA. It is as if we took the tail end of the G scale ♩ and moved it to the head or beginning of the scale, ♩ so that it ends on E or LA. And then since scales begin and end on the same letter, we could add the starting E:

**Listen to the effect of this change.** Teacher plays the scale. **It creates the same sort of haunting lonely effect we noticed in so much of the minor music we listened to and talked about.** Optional: Repeat this whole procedure with the following song, "Old Abram Brown"

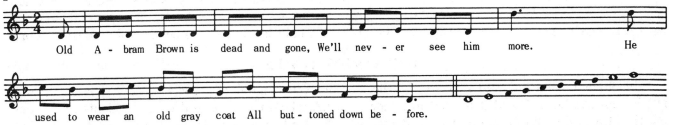

Old A - bram Brown is dead and gone, We'll nev - er see him more. He

used to wear an old gray coat All but - toned down be - fore.

Music by Benjamin Britten, Words from "Tom Tiddler's Ground" by Walter de la Mare. Copyright 1936 by Boosey & Co., Ltd., renewed 1963. Reprinted by permission of Boosey & Hawkes, Inc.

Notice in the song Old Abram Brown, that there are many LAs (D), and that although the key signature suggests the F scale, there is a complete descending scale in the song from high to low D (LA). Here again, no notes have been changed, added or deleted from the F scale. But instead of beginning and ending on F (DO) this scale moves from D to D. The TI-DO has been lopped off the top of the scale and tacked on to the bottom, and sealed with a starting LA.

F Major Scale

do  ti  la  so  fa  mi  re  do  ti  la

la  so  fa  mi

He used . . .                                                    re  do  ti  la

So the SCALE is what makes music minor. But what is it about the scale? Let's measure the steps to see how the minor scale is constructed. Use the keyboards.

Place your finger on E. Now measure the distance to the next note, F♯. A half step to F, another half step to F♯. The first interval is a whole step. Finger on F♯, measure the distance to G. A half step. Already this is different from the formula for the major scale.

**Finger on G, measure to A.   A whole step.**
**Finger on A, measure to B.   A whole step.**
**Finger on B, measure to C.   A half step.**
**Finger on C, measure to D.   A whole step.**
**Finger on D, measure to E.   A whole step.**

2 – 3         5 – 6

half step    half step

It is not necessary to memorize the exact formula for this minor scale, as long as students understand that the formula for the minor scale is different from the formula for the major scale. IT IS THE SCALE FORMULA WHICH MAKES MUSIC MINOR.

There are many things to note from this conclusion.

1. How have we said scales are named? By the first note. In this case E. And we have said this is minor music so the scale would be named E MINOR.

2. Even though the key signature is one sharp (F♯) the scale is not the G MAJOR SCALE, and the key is not G. Therefore it appears that a key signature can belong to and indicate more than one key. Can you state more accurately just what a key signature does indicate? Two scales, containing the same notes in the same order. One major, one minor. Only, the major scale goes from DO to DO and the minor scale from LA to LA. Not only do they have the same notes in common, they share the *same key signature.*

3. We might compare this to the same last name. And that leads to another point. If these scales have the same "last name" can we not say they are RELATED? In fact, that is what the E minor scale is to the G major scale—the RELATIVE MINOR SCALE. Why related? Because they have the same key signature, the same "last name." Also could we not say that because they have the same notes, they have the same blood in their veins, the way relatives do?

## The Relative Minor

Who could say how we could change any major scale into its relative minor? Just take the "TI-DO" off the end of the major scale and place it at the beginning. Since the scale now ends with a LA, we'll begin it with another LA. Now we have the relative minor. Let's dramatize it. We'll make the scale of F♯ major. All the notes are sharp except B. Jean, you take the F♯ resonator bell, Mary take G♯, Ann A♯, Sandra take B, Al take C♯, John take D♯, Frank E♯ (it will have the enharmonic name F on it) and Ted take F♯. Line up in scale formation:

We'll hang signs about their necks with the syllable names on them:

What syllable will end the scale if we change it to minor? LA. John, holding D♯, is LA. Frank and Ted, who are TI and DO will move to the front of the scale.

We need another LA to start the scale. What note is it? D♯. Since we need only one DO, why not ask Jean who is holding what was the starting DO to switch now to LA. She takes a D♯ bell.

To make it really accurate, Frank and Ted exchange their higher TI and DO for the lower octave E♯ and F♯ bells. **Now we have the relative minor scale built on the LA from the F♯ major scale, D♯. What is the name then of the relative minor scale of F♯ MAJOR? It is D♯ MINOR. Now let's do a flat scale.**

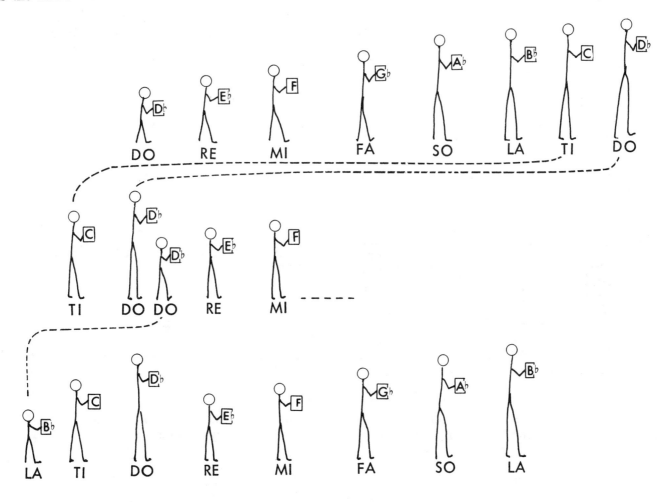

D♭ MAJOR SCALE changed to its relative minor, B♭ MINOR.
TO CHANGE ANY MAJOR SCALE INTO ITS RELATIVE MINOR, MERELY MOVE THE TI DO
FROM THE END TO THE BEGINNING OF THE SCALE AND ADD THE STARTING LA.

Music sometimes hops back and forth from its major key to its relative minor. Examples of this
are: We Three Kings (Her: 92), God Rest Ye Merry Gentlemen (Her: 174), Czech Folk Song, When
Johnny Comes Marching Home (Her: 179) fl.

GOD REST YE MERRY GENTLEMEN                                                                England

CZECH FOLK SONG

### Finding the Relative Minor of a Major Scale

What is a quick easy way to discover the name of the relative minor key of any major key? The
important note is LA. THE RELATIVE MINOR WILL BE THE "KEY OF LA."

How can we find LA quickly? Several ways:

1. Count three scale letters down from DO, including DO—DO TI LA (Since this involves three letters or three degrees of the staff, it is referred to as a third.)

2. Count 1½ steps or three half steps down from DO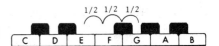
   G MAJOR (DO)—E MINOR (LA) G down to F♯, F♯ to F, F to E

3. Think a perfect 5th (or DO to SO) up from DO, and go up another whole step:

   A♭ - E♭, whole step up to F

   DO  SO                    LA

   When determining LA, if you don't have the scale spelled out in front of you, so that you can single out LA easily, the best way would be to picture the key signature on the staff: Find these relative minor keys.

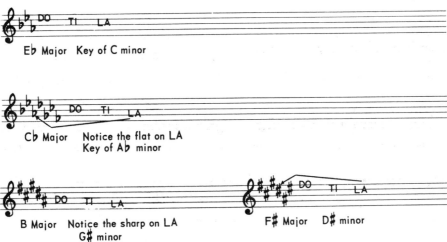

   You may remember that we had some ways to help us know quickly whether a key had flats or sharps in it (see Chapter 8). But in this process of determining relative minors, there is no such help. A major key can have *flat* in its name (E♭) and yet its relative minor will begin on a plain letter (C minor). Another major key will have *flat* in its name (C♭) and so will its relative minor (A♭ minor). A major key may be a plain letter (B) yet its minor will have a sharp in its name (G♯ minor). Another major key will have sharp in its name (F♯) and so will its relative minor (D♯). There is no short cut. We'll just have to keep a sharp look-out (!) to see if LA has a sharp or flat on its degree in the key signature.

   Every key signature then, really represents two scales or keys, one major and the other its relative minor.

   We know how to look at key signatures and to determine the key, by finding DO. To determine the minor key for the signature we have merely to find LA, by any of the methods outlined. Usually, this will mean, first find DO. Then from DO, determine LA.

   In the case of minor keys with sharps in the signature, there is a short way. Remember how in the case of major keys we count up one scale degree or one half step from the last sharp to determine the key. It is possible to count DOWN one scale degree (in this case a whole step—TI to LA) from the last sharp. This will be LA and the name of the minor key.

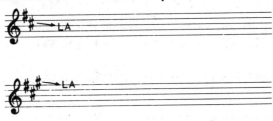

Name the Major and Minor Keys for the following Key signatures:

Answers: C♯ major, A♯ minor; A♭ major, F minor; D major, B minor; C♭ major, A♭ minor.

Well then, you ask, if a key signature does indeed indicate two different keys instead of one, how do we tell which key the signature intends? Do you remember the list we compiled of indications that the music we are looking at is in minor? We said:

1. many LAs in the music
2. sometimes SO is sharped; sometimes FA and SO both are sharped
3. there is not the frequent occurrence of DO-MI-SO passages in the melody—a characteristic of MAJOR
4. the music ends on LA.

All of these will tell us if the music is in major or minor; but the quickest and surest is by looking at the last note. Just as music in major almost always ends on DO, music in minor almost always ends on LA.

Which two keys do each of the following signatures indicate? Then, by looking at the "last" note before the double bar which we will assume to be the ending note, determine which of the two keys is the one indicated.

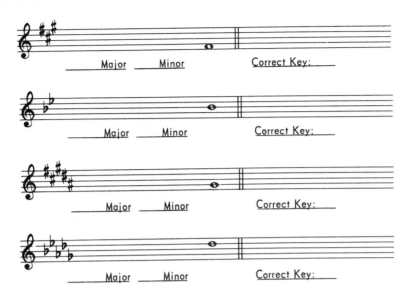

Answers: F♯ minor, B♭ major, G♯ minor, D♭ major

## THE TONIC NOTE AND THE TONIC TRIAD

In minor we have found a new leader. Instead of DO, it is—? LA. But once you digest this new fact, you can be reassured that most of the other familiar facts still apply: Everything you know about DO as it applied to major, is true about LA as it applies to minor. In minor, LA is the tonic.

LA starts the scale, ends the scale

LA ends the song

LA names the scale, names the key

LA is the tone-center, gives the key feeling

LA IS TO MINOR WHAT DO IS TO MAJOR.

Since LA is the Tonic, what then would be the Tonic Triad? What would we sing to get key feeling in this key for instance? Since a triad consists of three notes, every other note, taken from the scale, in this case space-space-space, it will be F-A♭-C. The tonic triad in minor is This is a bit more difficult to sing by ear than DO MI SO, the major tonic triad. You may want to play both LA *and* DO to help give you the proper minor key feeling. We'll see a little bit later (p. 158) why this is so, and exactly how the minor tonic triad is different from the major tonic triad.

## A VARIATION: THE HARMONIC MINOR SCALE

There is another characteristic about minor which we noticed earlier but haven't discussed further. We noticed that sometimes in a minor song, SO would be sharped. An example was the song, "Go Down, Moses." If SO is sharped, what does that do to the minor scale?

1. **The sound is changed. Perhaps the strangest sounding part of the scale is FA-SO-LA. Strange but pleasant, because much folk music and popular music uses this progression of tones. But with SO**

sharped, that effect is changed. It is not so unfinished in effect, vague or haunting. How does it sound when SO is sharped—SI-LA? More finished—a good ending sound.

2.  Also, the intervals between FA and SO, and SO and LA are now changed. How are these distances changed? Between FA and SI? Larger. How many half steps. Measure: C-C♯ ½ step; C♯ to D ½ step; D to D♯ ½ step = 3 half steps.

**And from D♯ to E?** A half step.

Try singing the scale, as I play it on the piano. That interval from C to D♯ is not easy to sing. Listen to the scale. Does it sound familiar? What does it make you think of?

Oriental dancing girls.

A cantor singing in the synagogue.

Slavic peoples.

Let's listen to some music which fits the list you've just made. In all of these selections you will hear that very large interval from FA to SI

## ORIENTALE                                                                                                                        César Cui

## EILI EILI

God  my   al - might-y  God,_____   Why hast Thou for - sa - ken   me? _____
Fi - li  Ei - - li _____    Lo - mo  a  sav  to  ni? _____

## FATE THEME—CARMEN                                                                                                                    Bizet

## RAKÓCZY MARCH                                                                                               Berlioz

Because SI (SO sharped) is not always used in the minor scale, notice that it is not written in the key signature. It is one of those sharps referred to as an accidental. This has several advantages. The sharp is right there by the note to remind us when we sing or play. And when we look at music, the accidental sharp before SO is a good clue that the music is minor.

Why do you suppose such a change was made in the minor scale as you first learned it?

1. It gives a more final "The End" sound to the scale and to music which uses this scale.
2. It affects the chords which come from the scale and helps these chords to achieve a stronger "The End" effect.

Probably because it assists the harmony which comes from the scale, this version of the minor scale is called HARMONIC MINOR. And because the version of the minor scale which we first examined comes straight from the major scale in its natural form, it is called NATURAL MINOR, sometimes PURE or NORMAL minor.

It's true that the minor scale has variations whereas the major does not, but this doesn't change all the facts we've gathered about minor, its signature, its effect, etc. Each major scale has a minor scale called its RELATIVE MINOR, found on LA. It can be varied slightly as we have seen, to make the HARMONIC minor, but it is still the same relative minor.

Songs like these use the NATURAL form of the minor scale:

I'm Just a Poor Wayfaring Stranger (Her: 5)
God Rest Ye Merry Gentlemen (Her: 174)
Hatikva (fl.)
When Johnny Comes Marching Home (fl., Her: 179)

WHEN JOHNNY COMES MARCHING HOME                                    Lambert

When John-ny comes march-ing home a-gain Hur-rah, ___ Hur-rah ___ We'll
give him a hear-ty wel-come then Hur-rah, ___ Hur-rah ___ O the
men will cheer and the boys will shout, The la-dies they ___ will all turn out And we'll
all feel gay when John-ny comes march-ing home. ___

But others use the HARMONIC form:

Eili, Eili
Go Down, Moses (Her: 254)
Hungarian Dance No. 5—Brahms

## THE MELODIC MINOR SCALE

Some minor music doesn't use either of those forms! You remember that sometimes we noted that not only was SO sharped in a song, but FA. How does the scale look then?

fa sharp  so sharp
   fi       si

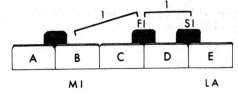

The distance between MI and FI is now 1 whole step, instead of the half step between MI and FA. The distance between FI and SI is now 1 whole step. The distance between SI and LA is now one half step, instead of one whole step between SO and LA in the NATURAL form. And the awkward interval of three half steps between FA and SI which occurs in the HARMONIC form is done away with.

RAKÓCZY MARCH                                                                                   Berlioz

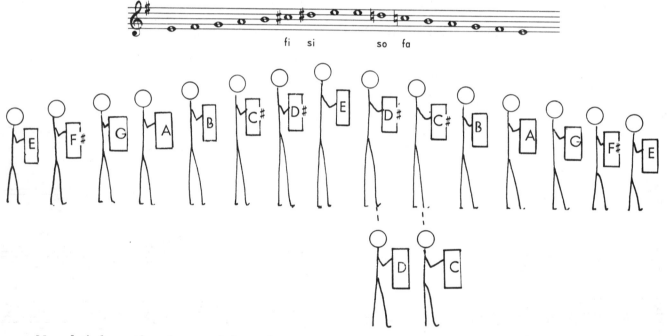

You might say the melodic line has been smoothed out. Maybe that will help you to remember that this variation of the minor scale is called MELODIC MINOR. It is the most complicated of the three variations. We have to remember to place two accidental sharps in this scale—FA sharped and SO sharped—but only in the ascending scale. When the scale descends, the accidental sharps are removed and SO and FA restored. Why? Well, listen to the sound. Sharps are an "up" sound and help the "up" feeling of the scale when it is ascending. But when it is descending, we want a "down" feeling which is helped when the sharps are removed. Let's spell it out with two sets of resonator bells. We'll need fifteen people. Play the scale up then down.

Now let's have the players of C♯ and D♯ in the descending scale exchange their bells for C and D respectively and hear the scale up and down again.

New let's play the songs  Charlie is My Darlin'  and  Hallowe'en  (p. 143) with each player playing his respective bell as I point to the notes. For  Charlie  we will have to change keys and bells.

CHARLIE IS MY DARLIN'                                                                        Scotland

## THE TETRACHORDS IN THE MINOR SCALES

These slight interval changes, caused by the accidentals, of course bring about the several variations of the minor scale, and therefore cause still another set of variations—that of the tetrachords. Like the major scale, the minor scale can be divided into two tetrachords, the bottom four notes of the scale, and the top four, each within the interval of a fourth—a perfect fourth. In the major scale, the bottom and top tetrachords are built exactly alike (see Chapter 7). This is not so in the minor scales, as you can prove to yourself by measuring the steps and half steps of each variation. You may notice something else of interest: all the changes in interval brought about by the accidentals and creating the several variations occur in the upper tetrachord. Each minor scale therefore begins similarly with an identical lower tetrachord, and then in the upper tetrachord branches out into the several variations.

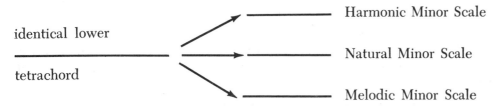

## THE TONIC OR PARALLEL MINOR SCALE

Not only do some songs hop back and forth from a major key to its relative minor, but sometimes a song goes from major to minor another way.

For instance, when I play Pop Goes the Weasel or America and make it minor instead of its usual major, I do it another way. I don't go from the major to its relative minor. Or take a song which has a minor verse like Go Tell Aunt Rhody.

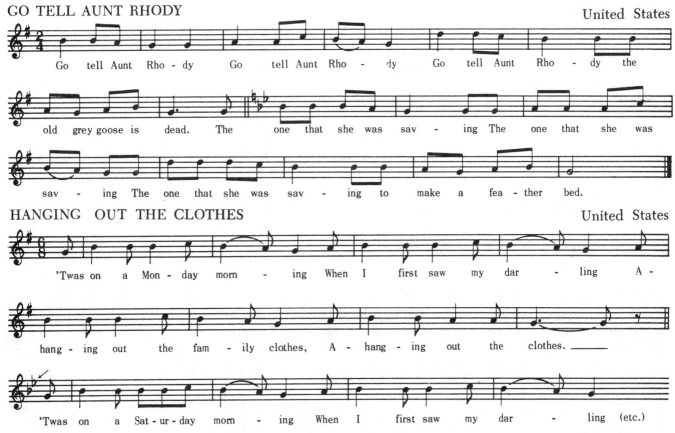

Or Hanging Out the Clothes. Let's look at the latter song and sing both verses including the verse for Saturday when they are all tired out. How has the Saturday verse been changed to sound tired out? Sounds minor. **Now notice the key signature—it is not the same as the signature for the rest of the verses—G major, so it cannot be a RELATIVE minor. What is the different key signature and what is the minor key? Ask yourself first what major and minor keys belong to two flats. B FLAT MAJOR. Go three half steps down. . . . G MINOR. Let's compare the minor scale on G to the major scale on G. For comparison's sake, let's number the notes of the scales:** *How are they different?*

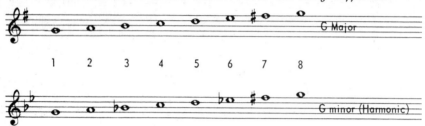

1. They have different key signatures.
2. The third and sixth notes are different in the two scales.

*How are they alike?*
1. They both are named G.
2. They begin and end on the same note, therefore G is the tone center for both scales. Therefore it can be said they have the same TONIC.
3. They have many notes *in common*; in fact only the third and sixth notes are different.

**How are the third and sixth notes different?** In the minor scale both are flatted.

*Several conclusions*
1. What is another way to change a major scale into a minor scale? Flat the third and sixth notes. Only, this way does not create a RELATIVE minor.
2. What these two scales G major and G minor do have in common is the same letter name and the same TONIC note. For this reason the minor is called the TONIC MINOR, and the two scales are referred to as PARALLEL; G MINOR is the PARALLEL MINOR OF G MAJOR. It is this parallel relationship we would use to sing or play Pop Goes the Weasel in minor; instead of G major it would be in G minor. All you have to do is flat the third and sixth notes.

### The Minor Tonic Triad

3. **Earlier we mentioned that the minor tonic chord might be harder to sing than the major. If we compare them, what difference do you see?** The middle note is different. In the minor it is flatted; it is 1 ♭3—5. **How then could we change any major tonic chord into a minor tonic chord?** Merely flat the third. Practice: change these major tonic triads into minor tonic triads.

G  B  D        G  B♭  D

(Answers at bottom of page)

How can we use this knowledge to accompany the song "Hanging Out the Clothes" at the piano? Play the G major chord at the piano for all verses except the minor verse, then flat the third of the tonic triad to make it a G minor chord for the minor verse.

Answer to practice question, above:

Suppose we wanted to accompany "Go Tell Aunt Rhody" at the piano in the key of G Major.

The tonic chord would be . . . ? 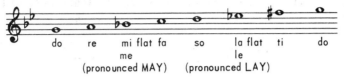 And to make it minor, flat the third: →

4. Since these two scales have the same TONIC we could say they use the same DO. If they do, what would *all* the syllables of the minor scale be?

| do | re | mi flat | fa | so | la flat | ti | do |
|----|----|---------|----|----|---------|----|----| 
| | | me | | | le | | |
| | | (pronounced MAY) | | | (pronounced LAY) | | |

## Tonic Minor Syllables

Now of course this is a completely different set of syllables for the minor scale. Some teachers prefer to use this approach to the whole concept of minor. Each has its advantages. What might they be?

*RELATIVE MINOR*

1. same key signature

2. the one scale comes right out of the other( in a "NATURAL" state); just go from LA to LA instead of from DO to DO
There is no second syllable language

3. the transition from major to relative minor in accompaniment is easy and clear (for instance, from G major to E minor)

*PARALLEL MINOR*

1. it seems more musical to refer to the tone center or key tone as DO and Tonic, rather than LA

2. the scale members would be numbered similarly from 1-8, and thought of this way

3. the transition in modes on the same tonic would be easily facilitated (for instance, from G major to G minor)

If the teacher were to approach the whole topic of minor from the parallel scale with the common tonic rather than from the relative minor, the easiest approach might well be through the MELODIC minor scale for which only one change need be made for its ascending form:

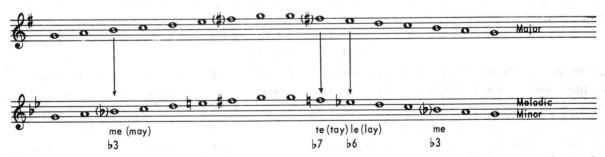

Then two other changes must be made for the descending form of the melodic minor scale, and what results is the same as the NATURAL minor scale, descending form. In the following illustrations the Major scale is compared to the other variations of the minor scale, all starting on the same tonic.

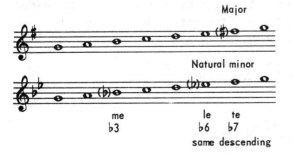

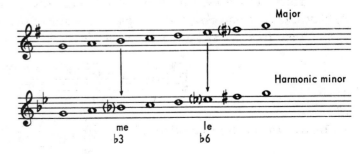

## DETERMINING THE KEY SIGNATURE OF A MINOR KEY

If you should want to notate something in a minor key—for instance, if you composed an original song and wanted to write it down in G minor, how could you know without spelling the whole scale out, what notes are in the scale, what the key signature is? It takes several steps. Since we know how to determine the key signature of major keys (see Chapter 8) the best idea would be to get back to the DO. Several ways were listed to get from DO to LA; use the reverse of any of those ways to get to DO and then determine the key from DO. For example, to determine the key signature of G minor:

1. Count up three half steps to DO—B♭.
2. Say the flats in order going one beyond the name of the key—B♭, E♭.
3. The signature for G minor is two flats, B♭ and E♭.

For sharps there can be an easier procedure. To find the signature for the key of C♯ minor for instance:

1. Count UP one degree (one whole step) to D♯.
2. That sharp is the last sharp of the key signature. Say the sharps in order—F♯ C♯ G♯ D♯, stopping on D♯ and that is the signature.

But the best way yet is this shortcut, similar to the device on pp. 101, 102.

If the minor key contains sharps, use this picture:     3  4  5  6  7  1  2
                                                        f  c  g  d  a  e  b

How many sharps in the key of d♯ minor? The number 6 is over the letter d, so the answer is 6 sharps. Which sharps are they? The letters in the picture give the order = f c g d a e

If the minor key contains flats, use this picture:     5  6  7  1  2  3  4
                                                       b  e  a  d  g  c  f

How many flats in the key of f minor? The number 4 is over the letter f, so the answer is 4 flats.

Which flats are they? The letters in the picture give the order = b e a d

If you don't know whether there are flats or sharps in the minor key you are working with, use one of the longer ways mentioned earlier.

## SUMMARY

To summarize some of the important facts about minor: How can we tell music is minor when we LOOK at it, but can't HEAR IT?

1. The music ends in LA.
2. There are usually many LAs in the music.
3. The pattern LA—DO—MI—the Tonic chord in minor will be much more prevalent than DO—MI—SO, the major tonic chord.
4. SO may be sharped.
5. SO and FA together may be sharped.

How can we tell music is minor when we LISTEN to it, but can't LOOK at it?

It usually conveys a strong mood or emotion which is not hard to recognize. Minor has a much wider range of emotions than just sadness; for instance, mystery, longing, haunting, spooky, etc. ALL MINOR MUSIC IS NOT SAD. Teachers should not teach that it is, or that major music is "happy." It IS probable that most sad music is minor.

## MINOR SCALE SONG

Unknown

The mi - nor scale once went like this but peo - ple found it hard to sing And

so they raised the sev - enth note a high - er lead - ing tone to bring At

last they made it go like this, it's eas - y now as an - y - thing.

From *First Solo Book,* by Diller and Quaile. Published by G. Schirmer, Inc. Used by permission.

*Songs in the NATURAL MINOR*

1. Johnny Has Gone for a Soldier
2. I'm Just a Poor Wayfaring Stranger (Her: 5)
3. God Rest Ye Merry Gentlemen (Her: 174)
4. Hatikva
5. Black is the Color of My True Love's Hair

*Songs in HARMONIC MINOR*

1. Go Down, Moses (Her: 254)
2. Eili, Eili
3. Coventry Carol
4. Joshua Fit De Battle (Her: 138)
5. Pat-a-pan (Her: 45)
6. Orientale—Cui
7. Hungarian Dance No. 5
8. Rakoczy March—Berlioz
9. Fate Theme—Carmen—Bizet

*Songs in MELODIC MINOR*

1. Greensleeves (Her: 10)
2. Charlie is My Darlin'
3. Hallowe'en
4. Rakoczy March—Berlioz

*Songs which move from RELATIVE MINOR to*
*RELATIVE MAJOR*

1. We Three Kings of Orient Are (Her: 92)
2. Greensleeves (Her: 10)
3. Czech Folk Song
4. God Rest Ye Merry Gentlemen (Her: 174)
5. When Johnny Comes Marching Home (Her: 179)
6. Fum Fum Fum (Her: 64)
7. Erie Canal (Her: 256)

*Songs with a verse in PARALLEL MINOR*

1. Hanging Out the Clothes
2. Go Tell Aunt Rhody (Her: 244)

The activities suggested in lessons like the ones on minor are not meant to be regarded as cute gimmicks. They are a way to make otherwise abstract symbols real, to personalize abstract figures, to involve the student in a learning experience which will make an impact on him. The student will remember and understand better if he actively has to exchange one bell for another in order to make a chord or scale or song sound right; if he plays a song into which a mistake has been purposely planted which he then has to correct by various motor-kinesthetic experiences; if he himself is part of a scale or other form in music; if he must rearrange *himself* in relation to other persons as well as rearranging a bell or a written symbol; if he can handle and manipulate musical symbols on the flannel board. These learning experiences give him the "WHY"; they help to clarify concepts.

# Chapter 13

# Larger Intervals

## WHAT YOU NEED TO KNOW

1. The staff
2. The scales
3. The tonic chord

   A brief reference to intervals is made in Chapter 6.

## BASIC FACTS YOU WILL LEARN

1. An interval: The distance between two pitches is called an INTERVAL.
2. An interval is named by the number of degrees or letters it encompasses.
3. Some intervals are referred to as PERFECT. This is so when each note of the interval is in the scale of the other. Another way to distinguish Perfect Fourths and Perfect Fifths from other forms of these particular intervals is that the Fourth and Fifth occurring in the Harmonic Series are perfect.
4. The Harmonic Series is a phenomenon of nature which illustrates that each single tone is really made up of a series of tones.

## WHAT THIS LESSON CAN LEAD TO

1. Better comprehension of the structure of music; therefore better reading and performing skill.

---

## INTERVALS DEFINED

If we should want to jump over a puddle we would have to measure the distance with our eyes and estimate whether and how to jump. If we throw something to somebody else, the way we throw is determined by our estimation of the distance. If we reach out to another person to give him something it has to be a distance we can reach. If we drive to a friend's house we have to know the distance in order to estimate our travel time. In that case our tool for measuring distance is the speedometer in the car. If we want to build a shelf or sew some curtains, we have to measure dimensions. In that case our measuring tool would be . . ? A yard stick or tape measure or ruler.

In music we measure several ways. If we are measuring time as it passes, what do we use? Beats. How do we measure distance in music, the space between notes? What is our ruler? The staff is one way, but a better way is the piano keyboard because it is an exact picture of steps and half steps, by which we can measure many larger distances in music. These distances have another name. The distance between two notes of music is called an INTERVAL.

What musical intervals do we already know? The shortest distance between any two notes on the keyboard is called a HALF STEP. The half step is an INTERVAL. And the sum of two half steps is another interval, the WHOLE STEP. We may have taken note of several other intervals without ever labelling them INTERVALS. Can you think of any?

1. When we build a scale it goes from a certain letter to the first reoccurrence of that same letter. How many notes away? Eight. That is an interval called OCTAVE.

2. When we built an Harmonic minor scale, we noticed an interesting wide *interval* between the sixth and seventh notes. It measured three half steps.

3. When we considered major and minor triads we compared the interval between the bottom and middle notes of each triad. Those are intervals called thirds. The number-name of the interval is determined by the number of degrees encompassed.

It seems that each person has his favorite way of organizing intervals for his own understanding and for teaching them to others. Some people prefer using the scale; most of the intervals can be found in the scale and it is an orderly logical organization of the intervals. Some start with the triad because it is such a common organization of notes in music. Some start with the biggest interval; some with the smallest. Teacher can vary the approach to intervals, always seeking the clearest most comfortable way. It might be useful to mention here certain things about some of the intervals.

1. The octave (eight degrees), because of its size, relationship to the scale and frequent occurrence in piano music, especially the left hand, is one of the easiest to recognize by sight, more difficult to recognize by ear than some teachers expect, and much more difficult to sing than music teachers and students alike expect. Its sound is confused most commonly with the Perfect Fifth.

2. Some regard the Perfect Fourth and Perfect Fifth as the easiest intervals to learn. Their distances make them easy to identify by eye and their sound is characteristic enough to recognize by ear and to sing. The trouble is, they are easily mixed up with *each other* for all the above reasons! Easily distinguishable from other intervals, they are difficult to distinguish from each other.

3. Thirds are easy for some of the same reasons as for Fourths and Fifths. They have a pretty, close sound. When both tones are sounded together at a fair volume especially in the middle or high range they cause a "beat" or vibration in our ears that can actually be uncomfortable. They are easy to recognize on the staff. When identified by ear they can sometimes be confused with Sixths. And it is quite difficult to distinguish among themselves the various thirds.

4. Among the hardest ways to begin a song is the sixth—SO-MI in major, or SO-ME in minor. It is difficult to sing and to recognize by ear. Perhaps this is because DO does not occur in the interval and it is hard to relate this particular combination of tones to a key-center and get your bearings.

5. Seconds are easy to see and hear but hard to distinguish among themselves, and sevenths and sixths are just plain hard in every way.

6. An effective approach is to use the triad as a base and to take from it first the octave and fifth, then

the fourth,  and then the thirds.

For these reasons an organized comprehensive approach to all the intervals will not be presented in the following pages. Refer to any good text on Dictation or Sight Reading for that. Although children and non-music majors can be taught to read, sing and recognize intervals successfully, it does seem to be a more advanced skill—this in the face of the challenge of our contemporary music which is more interval-oriented and less key-oriented.

To teach some concepts of intervals in general, what could be more effective than the games of the type presented by Madeleine Carabo-Cone in her writings.

## Make Up Your Own Variations On the Spin-A Dial or Bean Bag Games:

A. A giant grand staff should be on the floor—on paper or painted on, each line and space labelled with its letter name. We need a dial with numbers from 2 to 8 in both black and red. Every player starts on G of the Bass staff, or if just using the treble, on Middle C.

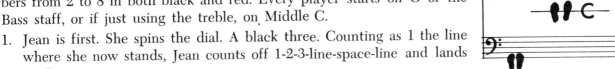

1. Jean is first. She spins the dial. A black three. Counting as 1 the line where she now stands, Jean counts off 1-2-3-line-space-line and lands on B.
2. Eric is next. He gets black 7. Calling his line G as 1, he steps off to 7 and lands on F.
3. Ann spins the dial next. She gets a red 6. She cannot move.
4. Jim gets a red 2. He cannot move.
5. Jean has her second turn. A black 7. She moves up from B as 1, stepping off each line and space till she gets to 7 on A.
6. Eric gets a red 4. He must go *backwards* from where he is on F, calling F 1, till he reaches number 4 on C.

And so on. Whoever reaches the top F first wins.

B. Use giant treble staff on floor with middle C. Each student stands on middle C and tosses a bean bag. He counts the degrees from middle C to where the bean bag landed.

1. Jean's toss landed on A. 6. Then, on squares or circles marked off around the periphery of the room, or on a playing board, she marks off 6 squares. Certain of the squares may offer bonuses or impose penalties (go back to middle C—no advance; or advance bean bag to D—4 more degrees so four more squares.)

  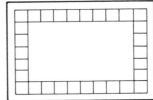

2. Tom's toss reaches the high F. He steps off the lines and spaces of the staff to discover it is eleven, then moves eleven squares on the board. There, a penalty says he must go back three squares. Whoever gets "home" first wins the game.

C. Each student has his own flannel board staff or staff drawn on large paper. He reproduces on this the interval he has tossed from middle C.

1. John tosses the bean bag to G. From C to G is a fifth, so he puts a note on middle C, one on G, and writes down a 5 for fifth.
2. On his next turn he tosses the bag to C. He reproduces the interval, writes 8.
3. After a fixed number of turns for each contestant, the highest total wins.

D. Take a Giant Step—as in the familiar game, a leader directs every other player in turn.

1. Jill, move up 4. Jill gives the number 1 to the middle C she is standing on and counts out four, moving up to F.
2. Bill, move up 2. Bill moves from middle C to D.
3. When the leader is not looking, stealing is allowed, but if the culprit is caught it's back to middle C. When they arrive at the top F they turn around and head back for middle C. First person to arrive back on middle C wins the game.

After some experience with games like these it is an easier matter for teacher to turn the attention of the students to a staff on the chalk-board and proceed as follows: **In our game, when you were told to move ahead 4, you started counting on whatever line or space you were standing and moved ahead, stepping on each line or space until you counted out 4. What obvious number-name could we give this interval?** A FOURTH. Of course. Using that as an example, name these intervals:

Sixth   Fifth  Third  Fourth   Seventh

**In each case, what determined the name?** The number of degrees (Lines or spaces) involved. A musical interval is named by the number of degrees encompassed.

Notice something else. Take the second interval in the example. Not only does it involve five degrees but say the letters of the musical alphabet from E to B. E-F-G-A-B. There are five letters. A musical interval is named by the number of alphabet letters encompassed.

## The Perfect Fifth

**Here is the beginning of Twinkle, Twinkle Little Star. What is the name of the first interval?** A FIFTH. Why? Because it covers five degrees of the staff. Also because it includes five letters of the musical alphabet. There can be more than one kind of fifth, but we are going to concentrate now on this kind of FIFTH, which is called a PERFECT FIFTH. There are a number of reasons why a Perfect Fifth is called that. We'll list them and then note some short cuts.

Use a keyboard and measure the distance from F to C by steps.

1.  It totals 3½ steps.

2.  The top note is in the major scale of the bottom note. If the fifth is not perfect, this will not be the case. For instance, C is a fifth from F♯, but C is not in the scale of F♯ so it is not a perfect fifth.

3.  Another reason is that the bottom note is in the major scale of the top note. If the top note were

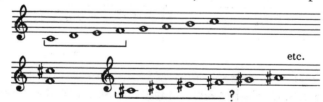

C♯, the scale on C♯ would not include an F so the fifth would not be called perfect. Measure it and you will see it is not 3½ steps.

4. Another interesting and complicated reason has to do with a phenomenon of nature called the Harmonic Series. (See end of this chapter.)
5. In any major scale we build, the fifth note will always be a perfect fifth from the first note. Check on Chapter 7 where all the major scales are spelled out. Here are just a few to serve as examples:

## Its Look

Now that's a lot of complicated calculating to do in order to recognize a perfect fifth. Here are some easier ways to recognize the perfect fifth by its look. Check the previous examples to verify the following:

1. If the bottom note is on a space, the top note is on a . . . . . space. Skip the next space from the bottom note and the fifth is on the next space.
2. If the bottom note is on a line, the top note is on a line. Skip the next line from the bottom note, and the fifth is on the next.

3. If the bottom note is flatted, the top note will be flatted.

4. If the bottom note is sharped, the top note will be sharped.

5. There is one exception: the combination of B and F.

What would be the main reason we would want to be able to recognize a perfect fifth when we see one? To know how it sounds. To be able to sing it correctly when we see it. How does a perfect fifth sound?

## Its Sound

1. Its the "outsides" of a major triad—it sounds like DO and SO. (It could be other combinations of syllables too, but that gets quite complicated.)
2. We could put a "middle" in it—a MI would fit between the DO and SO to make it sound like the major triad.
3. It sounds like the beginning of Twinkle, Twinkle.

**Test yourselves. Which of these intervals are the perfect fifths: Do this by look first, then I will mix them up and play them in a different order and see if you can recognize them by listening:**

Intervals 3–6–8 are Perfect Fifths

Here is a contest. We'll line you up in two teams. Using a flannel board for each team, I'll place some notes on the staff of each board. Each team member must place the proper note above the note already there to make a perfect fifth, go to the sets of resonator bells, play his interval correctly and then take his seat. The side which finishes first wins.

All this is Ear Training and Sight Reading of course. Also, find perfect fifths in songs in your song books:

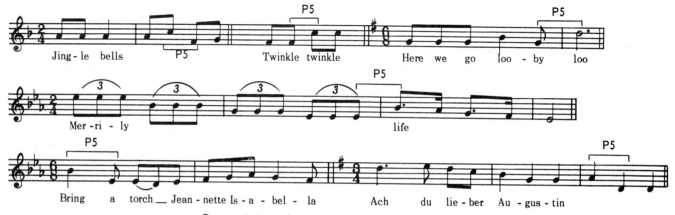

## Organizing Major and Minor Triads

Here is a useful way to organize triads, major and minor. Since the "outsides" of major and minor triads is a perfect fifth, this little drill will help in learning perfect fifths. It is most effective when played at the piano and recited out loud at the same time. In this way, we reinforce our knowledge through a variety of senses:

Visual, through our eyes; Tactile, through our fingers; Aural, through our ears; Intellectual, through spelling aloud, and Motor, by measuring the "feel" of a triad, the spacing, the distance. Be sure to use fingers 1-3-5 so that by skipping fingers 2 and 4 you impress on your learning the skipping of notes 2 and 4.

When the drill is started on F, the major triads are grouped according to their "appearance" and "feel."

1. The first three triads are all white-key triads.
2. The next three triads are all white-black-white key triads—a black note in the middle.
3. Then comes the maverick triad on B, like no other; and then another unique triad all on black notes.
4. The next three triads are all black-white-black triads—a white note in the middle.
5. The last triad is another unique triad, which ends on F and takes you right back to your starting note.

## Octave

We have already noted that a scale begins and ends on the same letter. How many notes are involved from the beginning of the scale to the end? Eight. How many degrees? Eight. The name of this interval means eight. Do you know other words having to do with eight? OCTET—eight performers; OCTAGON—eight sides. OCTAVE—an interval encompassing eight notes or degrees. An octave is easy to hear and fairly easy to recognize when we see it. Look at Chapter 7 with all the scales on it and decide what we can say about it.

1. An octave involves eight notes or eight degrees of the staff.
2. An octave is the distance between any letter and its first recurrence.
3. If the bottom note is on a line, the top note is on a space. No exceptions.
4. If the bottom note is on a space, the top note is on a line. No exceptions.
5. It has the appearance of a big jump—it covers lots of space.
6. If the bottom note is sharped, the top note is.
7. If the bottom note is flatted, the top note is.
8. If the bottom note is a plain letter (B), so is the top note.

### Its Sound

How does an octave sound?

1. It is a very big jump from somewhere near the bottom of our voices to somewhere near the top.
2. You can fit the whole scale between the two notes.
3. You could sing DO-MI-SO-DO from bottom to top or back.
4. It sounds like "Somewhere, Over the Rainbow" or "BA-LI hi."

Engage in games and drills similar to those suggested for the perfect fifth. Incidentally, the octave is another perfect interval for the reasons listed earlier. When it comes to singing the octave, that's a bit harder than just identifying it when it is played. Use the same aids we just listed.

## Perfect Fourth

**On the flannel board there is a D triad. Notice that like all chords we have built, we use every other note to make the triad. Suppose we wanted to use more than three notes but use only the notes in the triad. What would be the next two notes? Another D and another F♯. Very often to make a triad sound bigger and fuller a second DO is added at the top: Notice that the chord doesn't go every other note any more. The second DO is not just every other note away from the other notes of the triad. What is the name of the interval from the A to D? How many letters are involved? How many degrees? FOUR. Its name is FOURTH, PERFECT FOURTH. Put the top DO on these triads at the flannel board. The bottom DO will tell you where. Then we'll draw some conclusions.**

1. The perfect fourth covers four degrees, four letters.
2. It measures 2½ steps.
3. If the bottom note is on a space, the top is on a line; skip the next space from the bottom note and it is on the next line.
4. If the bottom note is on a line, the top is on a space; skip the next line and it is on the next space.
5. If the bottom note is sharped the top note is sharped.
6. If the bottom note is flatted, the top note is flatted.

7. There is one exception: the combination of B and F. What was the exception for 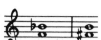 the perfect fifth? Also B and F.

## Its Sound

1. The sound of the perfect fourth is pretty easy to recognize. It seems to be saying "THE END." What syllables does it sound like?

2. SO – DO

3. What songs does it remind you of? Here Comes the Bride, Taps, Marine's Hymn, We Wish You a Merry Christmas, March of the Kings.

4. Try singing "THE END" from these different pitches:

5. Here is a melody composed only of pieces of scale and the perfect fourth. See if you can sight read it correctly. First, play DO. Sing DO. Sing SO-DO. Begin.

6. The following song, The March of the Kings, offers several factors to be noted:

    A. It is an excellent example of minor—what minor scale does it use? Harmonic.

    B. It moves mostly in scale line, with several intervals strategically placed—what intervals? It begins with a perfect fourth. There are also perfect fifths and some thirds. They usually comprise a tonic triad.

MARCH OF THE KINGS                         France

## The Harmonic Series

To look at a cake, we might not dream of all the ingredients which went into it. We can't see them. But if you've watched a cake being made, you know these ingredients are there.

It is one of the jobs of chemists to break down substances into all of their components. Here again, just looking at a substance doesn't reveal all the ingredients which make it up.

The prism is a dramatic example of this. A ray of light which looks colorless to us magically separates into many colors when directed through the prism. Where do the colors come from if they were not there all along, even though we do not see them in that ray of light?

So it is with a musical tone. Although it sounds like one single tone, it is really made up of a number of tones. These tones can sometimes be detected by the following experiment:

With your right hand depress these notes on the piano keyboard:

or three students can each depress one key. Then strike this D:

while depressing the damper pedal. Sometimes you will be able to hear resounding not only the D which was struck, but the other notes depressed on the keyboard. Because it is a fact that all these other tones are in the one tone struck and sounded. Notice that the first tone which occurs after the fundamental tone struck is an octave higher. The next tone is what interval? A fifth. What kind of fifth? A PERFECT fifth. And the next interval? A perfect fourth. There occur even more tones at other intervals, as illustrated, and all these tones are referred to as the HARMONIC SERIES. As you can see, these are the perfect intervals: octave, fifth and fourth as they occur in a phenomenon of nature. We can say that the fifths and fourths which occur in the HARMONIC SERIES are perfect; other fourths and fifths are not perfect. What would the harmonic series be if F were sounded?

Harmonic Series on F

This is a good time to point out that many of the laws of music as you have learned them in this book are not the invention of man, but the marvelous creation of Nature. The Circle of Fifths is another good example. (See Chapter 7 for mention of this and tetrachords.)

## SUMMARY

The *concept* of intervals is not difficult to learn. What is harder is the spelling and structure, and hardest still is aural recognition and the vocalizing of them. Whatever part of this the non-specializing student is able to do should be recognized as an achievement.

## SUGGESTED ASSIGNMENTS

1. Spell all the intervals you know from given notes. For instance, from F:
2. Label them.
3. Try to sing them.

P5    Oct.    P4    half step  whole step

Chapter **14**

# The Primary Chords

## WHAT YOU NEED TO KNOW

1. All about major scales
2. All about minor scales
3. All about key signatures
4. How chords are built
5. How to build a Tonic chord
6. It helps to have had experiences chording with bells; and with the autoharp, playing by ear, or rote, or from chord markings

## BASIC FACTS YOU WILL LEARN

1. The primary chords are the three most commonly used chords of a key.
2. The primary chords are built on the first, fourth and fifth tones of a scale. All the notes in the chords must come from the scale.
3. The 7 after the letter name of a chord (G7) represents an additional note added to a triad. This note is seven degrees above the bottom note of the triad.
4. In a major key the three primary triads are major. In a minor key, only the 5-chord is a major triad; the 1 and 4 chords are minor.
5. This means that the 5 chord in a major key will contain exactly the same notes as the 5-chord in the parallel minor key: i.e. the 5-chord in G major contains the same notes as the 5-chord in G minor.

## WHAT THIS LESSON CAN LEAD TO

1. Greater freedom and skill in reading music; and in harmonizing or chording an accompaniment.

---

## DISCOVERING THE PRIMARY CHORDS

Teacher can motivate several ways:

### Planned Mistake

Teacher says, let's sing "Silent Night." Find the C chord on your autoharps and be ready to play. Teacher accompanies at the piano and plays pretty loudly, always on the C chord, at places in the song where the C chord obviously doesn't belong. We'll hope they don't go through the entire song before the students protest loudly that something is wrong. This song needs more than one chord!

## Pose a Problem

Mr. Teacher, we want to accompany "Silent Night" (fl., Her: 223) on our autoharps, but the book we are using doesn't tell us which chords we should use. How can we find out which chords to use?

Here is a way you can always determine for yourselves which chords to use when the song does not indicate the harmonies. To begin, review what you know about the Tonic chord:

1. It is a very important chord
2. It is built on DO
3. It takes every other note from the scale until the notes make a 3-note chord called triad
4. It goes space-space-space or line-line-line
5. It will almost certainly end the song and probably begin it
6. Certain songs like rounds are 1-chord songs which will sound fine with just the Tonic chord, but most other songs need more than just the tonic.

Since you mentioned that notes are taken from a scale to make chords, suppose we put a C scale

on the flannel board. Teacher uses whole notes. **Jim, will you come up and take the notes which make up the "family" of the C chord and arrange them into a chord?**

**Put their syllable names to the side of each note. Meanwhile, these three students come up and take the resonator bells corresponding to the notes in the C chord.** These students could stand in a group or in order from shortest to tallest to make a "picture" of the chord. Or be very pictorial and have C kneel, E sit in a chair behind C and G stand behind E. **We'll sing the song, Silent Night again accompanying ourselves with the bell chord and the autoharps.**

**Since you've found the C chord did not always fit, let's experiment with the autoharp a little bit. Why don't you try the chord-button right next to the C button? If your left pointing finger is on C, the next button will be right under your third finger. What is its name? G7. Now as we play the C chord and sing the song, be listening for the first place in the song which doesn't sound "right" with the C chord. At that place, all bells stop playing, and autoharps try the G7.**

When everybody gets to "All is calm," hands fly up to indicate this is the spot. The bells drop out and the autoharps try G7. That's it! But G7 can't continue on "All is bright" and everybody hops back to the C chord.

Let's see where the G7 chord comes from. Since the chord named C-Chord is built upon C, it seems logical to assume that the G chord will be built upon. . . ? G. We've already used the G from our scale—where is it? In the C chord. Here is another G. Ann, come up and build a G chord on our flannel board. Put the syllable names beside the notes.

We'll have three more students come up to the second set of resonator bells and select the bells for the G chord.

You make yourselves into a picture like the C chord players have done. Now play a steady beat with the autoharp G chord; we'll see if you match. They do. But what does the 7 after the G mean? The bells sound fine the way they are.

Chords can have any number of notes in them. It is called a TRIAD if the chord has three notes, but it can have four notes and five and more. How do we always build chords? Every other note. And where do we get the notes? From the scale. If we were then to add another note to the G chord what note would it be? F. Take it from the scale on the flannel board, Meg, and put it in the chord. Marilyn, take the F resonator bell and join the G7 team.

Now follow the pointer closely and count with me. I am going to start on G and count all the lines and spaces up to F. What number is F? Seven. That's why there is a 7 next to the G if another note is added to the triad.

Now let's put these two chords to Silent Night. When they get to "Round yon virgin" the Tonic (C-chord) doesn't sound right. **Try the G7.** That doesn't sound right either. (Teacher can help here with some pointed playing and singing, and an exaggerated expression of pain on his face.)

Well, let's move down another button on the autoharp to the F chord. Try that. It sounds right.

Let's build the F chord. We know we'll start on. . . . . ? F. I'll put another F in the scale since we used the F that was there in the G chord. Katie, build the F chord on the flannel board. And three more students get the proper resonator bells and make a "picture" of the F chord. Notice that we've used up in the three chords all the notes that were in the scale.

Does this suggest anything to you? When seeking the proper harmony, chose the chord which contains the melody note you want to harmonize.

See now if you can work your way through the entire song, singing and playing all the instruments.

SILENT NIGHT                                                                    Mohr-Gruber

It turns out this song needs three chords to sound right: the C-Chord, G7 and F. You'll find these three chords fit a lot of songs. Try fitting them to:

1. Jingle Bells (fl., Her: 149)
2. Home on the Range (fl., Her: 84)
3. Old Folks at Home (fl., Her: 237)
4. Yankee Doodle (fl., Her: 91)
5. Auld Lang Syne (fl., Her: 60)
6. Marine's Hymn (fl., Her: 30)
7. Brahms Lullaby (fl., Her: 222)
8. Twinkle, Twinkle (fl., Her: 41)
9. Magic Flute Trio (flute book)
10. Happy Birthday (fl., Her: 210)
11. There's a Little Wheel a Turning (fl., Her: 255)
12. Joy to the World (fl., Her: 51)
13. Angels We Have Heard On High (Her: 47)
14. On Top of Old Smoky (Her: 123)
15. The Battle Hymn of the Republic (Her: 26)

Teacher can try some variations in the participation activities:

1. Make paper soldier hats à la Carabo-Cone and in the fold, place a large card with one syllable

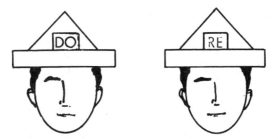

name from the scale. Spell another scale besides C on the flannel board and build the chords. Then each wearer of a hat goes to the resonator bells, selects the proper bell for his syllable. And the bells group themselves by families or teams and play at the proper time to accompany one of the three-chord songs. For instance:

DO picks E♭, RE picks F, etc. DO, E♭ and MI, G and SO B♭ form a family to make the E♭ chord, etc.

2. Use chord trays (made by manufacturers of rhythm band instruments). **George, get the resonator bells which make up the E♭ chord and place them in the chord tray. Get a triple mallet and be ready to play the E♭ chord. Meg, you get the bells for the A♭ chord, and Mary-Lou the bells for B♭7. Now we'll set the chords to Marine's Hymn. As you all sing the song, I'll point to each chord when it's the right time to play. The second time through you try to determine by yourself when you should play.**

## Building Primary Chords from the Scale

**Again, tell us how we build chords.** By taking every other note from the scale. **On what member of the scale is the Tonic chord built?** On the first—on *one*. **We can build chords on any note of the**

scale, but which other members of the scale have we used to make the chords we've used? Four and Five. FA and SO. In the key of F, it is the B♭-chord, and the C-chord. But we can also refer to them as the 4-chord and the 5-chord. It appears these chords are very frequently used, so much so that they are

referred to as PRIMARY chords.

As you can see by the list of songs (p. 175) a great many folk songs use only these three chords, the primary chords; so do some hymns and Christmas carols. Even musical masterpieces do.

3. I'll put the F scale on the flannel board and then I want Brenda to build the three primary chords from this scale. These three students each get a chord tray and place the proper resonator bells in the tray and each stand under the correct number sign for your chord which I will place up front on the wall. Autoharp players, you select the correct chords for the F "family." You'll notice that the chord buttons on the autoharp are placed next to each other in a "family" or group.

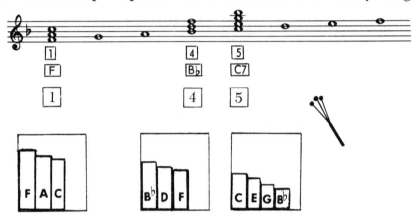

4. I am going to write some chords on the chalk board. Practice this silently until you feel you can play it. Each player will play one chord tray with a triple mallet or one chord on the autoharp. Decide which autoharp will play F, which B♭, and which C7. 4 F B♭ B♭ F / B♭ F G F / C7 F B♭ F / C7 F C7 F Now be ready to play. One-two, ready begin.

This time try playing all three primary chords on each autoharp. You'll find the family falls under your fingers like this:

  B♭                C7                  F
  4th finger    3rd finger    pointing finger

Now see if you can do something harder. Lucy, go to the chalk board and put the correct number under each chord letter-name. I am going to put a new scale on the flannel board. Marilyn, see if you can build the correct primary chords on the new scale on the flannel board.

Chalk board: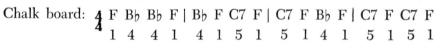

Flannel board: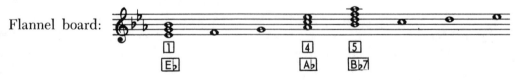

Will those playing the chords in the trays return the resonator bells to their containers. Then give the chord tray to others, and the new players go fill the chord trays with the correct resonator bells for the new key. And George, I'll erase the chord names currently on the chalk board, and you go to the board and place above the numbers the correct letter names for the new key.

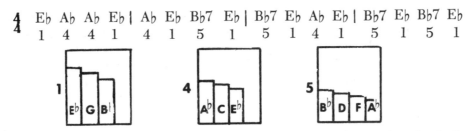

Can the autoharp play these chords? No, these are not on the autoharp. Just the bells can play this time. Practice silently, then be ready to play. Begin.

## Real Music Appreciation

Now what you've played is what we played before but in a different key. It is just what the Polish composer, Chopin, wrote for the middle part of a piano piece he called Nocturne. (see below) **Listen.** Teacher should play it at the piano, or a good recording. At first he should play just that part which the students have played, maybe more than once. Then he can let them hear the whole composition which is simple and takes less than five minutes.

Excerpts of music to illustrate the use of the primary chords are inexhaustible. These *are* the primary chords, the *chords used most*. However these three excerpts are very chordal in nature, so that you can see them clearly and hopefully hear the primary chords clearly. The excerpts are simple enough

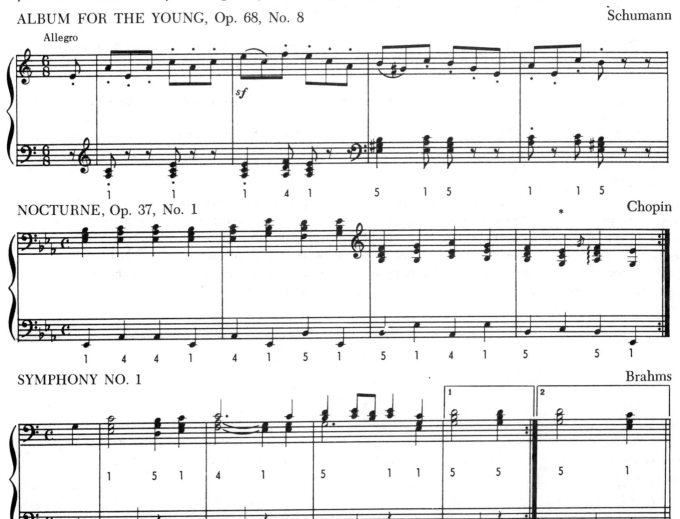

ALBUM FOR THE YOUNG, Op. 68, No. 8                                                              Schumann

NOCTURNE, Op. 37, No. 1                                                                         Chopin

SYMPHONY NO. 1                                                                                 Brahms

that each can be analyzed—spelled out, identified and marked, played by all on some instrument and then listened to in its original form within its original context. Teacher can hope then that not only will students understand more clearly the primary chords, where they come from, how they are made and used; but that they will have a satisfying listening experience, one that stems from knowledge, involvement and one that provides true pleasure—"appreciation." Is there a better way to teach real music "appreciation" than this technique? What we have played ourselves we have strong feelings about, we are involved in it, we are more likely to like it, and certainly be familiar with it. We know more about how it is put together and have been through the process of mastering it. It is not a superficial experience; a part of ourselves is invested in it.

An experience like this impresses on the student both the composition and the facts he is learning about the Primary Chords. Try the Schumann excerpt with bells and autoharps. For the Brahms use autoharp, on the melody line use bells or piano, recorder or flute and for the left hand notes, use piano or string bass, or Orff tympani. Some of Finlandia ( (Her: 94) can be played on the autoharp using only the primary chords: F C F Bb- F C F (d) C C F. Teacher should always follow up by playing a recording of the composition or an appropriate excerpt from it.

Incidentally, in spite of all the infinite variety of music, there is really only one way to end a piece, to say "the end." In music, the equivalent of "the end" is the 5-chord (or 5-7 chord) followed by the 1-chord: 5-1.

## THE PRIMARY CHORDS IN MINOR

Sometimes when I have directed you to find the G button on the autoharp, you have pressed a G button which didn't fit and I've told you to find another one. The one that didn't fit was labelled G min. Knowing what you know now, what do you suppose *G min* means and why didn't it fit?

Of course, *min* stands for MINOR and if we were playing a song in G major the G *minor* chord would not belong. Do you remember what we learned about the Tonic chord in a major key and in a minor key? (Chapter 9) They are different. What note in the triad makes the difference? The middle note. To make the major triad minor, flat the middle note—make it one half step lower. (See the Tonic chord in MINOR, Chapter 12.) The tonic chord in a major key is called a major triad; the tonic chord in a minor key is called a minor triad.

Let's review this and prove it out. We'll set up two flannel boards; one with the G major scale and one with the G minor scale. What is the key signature for G major? (If the students have forgotten how to determine key signatures or are uncertain, it is not necessary for this lesson that they answer this. The teacher can just write out the correct signatures.) F sharp. And for G minor? Bb and Eb.

George, you go to the G major scale and build the chords on 1, 4 and 5. Frank, you do the same for the G minor scale. Here are extra whole notes you will need. And in these chord trays, Meg you get the corresponding resonator bells for the 1-chord in G major, Lew the 4-chord, Brenda the 5-chord. Brenda, include the extra bell which makes the 5-chord add the number 7 to its name.   Mary-Lou, you get the bells for the 1-chord in G minor, Archie for the 4-chord and Sue for the 5-7 chord.

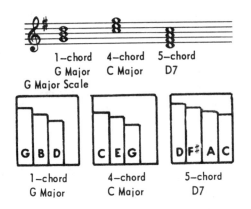

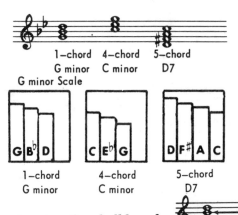

Now let's take each one-chord and compare them. I'll write them on the chalkboard:

Meg, you play your chord with the triple mallet. Mary-Lou, play your chord. We can hear that the chords are different and see that it is the middle note which makes the difference. In minor, the third note of the tonic triad is flatted; it is one half step lower. The G major triad will fit a one-chord song that is major. Let's sing "Are You Sleeping?" while Meg accompanies us with the bell chord:

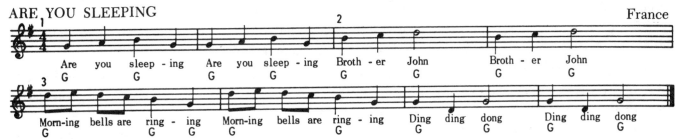

But if we sing a one-chord song that is minor, the G minor triad is better. Mary-Lou you accompany us as we sing "Hey Ho":

In fact if we try the G major chord to this song it would sound awful. Try it. Now let's compare the 4-chords. Lew, play your chord. Archie, play yours. Again, we can hear and see how the chords are different. Because there is an E♭ in the G minor scale, there must be an E♭ in the C chord from G minor, but the C chord in the G major scale does not have this E♭. Again the middle note makes the difference. Listen to how beautiful and how right the G minor and C minor chords sound in a song like "Black is the Color," by John Jacob Niles.

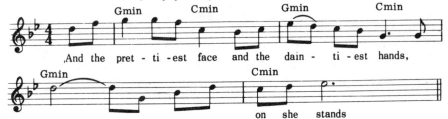

In this key it gets too high for singing. Substitute xylos for the voice. Now try it in this key with auto-harp and bells on the voice part as you sing.

BLACK IS THE COLOR                                                       Niles

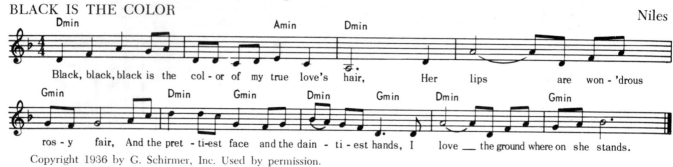

Copyright 1936 by G. Schirmer, Inc. Used by permission.

But for Jingle Bells, we'll want G major and C major triads. Try G minor and C minor triads and see how wrong it sounds with Jingle Bells.

And note how in "On My Journey Home" the minor 1 and 4 chords underline the minor quality of this song.

ON MY JOURNEY HOME                                              Traditional Hymn

When we compare the 5-chords we see something interesting:

The 5-chords are exactly the same! So when we sing a part of a song which is harmonized by the 5 chord, it wouldn't indicate whether it is minor or major until the 5 chord moved on to the tonic. Start in the middle part of "Swanee River": It's high in this key, so I'll play it at the piano. You could sing this part an octave lower.

This measure does not indicate until here that the song is major.      This measure reinforces major.

**Start in the middle of the "Coventry Carol":**

There is no minor chord until here. (But of course the melody shows us it is minor.)

Use the primary chords from G minor to harmonize all of Go Down Moses and Pat-a-pan. Do some of the following songs too. Use autoharps and the bells in chord trays. You'll notice again that the primary chords are grouped as a "family" on the autoharp.

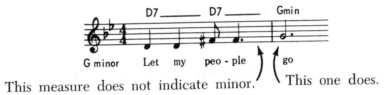

This measure does not indicate minor.     This one does.

    Birch Tree (flute book)
    Erie Canal (Her: 256)
    March of the Kings (see Chapter 13 on INTERVALS)
    Hatikva (see chapter on MINOR) (fl.)

    Almost everybody seems to be fascinated by chords. How does the piano player know which notes to play together? How does he change so quickly? Now you can see it is not quite so much of a mystery. Now *you* know something about chords too. You can even play these chords at the right places yourself.

## SUGGESTED ASSIGNMENTS

1. Refer to major songs, anywhere in this book or other books, and try to accompany them on an autoharp, guitar or piano, using the primary chords.
2. Refer to the minor songs listed at the end of Chapter 12 and try to accompany them on an autoharp, guitar or piano, using the primary chords.

Chapter **15**

# Other Scales

## WHAT YOU NEED TO KNOW

1. The Major scale—its syllable names
2. Key signatures

## BASIC FACTS YOU WILL LEARN

1. There are other scales besides major and minor.
2. The pentatonic scale is a five-note scale, omitting two very powerful notes, FA and TI. There is a resulting vagueness or unfinished sound.
3. Many songs use this scale; some we know well.
4. It is interesting to note that in notating the song in the pentatonic scale, it is the custom to retain the key signature of the major scale, even though all the flats or sharps in the signature won't be used.
5. The whole tone scale consists of six tones, each a whole step from the preceding note. It too has a vague unfinished effect.
6. The chords produced by this scale are all the same in sound and structure, even when turned up-side down (inverted).

## WHAT THIS LESSON CAN LEAD TO

1. Greater understanding of music familiar and unfamiliar.
2. The use of a growing array of musical material for self-expression.

## THE PENTATONIC SCALE

Let's sing and play a song we know well, Li'l Liza Jane (fl., Her: 272). **You can sing or play your flute.**

LI'L LIZA JANE — United States

You've a gal and I got none, Li'l Li - za Jane; Come my love and
be my one, Li'l Li - za Jane. Oh, E - li - za,
Li'l Li - za Jane Oh, E - li - za, Li'l Li - za Jane.

After the music has been performed, teacher asks, **What is the key?** Look at the key signature. F Major. **That means this song uses the notes in the F major scale, doesn't it? Let's just check. This scale** will start and end on . . .? F. And what else must we remember? The B♭. George, you put the notes of the F major scale on the flannel board, and the syllable names, while the rest of us compile a picture of the notes in this song. Each person tell us a note in the song. I'll put them on the staff. A G F C D . . .

Any others? No. 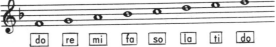 Then does this song use all the notes of the F major scale? No.

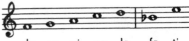

Which ones does it leave out and what are their syllable names? FA and TI.

Of course a song does not have to use every note in the scale, but it isn't just an accident that these particular notes are not in the song. There are many songs which leave out the same notes from a scale. Is it really a major scale any longer? Not really. How is it different?

1. It has only five notes.
2. It leaves out FA and TI.

Let's change the scale on the flannel board. George, you remove the notes, and Mary-Lou, you remove the syllable names.

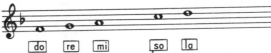

Let's listen to how it sounds.

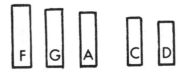

Robin, you take the proper resonator bells for this scale and set them up with empty spaces for the notes we removed from the scale.

F   G   A       C   D

Here is where our Orff instruments are so useful. Gene take a xylophone and Annette a metallophone and remove the proper bars. Now play this five-tone scale. This time we'll sing with you. Play it up and down twice. What can we say about its sound?

1. It doesn't sound as if it comes to an end.
2. It sounds oriental.
3. It sounds vague.

Yes, the two notes which are left out of this scale are rather powerful notes—listen. Teacher plays each of those notes with the V7 at the piano. What needs to follow? Everybody sings—almost shouts!—DO! That's why the scale sounds sort of unfinished—the two tones which are left out are two very "active" tones which almost demand that DO follow.

There is a name for this five-tone scale—PENTATONIC, meaning five tones. One could also interpret the name to mean five *tonics*—five independent tones. Its kind of vague, haunting, lonely effect has been very appealing to many peoples over the years. The Scotch have composed many songs using the Pentatonic scale. What are some Scotch songs? "Comin' Thru the Rye," "Auld Lang Syne," "Wi' a Hundred Pipers." The Japanese and Chinese use the scale. Many American cowboy songs use the scale: "Liza Jane," "Lone Star Trail," "Dogie Song." Our Negro spirituals employ the scale: "Water Boy," "Swing Low." It appeals to the primitive in people everywhere, and the child-like: Other songs: "Mighty Like a Rose," "Camptown Races" and another Stephen Foster song, "Old Folks at Home."

A lovely thing about the pentatonic scale is that you can make up tunes quite freely with several tunes all going at the same time without playing notes that clash. Let's try. We'll use all our sets of resonator bells, and all the Orff xylophones, metallophones and glockenspiels. Prepare them by removing all the Es and Bs. Glockenspiels, you play Practice with your fingers silently. Metallophones, with a mallet in each hand, play Practice the two parts together. Xylophones, with two mallets play Resonator bells join them. Everyone else take a xylophone or your flutes and we'll play "Swing Low" (fl., Her: 98) to this accompaniment.

This time make up your own ostinato for "I'm Goin' to Leave Ol' Texas." The bass xylos play The metallophones play The glockenspiels come up with The resonator bells chord: Two mallets in right hand one mallet in left hand. One glockenspiel player plays at random: It fits. Sing the song as you play. It all sounds good.

Not only can we make a pentatonic scale on these instruments which we are using, but another of our instruments has a pentatonic scale built right in. Who knows? The piano! Play the black notes. Start on F♯. F♯ G♯ A♯ C♯ D♯. That's like the F♯ major scale with FA (B) and TI (E♯ left out).

Do Trot, Pony, Trot as we have performed it from our song book before. Look it over and notice it really uses the pentatonic scale.

TROT, PONY, TROT

China

Piano parts to add ①
   right hand       ② Play any black keys you wish.

left hand

"Trot, Pony, Trot" from DISCOVERING MUSIC TOGETHER, Book 3, by Leonhard, Krone, Wolfe, and Fullerton. Copyright © 1966 by Follett Publishing Company. Used by permission.

Let's sing and play "Lotus Blossom." If you extract the notes from this song you'll find it uses the pentatonic scale also. We have played this song many times arranged for rhythm band, from our rhythm band scores by Vandevere. Listen to it now as it is sung by a chorus of children on this recording of the opera "Turandot" by Puccini. Since this is a story about a Chinese princess the composer Puccini used the pentatonic scale to create the oriental effect we noted earlier.

LOTUS BLOSSOMS                                                                                                                China

Here I bring you sweet scent-ed flow'rs   Sweet are they from dewy bow-'rs
Per-fumes light as sum-mer air   Fra-grant flow'rs of our friend-ship true
These I bring to you from my bow'r, bloom-ing fair   Fra-grant flow'rs of our friend-ship true.

"Lotus Blossoms" from DISCOVERING MUSIC TOGETHER, Book 4, Leonhard, Krone, Wolfe, and Fullerton. Copyright © 1966, 1970 by Follett Publishing Company. Used by permission.

Here is a list of pentatonic songs, repeating those already mentioned and adding some others:

*Scotch*
Auld Lang Syne (Her: 60)
Old MacDonald Had a Farm (Her: 66)
Comin' Thru the Rye
Adieu to My Comrades

*Cowboy*
O Bury Me Not on the Lone Prairie (Her: 267)
Lone Star Trail (Her: 82)
Dogie Song (Her: 2)
Night Herding Song (Her: 203)
I'm Goin' to Leave Ol' Texas Now

*Chinese and Japanese*
Sakura
Trot, Pony, Trot
Lotus Blossom
Japanese Rain Song
The Sparrows' School
Haru Ga Kita

*Negro*
Swing Low (fl., Her: 98)
Water Boy
Cotton Needs a Pickin (Her: 161)
Steal Away (Her: 270)
Every Time I Feel the Spirit (Her: 144)
Nobody Knows the Trouble I've Seen (Her: 189)
Somebody's Knockin at Your Door
Get on Board Little Children (Her: 7)

*American*
Camptown Races (Her: 72)
Liza Jane (fl., Her: 272)
Mighty Like a Rose
Old Folks at Home (Swanee River) (fl., Her: 237)
Old Brass Wagon (Her: 262)
Jesus Walked this Lonesome Valley (White spiritual) (Her: 247)
All Night, All Day (Her: 28)
There's a Little Wheel a Turning in My Heart (fl., Her: 255)

Pentatonic songs can often be one-chord songs—songs which need only one chord on the autoharp or piano.

# RAIN SONG

Japan

Pit - ter, pat - ter, fall - ing, fall - ing, rain is fall - ing down,

Moth - er comes to bring um - brel - la, Rain is fall - ing down.

Pi chi, pi chi, cha pu, cha pu, ran, ran, ran.

From *Sing a Song* by Roberta McLaughlin and Lucille Wood, © 1960, Prentice-Hall, Inc. By permission of the publishers.

do re mi so la

# HARA GA KITA (Spring Has Come!)

Japan

Ha - ru ga Ki - ta  Ha - ru ga Ki - ta  Do - ko  no  Ki - ta
Spring has __ come, oh, spring has __ come! Oh, where __ has  it  come?

Ya - ma ni Ki - ta  Sa - to ni Ki - ta  No ni mo  Ki - ta
To  the __ hills and  to  the __ vil - lage  mea - dow  it  has  come!

By permission of Cooperative Recreation Service. Copyright © 1958 by Lynn Rohrbough.

do re mi so la

# THE SPARROWS' SCHOOL (Chi chi pa pa)

Japan

Fine

Teacher: Chi - chi - pa - pa chi pa pa  Teacher: I  am the tea-cher of the  spar - row's  school
Children repeat  Children repeat: He is
She is

Teacher: We learn to sing a song by lis - ten - ing  Teacher: We learn to step and flut - ter just like this
Children repeat:  Children repeat:

D. S. al Fine

T.: Sing a lit - tle song and sing it ver - y well  T.: We can sing it bet - ter, spar-rows, try a - gain.
C.:  C.:

Copyright © 1962, Wadsworth Publishing Company, Inc. From Nye, Nye, Aubin, and Kyme, SINGING WITH CHILDREN, Second Edition, Wadsworth 1970.

## THE SIX-TONE SCALE

How many of you swim underwater with your eyes open? **How does the world look?** All blurry. Bubbly. The picture keeps changing. Waving, distorted and twisted.

How about moving through fog—what is that like? Hazy, veiled, hidden. **Do you think we could** *hear* **such a picture? This is how one composer thought veils would look—in sound.** Teacher plays recording of "Voiles" by Debussy. **How does the composer do this? How does he get this effect?**

VOILES                                                                          Debussy

**We've discovered at other times that the scale selected by the composer controls this. Here are**

**the notes and the scale used by Debussy:**

**What is there to notice about the scale? How is it made?** There are only six notes. Not all of the musical alphabet is used. **This gives it its name—six-tone scale. If we measure the steps on the key-board, we find:**

| | |
|---|---|
| C -D | one whole step |
| D -E | one whole step |
| E  F♯ | one whole step |
| F♯ -G♯ | one whole step |
| G♯ -A♯ | one whole step |

Here is an interesting alternate procedure for discovering the structure of the six-tone scale:

**Let's use all the notes between C and the next C—all twelve notes.** Teacher writes the chromatic scale on the board. **We'll need twelve bell players to play the notes. Line up in the order of the notes of the scale. In the chromatic scale how far apart are each of the notes from the next?** Half steps. **Play the scale as I tap your shoulders.** They play. **Now I'll tap some shoulders, and skip some.**

Those I skip please sit down. Those I tapped please announce the name of your note and play your bell. C D E F♯ G♯ A♯. Teacher draws arrow to those notes in the scale on the board. **What can we say about the notes still here?** They go every other note. **They are the notes in the six-tone scale. What can we say about the distance between these notes, if originally the scale moved by half steps and we have kept every other note?** They must be a whole step apart from each other. **They are.**

This scale consists entirely of whole steps. That is why it is also known as a **WHOLE-TONE SCALE.**

**Let's listen to the sound of this scale.** Teacher distributes the six resonator bells to six students standing in a row and points to each student to have the scale played in order up and down. **What's the effect?** It sounds vague, unfinished. **Notice something else about this six-tone scale: if we continued the scale in whole steps beyond the six notes, it begins to repeat itself. Even though it is moving only in whole steps. Suppose the six players make**  a circle. **Now start playing the scale with C and keep playing around the circle. Now play the six notes but start on A. On E. On F♯ and play several times around the circle. It sounds everywhere the**

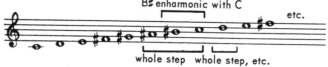

B♯ enharmonic with C    etc.

whole step   whole step, etc.

same. The scale seems to go around in circles—vague, endless, monotonous, unfinished. There is no finishing place, no strong TI-DO "The End." No one starting place, or a strong central note like **DO** around which all the other notes gravitate. This accents that vague unfinished effect.

## Chords from this Scale

**So why would a composer use such a scale? And when?** If he wants a misty blurry effect as in "Voiles." **What else do you think it would be appropriate to portray by means of this scale?** Fog, drizzle, mist, dreams, floating. . . . **Examine the chords which come from the scale. Start on C. How do we build chords?** Every other note from the scale. **Name the notes which are in the chord on C.**

C E G♯ . Even the sound of the chord matches that of the scale—vague, endless, unfinished. **Measure the distance from C to E.** Four half steps. Some of you may know this as a Major third. **From E to G♯.** The same—four half steps, a major third. So even the chord offers no variety. **Check the other chords.** They are all the same as the chord on C—two major thirds.

enharmonic   enharmonic

Here is something even more interesting about these chords. **Suppose we take the chord on C**

M3 **and place the bottom on the top** enharmonic M3 . **Now measure the intervals again.** Still two major thirds. Like the scale, the chords are everywhere the same. There certainly is not much chance for variety, which probably accounts for the fact that this limited scale is not much used.

Here is another approach to the scale, which is nothing more than a re-arrangement of the order of the steps. It is a more "straight," head-on approach. It isn't as much fun—for teacher or student.

**Teacher points to scale on the board:** 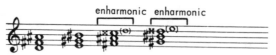 **How does it look different?** It has only six notes. **If we measure. . . .** All whole steps. **If we continue the scale and begin**

it again, we find it always progressing in whole steps. **What is the effect of its sound?** Vague, unfinished. . . . **Why would a composer use this scale? When?** When he wants such an effect as fog, mist, veils. The composer Howard Hanson uses the whole tone scale in his composition "Mists" which is from his work "For the First Time." Mozart used it, but as a joke. It is in the selection "A Musical Joke" in the violin cadenza as an example of a scale that gets off the track.

## CONCLUSION

Each of these scales creates a certain mood, is used for special effect. We noted this about minor scales too. Even with these unusual scales, we haven't covered all the scales which may exist. People continue to make up new ones. You could make up one. It might be that one of the scales you "made up" would be exactly like scales the Greeks used many centuries ago. *They* called them MODES.

What the Greeks declared about their ancient "modes" or scales is true about our contemporary scales: each scale does have its own characteristic quality or mood.

The important fact to be learned here is that much depends upon the kind of scale the composer selects—the melody, the harmony—the mood—all this is determined by the selection of the scale.

# The Bass Staff

*Chapter* **16**

## WHAT YOU NEED TO KNOW

1. The treble staff
2. Keys and signatures

## BASIC FACTS YOU WILL LEARN

1. The music for low-pitched instruments and voices is written on a staff called the bass staff. It looks like the treble staff but has a different clef or identifying sign.
2. The names of the lines and spaces of the bass staff are all different from those of the treble staff.
3. This is understood more clearly when one sees that the treble and bass staves are all part of one great staff called the Grand Staff. Middle C separates the two staves but is not a part of either.
4. Grown men and older boys sing music written on this staff. Instruments like the bass xylophone, string bass, bassoon and cello read from this staff. The pianist's left hand "reads" from this staff.

## WHAT THIS LESSON CAN LEAD TO

Facility in using Bass Staff.

---

## BASS STAFF

Teacher can try different ways of presenting the bass staff.

### Set a Trap

**Boys, here is a special descant for you to sing to our song, Hey Ho (Her: 186). Just two notes.** Teacher sings to illustrate. **Some of you have deep low voices so this will fit you fine. It's too low for the girls. They'll sing the melody. Ready, sing.**

What are the names of the notes the boys sang? Not easy to figure out, is it? All those leger lines. Can anyone think of a better way to write those notes? Make a whole new staff. Don't forget to leave C on its private line . . . . and then on into the lesson on Bass staff.

## Pique the Curiosity

Start a song in a range much too high, for example When Johnny Comes Marching Home Again in C or D minor. Protests and laughter. **All right, I'll put it lower.** Teacher plays here:

This should stump even the female "blues singer!" But who is able to sing it in this range? **The boys.** Their voices are lower and deeper. Boys, let's hear just you. The boys sing it through. **Help me write it down. It's in the key of A minor. What is the signature?** No sharps or flats. **I'll start you by telling you the first two notes are A below middle C and E. Even finding where to write E is a problem!**

Isn't there an easier way? Yes, there is another staff for low notes we can use. The same music will look like this:

## What's different?

1. No leger lines now.
2. The names of the lines and spaces aren't right—or at least they are not what we have been learning.
3. The sign at the beginning of the staff is different.

. . . and then on into the rest of the lesson.

## Pose a Problem

We have a beautiful new instrument, a bass xylophone. Its tones are very low, mellow and deep. I'll teach you a simple descant to play on the instrument for the Bells of St. Mary. The rest of us will sing the song or play it on xylos and resonator bells.

The descant and song in this arrangement are in the key of C. What will be the signature? No sharps or flats. We start on the biggest bar, the last one to the left and jump up to the smaller C. Then come evenly down the scale like this: C-B-A-G-F-E-D-C. Practice again. The notes are all eighths and the descant begins with the octave jump: C̲ C̅ B A G F E D | C̲ C etc. Now we'll play it to the song.

```
               G –  | C–C  – – D – | E–E  – – G – | A–A  – – B –
C̲C̅BAGFED | C̲C̅BAGFED | C̲C̅BAGFED | C̲C̅BAGFED | C̲C̅BAGFED
```

```
C–C  – – A – | G–G  – – E – | F– F –    etc.
C̲C̅BAGFED | C̲C̅BAGFED |
```

Watch me write it on the board. The highest C on the bass xylophone is middle C . How

shall we write the low C—where does it go? We'll just have to lower a rope ladder of leger lines till

we find it: 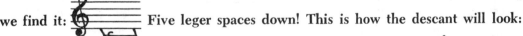 Five leger spaces down! This is how the descant will look:

Not very easy to read! If I were suddenly to point at the fifth note, could you name it? Many couldn't without counting down! We had better letter the notes. Is there any other way to write this? Do we have to do it this way? Look.

What have I done? Made another staff out of the leger lines. **Notice that I didn't include the middle C line.** Middle C usually has its private personal portable line. Is it a complete staff? No, I'll add the necessary lines. What will be their names? Count down—B—A—G

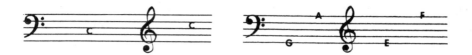

This staff looks like the one above it—it has five lines and four spaces, but is it the same? Look carefully. The names aren't like the other staff. For instance, the Cs we are playing are found on the second space, not the third. The bottom line is G, the top line is A—different from the staff we know:

What is the name of the staff we are most used to? Treble staff. And the sign that identifies it? G Clef or Treble Clef. Is this other staff a treble staff? What instrument is playing the notes we wrote for it? The *bass* xylophone. Does that give you any hints?

This other staff is a bass staff. It is for low instruments and voices. Can we use the same identifying sign, the same clef? No. Instead we use this sign 𝄢 which evolved from an old-fashioned F, 𝄢 .

Notice the two dots are on either side of the fourth line up, which you'll notice is F, and this clef is called the F clef or Bass Clef.

Why do the lines and spaces of the bass staff have different names from the treble staff? Did some mean person do it just to make things harder? No, you saw how the staff was made from the leger lines just as they are added below the treble staff. Do you remember seeing this before? You may recognize this as the Grand Staff—the treble and bass staves (plural of staff) combined (see Chapter 5). And if we begin lettering at the bottom with the beginning of the musical alphabet you will see again how and *why* the lines and spaces have different names in the different staves.

Our problem is to learn the new names of the new staff. Who needs to especially? Boys and men whose voices are lower than female voices. Players of the bass xylo. What other instruments? The bassoon. The string bass. The piano! Yes, imagine, the left hand reads one set of names and the right hand another set.

1. You can spell words as you've done before:

2. You can take Dictation. It will have to be very easy. For instance, here is the scale of A Major in the bass staff—we'll keep it here on the chart where you can all look at it when you need to. This

is high A or DO and this low DO. (Teacher plays on piano or bass xylo.) Look at the scale as I play to help keep your bearings. Teacher dictates patterns like these:

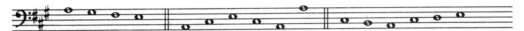

The students write at a board, or work at a flannel board or at their own papers.

3. Try reading. These patterns are for the boys. Sing on DUH or syllables. It's all right to refer to the scale on the chart.

Here are some patterns for the bass xylo to read. We'll have you take turns. Find the low G and higher G.

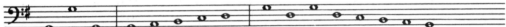

Everybody try singing these patterns on letter names.

I'll stay in the key of C. Hang on to Middle C as a reference.

Here is an excerpt from a piece Robert Schumann wrote called "Knight Rupert." It is part of a group of works he called *Album for the Young*. It begins in the bass staff and climbs right up into the treble:

This recording I am going to play has a cello playing a beautiful solo called "The Swan." It is from the *Carnival of the Animals* by Saint-Saëns. The notes for this instrument are written on the bass staff and you can hear the notes sing low and then rather high too. Another selection from the same work is a solo played by the lowest stringed instruments, the string basses. It is called "Elephants." Why do you suppose the composer chose these instruments to depict elephants? Because they are big clumsy lugubrious animals; so are these instruments as you can see by their picture, and the low low sound seemed appropriate. The string basses don't often have solo opportunities, but Beethoven gave them a chance to shine in his Fifth Symphony in C Minor. The third movement consists of three parts and it is in the middle part that the basses begin this way:

SYMPHONY NO. 5 IN C Minor, 3rd movt., Trio                                    Beethoven

Learning to read a whole new clef is not easy and the best way to do it is as the need arises. Of course it is up to teacher to make sure the need does arise, and then meet it with the kind of techniques just enumerated.

# Chapter 17

# More Advanced Rhythms

## WHAT YOU NEED TO KNOW

1. Basic note values
2. Meters
3. Ties, dots, rests
4. A background in relating words to rhythmic patterns

## BASIC FACTS YOU WILL LEARN

1. When four even notes occur to a beat they are called sixteenths. They use two beams ♬♬ or two flags. ♬

2. A sixteenth rest also uses two flags. ♯

3. ♩. ♪ and ♩. ♪ are both uneven long-short patterns. Their mathematical proportions are the same, (3-1); the amount of time each takes differs. Although they can be skipping patterns, they differ from the $\frac{6}{8}$ skipping pattern which is lazier and in a different mathematical proportion (2-1).

4. In syncopation, many notes come *off* the beat

*before* the beat
*after* the beat
*in between* the beat
*ahead of* the beat

but not       on the beat
or          with the beat

5. A typical syncopation pattern and picture is short — long — short.

♪     ♩     ♪

♩     ♩     ♩

♪     ♪     ♪

6. Two common tools for making syncopation are the TIE and REST.

♪♩   ♪♩♪♩   ♪

♪♪♩ ♪   ♪

7. In syncopation, the first note is of lesser value.
8. In syncopation, a shifting of the accent occurs.
9. A triplet is a musically correct but mathematically imperfect way to indicate three even, equal notes to a beat.
10. A triplet must be executed evenly, not rushed.
11. There are several ways to indicate a triplet:

The slur does not have to be present, but the 3 is essential.

## WHAT THIS LESSON CAN LEAD TO

1. Greater skill in reading and performing music.
2. Listening with greater comprehension and enjoyment.

---

## SIXTEENTHS ♪♪♪♪

Let us begin with a song we have sung before, Angels We Have Heard on High. We'll do it from memory. Do you remember that we had finger cymbals playing on every beat? Xylos be ready to join us in the chorus.

If you were to notate the finger cymbals' part in actual notes, how would you write it? If you are not sure what note value it would be, move your feet as you listen again to the finger cymbals. They are quarter notes. Yes, your feet walk and the cymbals play on the beat or count. Now listen again as the xylophones play the "Glorias" of the chorus together with the finger cymbals. How many notes do the xylophones play each time the finger cymbals play their quarter note? I'm going to let you keep your answer to yourself as we investigate a bit further.

Now let's sing "A Railroad Rhyme." This song should not yet be in the view of the students. Use the sand blocks beginning on the words "train, train." What is the time value of the notes on "train" which the sand blocks are playing? Quarter notes. Yes, the beat and your feet tell you this. Let's make this train travel all over the United States. What names of places could we substitute for Lackawanna in the song?

| | | |
|---|---|---|
| California | Pocatello | West Virginia |
| Pennsylvania | Silver City | Cedar Rapids |
| Philadelphia | San Francisco | El Dorado |
| South Dakota | Mississippi | Amarillo |
| Carolina | Colorado | Sacramento |
| Indiana | Arizona | San Diego |
| Kansas City | Minnesota | |

What makes all these places fit the song? They all have four word-syllables. Yes. How many of you had four as the answer to the question on the previous song? The xylophones played four notes to each one "ping" of the finger cymbals. We could make a picture something like this:

Train            Train            Train            Train

Carolina         Carolina         Carolina         Carolina
• • • •          • • • •          • • • •          • • • •

What kind of notes are used for Carolina? Why can't they be eighth notes? Only two eighth notes go to the quarter—here we have four notes. At this point, if any student can tell the teacher the answer from whatever his experience may be, that is best. Otherwise, teacher must tell the students. There is always the mathematical approach, but if you will be working with young children they may not have learned such fractions yet, and some of us who are older may not be very good at mathematics! It is better to reserve the mathematical approach as a reinforcing or confirming technique.

## ANGELS WE HAVE HEARD ON HIGH
French-English Carol

## A RAILROAD RHYME
L. Vandevere

**If you look at either song** (books should now be opened or charts uncovered) **you will see how these four notes are written:** ♪♪♪♪. Usually they are all together, connected by not just one beam as eighth notes are ♫ but two ♪♪♪♪. This helps show us they all go to the one beat; to the quarter note. We can write this equation: ♪♪♪♪=♩. If ♩=♫ what other equation could we say? ♪♪♪♪=♫♫ These notes are called SIXTEENTH notes. Four SIXTEENTHS = 1 quarter.

## Proving ♫♫♩=♩

1. Let's prove it by chanting the words from the Railroad Rhyme.
   This group chant    TRAIN            TRAIN
   This group chant    RAIL-ROAD        RAIL-ROAD
   This group chant    CALIFORNIA       CALIFORNIA        Ready, begin.
2. This time instead of chanting, snap your fingers on **TRAIN**, slap your palms on **RAILROAD**, pat your knees on **CALIFORNIA**. Ready, go.

   L    R    L    R
3. Can you *be* all the words at once? Tap your left foot for **TRAIN**. Tap your left hand for **RAIL-ROAD** and tap your right hand for **PENNSYLVANIA**. This is hard and not everybody can do it.
4. This time make a round. First everybody snap your fingers for 4 **TRAINS** then clap four **RAIL-ROADS**, then patsch (pat your knees) four **COLORADOS**. Now we'll divide you into three groups. This group start. After they have snapped four **TRAINS**, the second group begin snapping **TRAINS**. When they have snapped four **TRAINS**, the third group begins. Each group go through this twice. See if you can do it without getting lost or mixed up.
5. This time we'll use instruments and play all together. This group play finger cymbals on **TRAINS**; This group play tom tom on **RAILROAD**; this group play sand blocks on **PHILADELPHIA**.
6. This time do it as a round.
7. The possibilities are endless. Make up your own.

   If you know your mathematics, answer this. If we wanted to divide $\frac{2}{8}$ into four equal parts, it would be $\frac{2}{8} = \frac{?}{16}$ $\overset{Ans.}{\frac{4}{16}}$ **Reduce it to a common denominator and it would be** $\frac{4}{16} = ?$ $\overset{Ans.}{\frac{1}{4}}$

## Hearing and Reading ♫♫

If we wanted to write only one sixteenth note, we wouldn't use a whole beam ═══ but . . .? Flags or tails. ♪ And for a rest, do you remember that for the eighth note ♪ we kept the flag, but turned it around like this ⅄. How then do you suppose we write a sixteenth rest? Yes, two flags, just like the note ♪= ⅄. Sometimes instead of using any four-syllable word, the action words "hurry hurry" are used.

   ♩      ♩      ♫      ♫♫
   Walk  walk  run  run hurry hurry

Sing some of the following songs to yourself by ear and find the words which go to four sixteenths.

Swing Low(fl., Her: 96)          coming for to
Kookaburra(Her: 168)            Kookaburra or merry merry
This Old Man(fl. Her: 265)      give the dog a
Old Brass Wagon(Her: 262)      circle to the
Hey Ho(Her: 186)                money have I
Cape Cod Chantey(Her: 133)    bully bully

What names of persons go to ♫♫ ?

| Juliana | Salvatore | Aloysius |
| Marianna | Alexander | Henrietta |
| Emmalina | Annabella | Isabella |
| Margaretta | Evalina | Fredericka |
| Consuelo | Maximillian | Katerina |

Can you sight read these rhythms? Use words and your feet to help you. Talk it through or walk it through first, then clap or tap.

Which of the above measures am I drumming? (Dictation) We'll take turns drumming a measure for others to identify.

Look at the last four measures of Polly Wolly Doodle. Try to sight read the rhythm. Then get DO from the key signature—use your xylos for the pitch, and softly sing the pitches on syllable. Now try singing the syllables aloud to the rhythm.

POLLY WOLLY DOODLE                                                                    United States

Oh, I went down South for to see my Sal sing-ing Pol-ly Wol-ly Doo-dle all the day My___

Sal she is a___ spun-ky gal Sing-ing Pol-ly Wol-ly Doo-dle all the day.    Fare thee

well,     Fare thee well,     Fare thee well my fair-y fay,     For I'm

goin' to Lou-si-an-a for to see my Su-sy-an-na, Sing-ing Pol-ly Wol-ly Doo-dle all the day.

## DOTTED EIGHTH AND SIXTEENTH

### Derived from ♩♩♩♩

Let's take a different combination of sound effects from the Railroad Rhyme song. This group be Train ♩; this group be Mississippi ♩♩♩♩; this group be chu-ca ♩.♪. (The students are not to see the written musical equivalents.) Chant them together eight times. Begin. How does "chu-ca" compare to "Mississippi"? We know Mississippi is represented by ♩♩♩♩. "Chu" takes up all of the word except the last word-syllable. It takes up all the notes except the last note. That would be what kind of note? A sixteenth. Let's write it here: ♪. Then what does "chu" equal in terms of notes? The other three sixteenth notes. Chu = ♪♪♪ ca = ♪. But all three of those sixteenth notes aren't sounded. How can we indicate this? One way is to tie them all: ♪♪♪. Another way is to add them all up into one note. $\begin{matrix} ♪ & ♪ & = ? & ♪ \\ ♪ & ♪ & = ? & ♪ \end{matrix}$ So the musical picture of "chu-ca" is ♪ ♪. They can be put together on one beam like this ♪.♪.

### Derived from ♫

Or here is another way to get to the same point. Starting back with "Chuca:" One "chuca" goes to each "train." Each "train" gets one beat so each "chuca" gets one beat. How do we write it in music when two sounds go to one beat? Two eighths: ♫. But are they even? Does it go "chu-ca" "chu-ca"? No, it goes "chu ————— ca chu ————— ca. Which is the longer of the two notes? The "chu"—the first of the two notes. How can we indicate this in the musical symbols? I really don't expect you to know. Let me show you. What we need to do is to make the first note longer and the second note shorter. A way to make the second note shorter is to cut its value—add a flag: ♪. A way to make the first note longer is to add a dot: ♪.    Result: ♪.♪

## Mathematical Explanation

Or for a more accurate mathematical explanation: picture each of these chu-ca eighth notes in terms of the notes of Mississippi—Sixteenth notes. Now to make the first note longer, steal—yes *steal* one of the sixteenth notes from the second eighth note and add it to the first. The first note can be represented, as we saw before, by one note equaling the three sixteenth notes, or the dotted eighth, leaving the remaining sixteenth note all by itself at the end of the "chu-ca".

## Comparing to Other Related Rhythms

**Now let's chant again the chu-cas and play them with sand blocks.**

chu-ca  chu-ca  chu-ca  chu-ca

**We've already said they're uneven. What words can we use to describe them? Long-short Long-short. What action could we do to the sound? Sand blocks play again to help us. Gallop, Trotting, Skipping. We've said the same thing about another rhythm pattern. Can you remember? The dotted quarter and eighth . Yes.**

*How are these two patterns alike?*
both galloping or skipping patterns
both have the same proportions

*How are these two patterns different?*

takes two beats        takes one beat

There is another skipping pattern, in $\frac{6}{8}$ . Although they all fit skipping, the $\frac{6}{8}$ pattern for skipping is a lazier, more st-r-e-t-ch-e-d out action; the others are sharper and more angular. The mathematical proportions explain why:

Lots of songs use the jaunty long-short pattern.

Find the pattern in the following songs:
Charlie is My Darling (Chapter 12)          Erie Canal (refrain)
Battle Hymn of the Republic                 Alouette

BATTLE HYMN OF THE REPUBLIC                                    Howe-Steffe

ERIE CANAL (Refrain) — United States

Low bridge, eve-ry-bod-y down, Low bridge 'cause we're com-ing to a town And you'll al-ways know your neigh-bor, You'll al-ways know your pal, If you ev-er nav-i-gat-ed on the Er-ie Ca-nal.

ALOUETTE — French-Canadian

A-lou-et-te, gen-tille A-lou-et-te, A-lou et-te, Je te plu-me-rai.
Je te plu-me-rai la tête Je te plu-me-rai la tête Et la tête Et la tête Oh

## SYNCOPATION

It is good teaching and necessary for effective learning to vary the approach to a topic. Sometimes the mathematic structure precedes learning experiences; more often it should follow the exploring, discovering activities. The same teacher with the same students and the same topic should vary the approach. But if ever there was a topic where the "feel" and the experience should precede the theoretical equation, it is syncopation.

Foot stamping, sometimes frowned upon in the formal classroom and conservatory, but wholly acceptable to the jazz musician, and to many instrumentalists here should come into its own. The foot stamp is the beat, and in syncopation, the beat is vital, the beat is EVERYTHING.

### Feel Your Way to Syncopation

Let's start with some echo rhythm patterns. We'll use foot stamping (or toe tapping), patschen (slapping the knees), finger snapping, and clapping. Whatever I do, you repeat after me like an echo.

1. stamp stamp patsch patsch snap snap
2. stamp stamp patsch snap patsch snap
3. clap clap clap clap stamp snap
4. patsch snap snap / stamp stamp stamp stamp
5. stamp stamp clap / stamp stamp

stamps: cymbals, drum
claps: sticks, shakers

Keep up this last one. Add just a few instruments.

Without losing the momentum, but emphasizing a steady beat—fight the natural tendency to accelerate—teacher should go to the piano and play through several selections containing the pattern they are clapping: Liza Jane (Her: 272), Czech Dance Song, Czech Folk Song, Somebody's Knocking at My Door, Sometimes I Feel Like a Motherless Child, Nobody Knows the Trouble I've Seen (Her: 189), theme from Cesar Franck symphony. Sing if you know the words. The whole room should be jumping! There are usually broad grins. Imagine being *allowed* to do this in a music lesson. Unfortunately too often, something as lively and "swinging" as this is regarded as forbidden fruit, not to be found in a "music lesson." Teacher brings the activity to a close. One-two and HALT!

What makes this music so much fun? The beat. It swings. Teacher is likely to get a list of terms using the latest jargon. But everybody likes it; almost everybody can do it—when it is a rote experience. Reading it is another matter.

What is the name we give to this kind of rhythm? It has a special name. **SYNCOPATION.** How else could you describe the syncopation you have been clapping and playing and singing besides the list we just mentioned? Compare what your foot was doing with the claps or sticks. They weren't always together. They don't play at the same time. Sometimes the claps come with the stamp, the stick with the drum, but sometimes, what happens? The stick comes *after* the drum. Or *before* the drum. Or *in between* the drum beats. But not *with* the drum beat.

### What Makes Syncopation

If we were to use the words long and short for the pattern we clapped and played with the stick, how would the words go? Short - long - - short, short - long - - short. Clap and chant. I'll put it on the board this way: S Long S,  S L——— S. If we have used only quarter and eighth notes, how would the notes fit with this code we have on the board? (Which is the shorter note, eighth or quarter?)

What kind of note would you say the drums are drumming and our feet stamping? Quarter note. Let's do the patterns again and answer this next question. Where do the quarter notes come and where

CZECH FOLK SONG

CZECH DANCE SONG

HUNGARIAN FOLK SONG

**SOMETIMES I FEEL LIKE A MOTHERLESS CHILD** — United States

Some-times I feel like a moth-er-less child _____ (Repeat)

A

long way_____ from home _____ A long way_____ from home.

**NOBODY KNOWS THE TROUBLE I'VE SEEN** — United States

No-bod-y knows the trou-ble I've seen, No-bod-y knows my sor-row

No-bod-y knows the trou-ble I've seen Glo-ry hal-le-lu-jah.

**SOMEBODY'S KNOCKING AT MY DOOR** — United States

Some-bod-y's knock-ing at my door Some-bod-y's knock-ing at my door

**THEME FROM SYMPHONY IN D MINOR** — Franck

**2 THEMES FROM SYMPHONY NO. 5 (New World)** Dvorak

etc.

shall we write them in this pattern on the board? We've already answered it once when we compared

the sticks and drums, but do it again.

S Long S S L S

The drums and cymbals, playing quarter notes are the beat. The beat and the short and longs don't always coincide, do they? The syncopated pattern is *off* the beat or *before* the beat or *after* the beat or *in between* the beat. But not always *on* the beat or *with* the beat. This is what makes syncopation.

## Hearing and Reading Syncopation

You can tell when you hear it. Raise your hands or stand up when you hear that short - long - short pattern with the notes in between the beats. Tap your toe on the beat because if we are going to detect notes which are *off* the beat, let's make sure we know where the beat is.

Because it is difficult to truly detect a particular rhythm pattern while listening if it comes and goes very quickly, the teacher would be wise to improvise at the piano or on the tom-tom a series of rhythms in which each pattern occurs for several consecutive measures. For instance:

That way a fair portion of students can really detect it. And if they can detect it, they can identify and write it. Teacher should try dictating the same series of patterns and others like it for writing down. He should encourage—insist upon—foot tapping. He can place the syncopation pattern on the board for all to refer to: ♪ ♩ ♪. This is not a test of memory but a test of identification.

Do them backwards. Then do the reverse of dictation. Read those patterns. Clap them, patsch them, play them on sticks.

This has been a sort of "back door" approach to syncopation. It doesn't tell us everything about it. Of course, when it comes to our American popular music and jazz, there just isn't any way to write much of that down. So many notes come in just a little bit ahead of the beat, we just have to know how that is done. You've probably noticed that if a popular piece is played from the music just as it is written, it won't sound "right." The player has to add that little touch of "beating the beat!" to make it sound the way only our American popular music can sound. But when it comes to all the songs we were playing and singing earlier, largely folk songs, there *is* a specific way to write the syncopation pattern as you have seen.

## The Look of Syncopation

Let's look at it more closely. There is something unusual about its appearance. Can you state what it is? ♪ ♩ ♪ It's the way the eighth notes are arranged. We are very used to seeing eighth notes in pairs ♫. When we see one alone, there is usually a dotted note along with it. ♩. ♪ In ⅛ we see them in groups of threes ♪♪♪ or in long-short combinations ♩ ♪. But here in the syncopated pattern they are at either end of the measure so to speak, each one standing alone. It makes a special picture which will always indicate syncopation. Remember it, short-long-short. What other combination of notes would fit short-long-short? Suppose we couldn't use eighth notes. ♩ ♩ ♩ is also short-long-short. We have just doubled the value of each note. Suppose we cut in half the value of each note of the original pattern. ♪ ♪ ♪ Still short-long-short. All syncopation.

## Count Your Way to Syncopation

Let's approach it another way. This could be a first way, or a reinforcing approach. It is more mathematical. We'll do some counting, chanting, clapping and tapping. Teacher sets up a quarter note beat in twos. **Count and tap the beat, and when I point, clap the pattern I place on the board. Do each several times:**

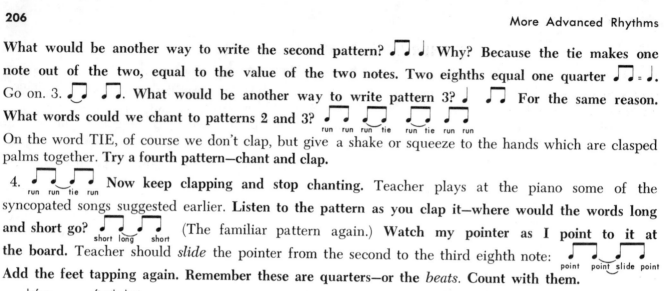

What would be another way to write the second pattern? ♫ ♩ Why? Because the tie makes one note out of the two, equal to the value of the two notes. Two eighths equal one quarter ♫ = ♩. Go on. 3. ♫ ♫. What would be another way to write pattern 3? ♩ ♫ For the same reason. What words could we chant to patterns 2 and 3? ♫ ♫ ♫ ♫
run run run tie   run tie run run

On the word TIE, of course we don't clap, but give a shake or squeeze to the hands which are clasped palms together. **Try a fourth pattern—chant and clap.**

4. ♫ ♫ **Now keep clapping and stop chanting.** Teacher plays at the piano some of the
run run tie run
syncopated songs suggested earlier. **Listen to the pattern as you clap it—where would the words long and short go?** ♫ ♫ (The familiar pattern again.) **Watch my pointer as I point to it at**
short long short
**the board.** Teacher should *slide* the pointer from the second to the third eighth note: ♫ ♫
point point slide point
**Add the feet tapping again. Remember these are quarters—or the *beats*. Count with them.**

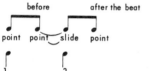

Repeat several times. Notice how nothing is happening *on* the second beat. The previous note is held. We can say there is a note sounded *before* the beat and *after* the beat, but not *on* the beat. What note could we substitute for the two tied eighth notes? A quarter: ♪ ♩ ♪
short long_____ short

Now where in *this* pattern can we indicate beat two? ♪♩ ......... ♪ Half way through the quarter
1       2
note. Remember that these two patterns are exactly the same: ♫ ♫ Notice the TIE in the first example, often used to make syncopation, but certainly ♪♩ ♪ not used for *only* that. The second pattern has the lonely eighth notes. Can you think 1   2 of a third way we might write this pattern so that the effect is almost the same, but not quite? We could use a REST.

The rest obliterates the second beat also, but by *silence* rather than sustained sounds. The TAs show the difference. Try it.

♫ ♫ } ta ta-a-ta
♪♩ ♪ }

♪♪ 𝄾 ♪ ta ta silence ta
1   2

Another way the same effect could be achieved is to literally remove the note from count 2. A flannel board and notes would be effective here so that the note can literally be removed:

♪♪♪♪ | ♪ ♪ take away ♪
                      the 8th

Now we know in music we can't ever just leave a blank space, but that we use signs to indicate silence as well as sound. If we replace an eighth note's worth of sound with an eighth note's worth of silence, the sign we need is - - ? an eighth rest 𝄾. flannel board: ♪♪ ♪ | ♪♪ 𝄾 ♪ Then we might say
place in
blank space

♪ ♪ 𝄾 ♪
clap clap rest clap
and the effect is just about the same as the previous pattern. However, suppose we are playing a flute, or piano or singing this pattern. How would ♪ ♪ 𝄾 ♪ be different from ♫ ♫? The tied note continues to sound—we will continue to sing or blow into the flute or hold down the piano key, but for the rest there must be silence—we will stop singing or blowing or lift our finger from the piano key.

## OTHER SYNCOPATION PATTERNS

Syncopation is not easy to read although when we just perform it instinctively or imitatively, it comes more easily then. Here are some harder patterns. You may want to pass them by if they seem just too hard. **Sing Jacob's Ladder** (fl., Her: 119) **in twos. Count, conduct ready sing:** WE ARE

1        2    1        2    1        2

CLIMBING        JACOB'S        LADDER

1        2    1        2    1        2 . . . **Within the two counts, how many word-**

syllables do you sing? Two. **Are they even?** No. **How is the long and short arranged?** Short-long. **Then can you arrive at the note values for those two notes? Where do they come in relation to the beats?**

 or substitute one note for the three tied eighths:

Double the value of the notes and the meter, and you'll have Jacob's Ladder the way it is more commonly written, still syncopated: We are ? – – – climbing ? – – –

1    2    3    4    1    2    3    4

We     are     climb - ing     Ja - cob's     Lad - der

We     are     climb - ing     Ja - cob's     Lad - der

### The Effect of Syncopation

Syncopation is sometimes described as a shifting of accents. The shortness of the first note seems to add a special accent to the second note: ♪ ♩. But our expectation is that the accent will come on count-one with the down-beat. Hence the surprise—and pleasure—to hear the accents shifted to the "and" of count one—to a place after one. We somehow expect something to happen *on* a beat, *on* a count, no matter how much does or does *not* happen *between* beats:

1        2    1        2

Cir-cle to the left     old brass wag - on

All we would have to do is rearrange these notes so that on some beats something does *not* happen: and we have syncopation. Or do it in reverse: Take a song that *is* syncopated and "*unsyncopate*" it:

1        2    1        2

Cir - cle left _____     old brass cart

Notice nothing happening on beat 2 except sustained sound, started *after* beat one but *before* beat two—syncopated. Straighten it out and what a dull song!

1    2    3    4    1    2    3    4

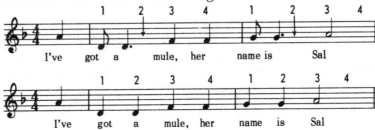

I've     got     a     mule,     her     name     is     Sal

1    2    3    4    1    2    3    4

I've     got     a     mule,     her     name     is     Sal

The rest of the song gets very syncopated, and more complicated.

Fif - teen      miles      on      the      E - rie  Ca - nal ____

Notice that in the shifting of accents the first note of the syncopated pattern will be of the lesser value—that's another way to recognize syncopation when you see it:

## The Effect of the Tie

In the next example, see how the TIE can complicate matters! Suppose we put together two measures of the basic syncopation pattern we've been working with: Count, tap and TA it.

Now see what one little tie can do: Count, tap and clap:

Every single beat except the first has been obliterated—nothing happens *on* any of them—there is always a sound sustained from *before* the beat, throwing the accent *off* the beat, so-to-speak.

You'll note two eighths with a TIE have to be used because we can't place a bar-line *through* a note: but if the meter were 4/4 it *could* look like this and at a quick glance we might not even notice this is a syncopated pattern except for the strange arrangement of eighth notes—those "lonely sentinels" at either end of the measure. The Cesar Franck excerpt has almost that pattern. If you are used to subdividing the beat aloud as you count: one — and two — and three — and four — and    or    one — de two — de three — de four — de    etc. then what is happening is that the tones are sounding on the "ands."

one  AND two  AND three AND four AND

The thing to remember most about syncopation is to relax and enjoy it—feel it—let it swing—make the room jump! And always keep the beat, just so you know what it is you are NOT playing on.

## SUMMARY

In syncopation the accent comes where it is not expected. Sometimes it is called a misplaced accent. The accent occurs on a part of the beat not usually accented. The accent is removed from its usual location. It is shifted. The accent comes *after* the beat, *before* the beat, *off* the beat, *in between* beats. Sometimes it disappears and there is silence where an accent was expected.

The TIE is often used to create syncopation; sometimes it is necessary, as when it is used across the bar-line to sustain a tone and obliterate the beat or count. The REST is often used to create syncopation in the same way, except with silence rather than sustained sound.

The eighth note, which we are used to seeing in pairs, appears in unusual arrangements, sometimes singly, sometimes like lonely sentinels on either side of a quarter note, sometimes tied or accompanied by a rest.

Syncopation is an uneven rhythmic pattern.

The spirit or bounce or beat of syncopation is almost more important than being able to count it out. Americans should have no trouble with a beat that is very much their own (but they do). We should notice from the music containing the syncopated patterns that syncopation is very much a part of Black music and therefore American music. It is an essential part of all our American popular music. It also appears in the art and folk music of many countries.

## THE TRIPLET

Let's start with our name game. We'll list again some of the names we've used which have only one word-syllable. Let's tap rhythm sticks on our desks to the names. Move your fingers. How do they move? Walking.

| John | Bert | Gail |
|------|------|------|
| Bill | Jean | Fred |
| Ted  | Jane | June |
| Hugh | Joan | Jill |

Now a list of names which have two word-syllables. Tap your sticks to one of those names and tell what action belongs. Running. We'll divide you in half. This side tap PEGGY (♪♩) and this side play TED (♩) on drums.

| Peggy | Katie |
|-------|-------|
| Robert | Richard |
| Humphrey | Winston |
| Betty | Phyllis |

Now a four syllable name. Those are harder to think of aren't they? How about Margaretta? Use

Evalina
Emmalina
Margaretta
Annabella
Alexander

shakers for that name. How would we write that name? ♫♫ Four sounds to one beat. Now make an orchestra. We'll play the three names together. One - two - ready, play. Teacher could improvise lightly at the piano.

How about this name? Teacher chants evenly: **JONATHAN  JONATHAN  JONATHAN. How many word-syllables to the beat this time? You chant  TED TED while I say JONATHAN. JON A THAN**
                                                                                                          **TED**

JON A THAN     Three word-syllables. Three notes to a beat. How shall we write that? Is there such
TED
a thing as a "third" note—or a "twelfth" note?! No. Two sixteenths and an eighth? ♫♪ That is entirely possible, but then we would have to chant the name in a slightly different way—JON A THAN.
                                                                                                            ♫  ♪

The first two syllables quite short, the last syllable longer. But I have been chanting the name very evenly. With a name like Margaret, we might be able to spell it in music this way: ♩♫ with the first syllable longer than the other two.

But I want you to think of a way we can write, in music, three equal notes to one beat. (If someone mentions ⁶⁄₈, ask for a way besides that.)

**There isn't a way! We know 1 beat  = ♩ = ♫ = ♫♫**  but music doesn't have a way to write three equal notes to one beat. Yet we know music uses such a pattern—take Row, Row, Row Your Boat! ²⁄₄ Mer ri ly Mer ri ly  Mer ri ly Mer ri ly or the hymn ⁴⁄ Once to - - eve ry | man and - - na tion. **The**
                                                                                    ♩        ♩ ♩| ♩      ♩.♫♩

1        2      1        2

**underlying beat of much "rock" music is made up of three even notes to the beat.**

ONCE TO EVERY MAN AND NATION

Words, James Russell Lowell
Music, Thomas John Williams

Some great__cause God's new Mes - si - ah Off - 'ring__ each the bloom or __ blight

And the __ choice goes on for - ev - er 'Twixt that__ dark - ness and __ that light.

Used by permission of Houghton Mifflin Company, Boston.

What happens, is that music "makes do." Usually so very mathematically correct, music has to improvise a way to write three even equal notes to one beat. What do you suppose the pattern is called? Here are some hints:

1. There is a play in baseball when the batter gets a hit and runs all the way to third base.
2. How about a three-wheel bike?
3. What do we call three babies all born at the same time from one mother?

The answers respectively are 1. triple     2. tricycle     3. triplets. And the last answer is the exact name in music for three even equal notes to one beat—TRIPLET.

How does a TRIPLET act? You know how it is when a third person is squeezed into the front seat of a car made only for two—there isn't really enough room, but each person just takes about a third of what is there. It's the same with the musical beat—there isn't any more space or time in the beat; it is just divided three ways instead of two or four.

## The Look of the Triplet

And how does a triplet look? An examination of the version of Wagner's Pilgrim's Chorus from Tannhäuser in the flute book shows us one of several ways to indicate a triplet. The number 3 is important. That is what tells us the notes make a triplet. ♪♪♪ ♪♪♪     ♪♪♪ ♪♪♪ These are all ways to indicate a triplet. Notice that three eighth notes are "holding hands" on the same beam ♪♪♪ . Do you know another time when three eighth notes appear on the same beam? Yes, in §. But in § the 3 is not necessary—a very important difference. It wouldn't hurt to review the chapter on § at this time. (See Chapter 4.)

See what would happen if the 3 were not written in. Count the beats indicated by the notes: 3½ beats in a measure which has room for only three beats. It's that extra eighth note crowding in. A triplet to one beat will always consist of notes of a denomination which ordinarily go two to a beat. In this case two eighths equal one beat. Therefore the triplet will consist of eighth notes, but one more—three. There can be other kinds of triplets but all that is quite advanced.

A triplet is a musically correct but mathematically imperfect way to indicate three even equal notes to a beat.

## Hearing and Reading Triplets

See if you can convert these names into the correct musical symbols—write at your seats or on a flannel board. TED  JONATHAN  MARGARETTA  PEGGY  Chant them with me and note how

evenly and steadily we must say these names. They translate into

Listen as I drum. Which name am I drumming? Teacher chooses one and drums repeatedly and steadily. The students now take turns drumming one name—then a combination of two names for recognition. This is dictation again.

We can even make the name triplet have three syllables: tri - pl - et tri - pl - et. Use the term "walk"

and "tri - pl - et" to "read" this rhythm: Be very steady.

There is a tendency to rush the triplet and get to the last note too soon. That makes the third note longer than the others.

This would be a very good time to play on our flutes the Pilgrim's Chorus as it appears in the flute book. Before we play, let's read it through by speaking. This is reading, of course. Speak through ONCE TO EVERY MAN AND NATION.

PILGRIM'S CHORUS (Tannhäuser)                                                              Wagner

Finger your flutes this time, covering the proper holes in rhythm, but don't blow. After this silent practice we are ready to play.

Take a map and see how many places you can find whose names are triplets. There's a list at the end of this chapter.

You could now sight read music with triplets. Some of you take resonator bells—F A C and see if you can play this opening fanfare correctly. Chant to yourselves if necessary. It is the familiar opening to the hymn, God of Our Fathers. (Her: 200)

## The Triplet's Pledge

Since I enjoy the privilege of including an extra note in my beat, of the same note value as the other notes, as if there were no third note, I will treat that extra free-loading note just like all the others in the beat.

On my honor,
I will always be steady,
I will always be even,
I will always be equal,
I will never rush to the next beat,
I will never take more than the time allotted to the beat.

*Map Names*

| Lexington | Trenton | Carolina | Maine | |
| Greensboro | Princeton | California | Bern | |
| Syracuse | Dallas | Mississippi | France | |
| Roanoke | Gary | Pennsylvania | Ames | |
| Buffalo | Fort Worth | Indiana | Platte | (River) |
| Madison | Tulsa | Albuquerque | Bow | (River) |
| Rochester | | Amarillo | | |
| Arkansas | | Oklahoma | | |
| Little Rock | | | | |
| Birmingham | | | | |
| Bakersfield | | | | |

*Names of People*

| Barbara | Humphrey | Emmalina | John |
| Jonathan | Winston | Margaretta | Bill |
| Lionel | Betty | Katerina | Ted |
| Carolyn | Tommy | Evalina | Hugh |
| Lizabeth | Phyllis | Cinderella | Bert |
| Genevieve | Peggy | Rumpelstiltskin (!) | Jean |
| Margaret | Ethel | Concietta | Jane |
| | | Alexander | |
| | | Aloysius | |
| | | Maximillian | |

## COMPOUND METER

I suggested you might want to refer back to the chapter on ⅜. You may remember that one of the outstanding characteristics of ⅜ is that two pulses are felt in each measure, and each pulse is subdivided into three:  . But by using the eighth note as the beat note or unit of measure there is no mathematical inaccuracy—it all fits without the need of the number 3. However, what makes it fit into 6 is the spacing of the accent: 1 2 3 4 5 6 .

Listen to this well known Christmas song and count how many pulses you hear from one accent to the next. I'll emphasize the accent. Teacher plays.

**Before you answer, this time count steady eighth notes and see how many there are of them.** Teacher

sets correct tempo: eighth — eighth — eighth — eighth — now — count

If necessary teacher counts out loud with the students. **Is it possible? Twelve eighth notes?! And how many pulses? Four. There are four pulses in each measure, each pulse subdivided into three.** Is it very different from $\frac{6}{8}$? **No, only in the matter of pulses. What do you think the measure signature would be? Yes, it is $\frac{12}{8}$** . The only real difference from $\frac{6}{8}$ is that the accents don't come as often.

**Listen to this music and try to determine the measure signature. The subdivision into three will be easy to hear because the music gives it to us.**

SANCTUS     St. Cecelia Mass                                                            Gounod

**Can it be $\frac{9}{8}$? Yes, there are three pulses—three groups of three eighths.** Measure signatures like this are referred to as COMPOUND METERS because by pulses they break down into a smaller meter.

6 can be counted in two 1-2
9 can be counted in three 1-2-3
12 can be counted in four 1-2-3-4

Other examples of $\frac{12}{8}$ can be found in "Messiah" by Handel—the Pastoral Symphony and Come Unto Him, among others; and the horn theme of the Andante movement in Tschaikovsky's fifth Symphony in E minor. Other examples of $\frac{9}{8}$ are "Over the Bright Blue Sea" from H.M.S. Pinafore by Sullivan, and "Beautiful Dreamer" by Foster.

## SUMMARY

In this chapter we have dealt with some rather advanced rhythms, and it would be unrealistic to expect a majority of students to master them quickly. They are difficult! It is at this point that many fall by the wayside; even some of those training themselves seriously in music stumble over patterns like these.

Among those students who make no pretense at being music specialists, more will understand the material intellectually than will be able to execute the music practically. For many students the most we should expect in a short time is some understanding of how these rhythms look, sound and are constructed. But the actual execution of such rhythms may be too great a challenge. As a result, this is where the choral director finds it necessary to resort to rote procedures to get the music learned!

This is not to imply that the educational picture is then necessarily bleak; it is merely that the mastery of such rhythmic complexities as these is rarely achieved during one or two short courses, but takes a longer period of continued experience and maturation. Here in these preceding lessons can at least be provided clear useful explanations and procedures. Game-drills like those suggested in this chapter offer one way to bring about this maturation; continual opportunities to make music and to listen to music supply another avenue.

## Chapter 18

# Creativity

## CREATIVITY

Thousands of words have been written on the values of creativity. Creativity has been considered from many points of view: as a contribution to the nurture and growth of the "whole child," as an enrichment of education and adult life, as an avenue to or means of self-expression, for its psychological and therapeutic value of "ventilation" and expressing the emotions, as a means of helping the child in difficulty "find himself," for its aesthetic value and the chance to walk with beauty, as a social experience, as a motivating tool, as an avenue to realization of the complexity and skill of the art of creativity as a result of attempting it oneself—all of this and more is believed true about creativity.

But this is a book on Theory and specifically on how-to-teach the fundamentals of music. Creativity will be considered here for its value as a tool for grasping concepts of time, rhythm and melody in music, as a resource for the learning of the fundamentals of music.

Its value is enormous, and its potential relatively untapped. This is not to say creativity is not a part of the learning experience provided in education today, but more for the many fine reasons just listed, than as a teaching tool. Here are some examples of how creativity can be used as a tool for proving out and applying a newly learned fact.

### Rhythms

A mistake we teachers make is waiting until our students have acquired what we regard as a suitable number of facts and concepts before turning them loose to experiment or giving them a "real piece of music." For the disciplined, skilled and talented student who has a mature viewpoint and a long-range goal in mind, this may be acceptable. But the average student needs short goals, a series of small successes, frequent explanation as to the "why" of what he has learned, and continued opportunities to *use* what he is learning. Creative activity satisfies all these needs and the student should be provided with opportunities for such experiences as soon and as often as possible.

Back in the early chapters on Rhythms, mention was made of the Rhythm Band and rhythm band scores as marvelous tools suffering from neglect, malignment and ignorance. The minute a student has learned two or three note values ( ♩ ♩ ♪ ) he can use these in his own arrangements for percussion instruments. Before he even learned the note values he was able to create by consciously deciding *when* and *where* in a song he would play a triangle (every other beat, or only on the accent, etc.) and even *how* (trill three beats here 𝆺 , one stroke here ♩). Even here he is learning concepts of

| | |
|---|---|
| duration | — as above |
| timbre | — I prefer triangle to shakers |
| accent | — play only on loud beat |

meter          — the loud beats come every four counts

style          — I want to play the triangle loudly on every beat in this music, but gently only once at the end of each phrase in the Chopin Prelude in A major

PRELUDE IN A MAJOR, Op. 28, No. 7                              Chopin

form          — In Amaryllis there are three parts. The last is like the first. Each part is played lightly once and then more heavily a second time. I know this because I have a solo for the triangle in each light part. (excerpt of Amaryllis in Chapter 2)

As soon as students have learned these three note values, teacher can provide a chance to read them in a genuine musical situation—the rhythm band. Each student gets a part written only for his instrument using only those note values; and using his new skill and understanding he is able to interpret these signs and fit them to the music. The part may contain a rest or two—excellent motivation— a real reason, urgent and immediate, for learning about rests.

When he plays his part in concert with the other students playing their parts he experiences the thrill and joy of of playing in ensemble. Teacher can show him the picture of what that ensemble looks like— the complete score which the conductor needs. Now is the time. Teacher can say, why don't we all write our own score to a song?

Cymbals, let's hear where you think you should play. What kind of notes are they playing? On what words of the song? On what beat? I'll write it here on the board.

Sticks, let's hear you. There are several ideas—let's choose one. What kind of notes are they playing? (Dictation) Quarter—eighth, eighth ♩ ♫♩ ♫ . I'll write it on the score on the board. Drums, you shouldn't play very often because you are a noisy instrument. Let's hear you play. When do they play? On the first beat of each measure. What kind of note? Quarter. How do we indicate when they don't play? Rests. Like this ♩ 𝄾 𝄾 𝄾 . I'll add it to our score.

This is a joint creative project, giving everyone a chance to "break in," to get the feel of such a venture. It involves all their knowledge of rhythms (no matter how limited or extensive) and the skills of dictation and reading, all synthesized now into the meaningful and even aesthetic experience of creation.

Now why don't each of you try to write your own "orchestration"? Choose your own song and your own instrument. If you don't have such rhythm instruments available at home (and who does?) use bunches of keys, pot lids, pails and wastebaskets, pencils and rulers to experiment with sounds.

To reiterate, a creative project like this can be undertaken almost as soon as the barest knowledge is acquired, and should be. But teacher should do it again often as his students acquire more knowledge: the results will be more sophisticated, of course.

Add pitched and chording instruments to the arrangement: autoharps, guitars, ukes, bells, flutes, melodicas. Arrangements for such combinations of instruments (pitched and percussion) are published: Melody, Rhythm and Harmony by Lloyd Slind published by Mills; Melody Makers by Golding and Landers published by Van Roy, among others.

1. Playing from such arrangements would be a first step. This of course is reading.
2. Then, as before, a joint creative effort.
3. Then the individual creations.

And though there are surely many corollary benefits to such creative activities, the main goal of the theory teacher is to place the students in situations where they use and manipulate these tools of music with understanding and skill, with the added motivation of expressing their own ideas.

Teacher can have "research and question" sessions after the students have begun their individual work. These come about quite spontaneously OUT OF THEIR *NEED* TO KNOW. It is useful to insist that they put their questions into words; not come and show teacher the problem. The purpose is to attempt to answer and solve the problems with words and written musical illustrations. The students must learn to communicate with each other and the teacher in the language of music. It is an excellent measurement device for the teacher: he *hears* how his students think and communicate, he hears them use or mis-use the musical language.

The published rhythm band scores are before the group and they are examined closely to get the answer. Go to the source. How do we write Rhythm Band scores? Study some already written.

The questions which come up are excellent. There is rarely a stupid one. And when the question and research sessions are over and the individual scores are written, the students really do understand the tools of music they have used. They have had intimate and involved contact with them. Is the measure signature a fraction? (No). Is it repeated on every staff? (No). Which comes first, key signature or measure signature? Where are the flats written—is E♭ on the first line or fourth space? Which way do the flags on eighth notes go? When is it better to write an upside-down quarter note (beginning students don't even recognize this ⌐ as a quarter note, did you know?). The vertical aspect of music is better understood when the student composer discovers a score like this isn't readable by the conductor, because the beats aren't vertical.

Poor                    Correct

What is described so far is mainly a purely rhythmic creative experience, or rhythmic combined with very elementary pitch and harmonic symbols; for instance, letters for autoharp chords (G7) letters for bells (B G A G) or numbers for flutes (6 4 2 4) or letters for bass notes for left hand on the piano (G–D, G–D, or even the actual notes):

## Creating Original Songs

As students progress in the realm of pitch, melody and harmony, the possibilities for creative experience increase. For instance, the echo technique of Orff and others on the bells (listen to what I play and watch as I play it—now you play) are great for the ear and for basic concepts of high-low, left-right, short-long, etc. But it is desirable to go a step further and say "write it down." What did I play on the xylo? G A B G. You play it. *Write it down.* (Dictation and reading.)

Sing me your own original tune. (Creativity). What are the syllables? (Dictation). What is its rhythm? (Dictation). *Write it down.* (Creativity combined with theory).

Experience with creating original songs, words and music, reveals two areas of special weakness in the background of students.

1. Experience with poetry: what makes poetry—how should we recite it—accent and meter and rhythm in poetry—the difference between prose and poetry—poetry does not have to be a jingle, does not have to rhyme, but some poetry does.

2. The ability to detect by ear the natural inflection of words, the natural rhythm of phrases—BUILT IN inflection, BUILT IN rhythm. We can't really change this. There is usually more than one way words and phrases can go, but also many ways they cannot (see Chapters 1-3).

For the first weakness, the music and literature teachers ought to work together to provide opportunities for students to listen to teachers and professionals recite poetry, to talk about it, and to recite poetry themselves.

For the second weakness working with words as illustrated in this book, and the use of Orff techniques should certainly help. In addition, chant the words of poems and mark the accents with barlines:

| Peter, Peter, | pumpkin-eater | Had a wife and | couldn't keep her
| Once to every | man and nation, | Comes the moment | to decide.
| Hey ho, | anybody home, | meat and drink and | money have I none
| We three | Kings of | Orient | are
The | first No|el the | angels did | say
O | say can you | see by the | dawn's early | light?

The discerning and marking off of the meter and accents of his original poem appears to be the most difficult step of the creative procedure for the average student. More preparatory experiences with poems not his own should help.

The second most difficult step is to determine the actual rhythms, the note values of the words. If the accents have been correctly determined, the task is not so formidable.

Here are a few viewpoints and techniques regarding creating original poems and setting them to original music. With a group which is inexperienced it is more effective to maintain an attitude of matter-of-fact expectation that they can do it, an acceptance of what they offer, and an absence of criticism and rejection. Response is likely to be slow. Teacher must be patient. He should work first on the poem.

Sometimes it is good to list ideas on the board and have a discussion about the topic. He should encourage chanting; talking out loud. Teacher should try to accept any phrases and line offered, or parts of them. In the beginning almost anything—later on all want to be more selective. If it's necessary to prod with a word here or there, he can do so, although there is a debate about this technique. It's not wise to waste time on comparing or choosing or voting on a choice. That may come later. Teacher should show approval or pleasure whenever possible and try to encourage participation from as many as possible. Sometimes certain students will come to life who have never or rarely participated before. It is the tendency for a few to shine. It is hard to strike the right balance of encouraging them without allowing them to take over. In a group situation teacher shouldn't worry too much about reining in such students because their interest and talent will likely carry over into their free time activities. Sometimes a miracle will occur and "inspiration" will strike everyone at once, and out comes a whole line in unison! In such cases the "inspiration" will hardly have been unique or of great quality, but that may come. Meanwhile, the success of the immediate moment is total participation.

Usually in a few moments the poem is complete. Now comes the tune. Humming and singing out loud should be encouraged. If what comes out seems to be in an unsuitable range, teacher can just repeat it in a more appropriate one or say it's too high or too low, and move it.

With the uninitiated it can be expected that the second and third and fourth lines may be replicas of the first. When it happens teacher can just point this out and push for something different. The third and fourth phrases may echo the first and second. Sometimes this can be accepted, other times teacher guides toward ABAC or ABCD. Sometimes with just a note teacher can push them in a better direction. ("Better" is a subjective word. It's what *teacher* regards as better. *Best* is to keep out unless collapse is imminent!) Often the "miracle" occurs again and all will sing the same tune for a line spontaneously. The "expectedness," the predictability of such a line and therefore its banality is less important AT THIS TIME than the surprise, astonishment and delight of students who never dreamed of creating their own tune and words, but find themselves doing it. The quality will improve later— the students will demand it of themselves. They can do beautiful things as experience increases.

Even though the group has created words and music, teacher hasn't finished making demands yet. Of course if they stop here, it is still a fine satisfying creative activity, but if it is to be an experience in theory, they have yet to put to creative use the tools of music they are learning.

Let's write it down says teacher. If students have been chanting poems to determine meter and rhythm, this will be just another poem to treat similarly. Where do the accents come? Does it start with an anacrusis? Put a vertical line | before every accented word or syllable. Count, chant, clap, conduct. What is the meter?

Now within each measure utilize all the techniques used so often—get up and "walk" the words, move your fingers, tap and chant. The familiar questions—How many notes to a beat, are they even or uneven; how many beats to a note? Keep in mind that accents can come in the middle of a word and that one phrase can end and another begin within the same measure. A common mistake of students is to try to make the rhythm of the poem fit what they decide is the measure or the rhythm. The rhythm and meter of words and phrases is built in and we can't make it be what it is not. Let the words TELL *YOU*. Don't force an accent where it is not. Chant the words, beat and stamp. They'll tell *you*.

Often students make a private little decision not to compose in $\frac{6}{8}$—it *is* a more complex and challenging meter. Trouble is $\frac{6}{8}$ meter has a wonderful swing and will often prove to be the very meter a majority of songs have written themselves in! Many times a song can be notated correctly in more than one meter; for instance $\frac{2}{4}$ as well as $\frac{4}{4}$ or $\frac{2}{2}$; or $\frac{3}{4}$ as well as $\frac{6}{8}$. In some cases the trained music teacher will detect certain subtleties which make a song more suitable in one meter than in another—a point with which the beginner should not be troubled.

Now the tune. Does it end on DO as most tunes do? Is it major or minor—it may end on LA. Compare the starting tone with the last in order to know where the tune starts. Use syllables and dictation to write the tune down or pick it out by trial and error at the piano. What is the key, or more important, what is the signature of the key you've chosen? One of the common mistakes students make is to choose to start a song on a particular note, or to choose both to write in the key of C (none of that bother with flats or sharps, you know), and to start *on* C.

## Songs Write Themselves

Students think they will make it easier on themselves if they control the key and starting tone; instead they make problems. Let the song come. We can then put it in *any* key—one suitable to our range—a key where most of the notes will stay on the staff and thus within good singing range. Use syllables and instruments to help you notate the song. If you want to change the key later, syllables will make the task of transposing easy.

In this activity of creating and notating a song, words and music, there must be brought to play all the knowledge and skills this whole book has been about—a most worthy and satisfying culminating project.

It is possible to go even further and orchestrate the original song for pitched and rhythm instruments and chord it for harmonizing instruments such as autoharp, uke or piano. But always, students should be encouraged to utilize knowledge and skills rather than allowed to make it merely a rote experience. In this way, learning is made fun, learning is made easy, learning is fulfilling.

Creative experiences such as these provide additional incentive to learn the tools of music. We need these tools in order to express and preserve our own musical ideas. Creativity has been treated here as a means of motivating the learning of the fundamentals of music, and then as an avenue for utilizing the acquired skills.

The goal of this book has been to help teachers present the fundamentals of music to their students in an effective way; and to help students learn the fundamentals of music through experience with them. To the extent that we are all successful, students and teachers, will we produce more enlightened listeners and consumers of music, more competently equipped novice creators of music, and more skilled re-creators of music: those who interpret and perform.

## How Does the Composer Convey His Wishes?

The children are deep into composing an original rhythm band score. The questions fly. I want to hit the cymbal on the edge. How do I show that? Just say "edge." I want the wood block to play softly. You can just say "softly." The language of music is Italian. You could say "piano." But more and more, composers are using their own native language. (See p. 189, the excerpt by Debussy.) A Frenchman might say "doucement"; you could say "gently."

Here is a list of some of the terms you might want to use. Either language can be employed.

| Tempo | | Dynamics | | |
|---|---|---|---|---|
| **Grave** | solemn, slow | **Piano  p** | | softly |
| **Largo** | very slow | **Pianissimo  pp** | | very softly |
| **Adagio** | slow | **Mezzo piano  mp** | | moderately softly |
| **Andante** | walking pace | **Forte  f** | | loud |
| **Moderato** | moderately | **Fortissimo  ff** | | very loud |
| **Allegretto** | moderately fast | **mezzo forte  mf** | | moderately loud |
| **Allegro** | lively, fast | **sforzando** | > | accented, suddenly loud |
| **Accelerando** | gradually growing faster | | | |
| **Ritardando** | gradually growing slower | **crescendo** | < | growing louder |
| | | **decrescendo** | | |
| **Presto** | very fast | **diminuendo** | > | growing softer |
| **Molto** | very, much | | | |
| **Poco** | a little | **1.** | | first ending |
| **Piu** | more | **2.** | | second ending |
| | | | | fermata, hold indefinitely |
| | | **Da Capo** | | back to the beginning |
| | | **Fine** | | finish |

# Indexes

## General

## Index of Musical Excerpts

## Index of Songs

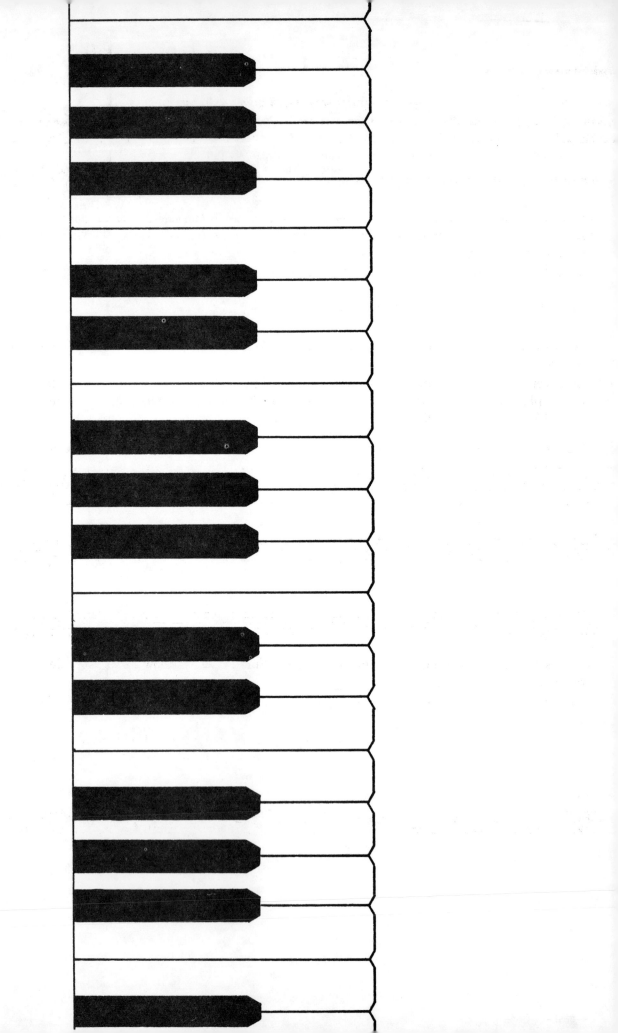